S0-CGP-188

SPORTS CONDITIONING

Other Doubleday books by Bill Libby:

KING RICHARD The Richard Petty Story
CHARLIE O. AND THE ANGRY A'S
LIFE IN THE PIT

SPORTS CONDITIONING

Getting in Shape, Playing Your Best, and Preventing Injuries

By Frank O'Neill
with Bill Libby

DOUBLEDAY & COMPANY, INC. GARDEN CITY, NEW YORK 1979

Library of Congress Cataloging in Publication Data

O'Neill, Frank.
Sports conditioning.

1. Physical fitness. 2. Sports. I. Libby,
Bill, joint author. II. Title.
GV481.053 613.7
ISBN: 0-385-14108-4
Library of Congress Catalog Card Number 78–68373

Printed in the United States of America
First Edition

For my children, whom I dearly love—Frank, Jr., Patsy, Michael, and Mark.

Frank O'Neill, 1979

FOREWORD

Sandy Koufax came by one day about twelve years ago, after he'd been pitching in the major leagues about twelve years. He was by far the best pitcher in the big leagues, but there was a lot of talk that he was about to retire. No one knew for sure. The great southpaw pitcher had been coming to see Dr. Robert Kerlan for treatment of an arthritic left elbow. My office of physical therapy was part of the great doctor's office of orthopedic medicine at that time, and he had referred Sandy to me for whirlpool baths, ultrasound treatment, and massage on his sore elbow. But it was becoming clear there was no cure for Koufax's condition and no way he could continue to pitch without constant pain.

"How's it going?" I asked him. "What are you gonna do?"

Sandy smiled, but it was a wistful sort of smile. "Well, I'll tell you, Frank," he said, "when I'm forty years old, I'd still like to be able to comb my hair."

That's all he said. But that's all he had to say. He went on his way, and I knew he was going away.

The next day, he announced his retirement.

Injuries are a part of sports, but care and conditioning can prolong life and increase careers. My job is keeping people fit. I'm a physical therapist in general and an athletic trainer in particular. I'm not a doctor; I can't do what a doctor does and I can't take care of you as a doctor would. But I work with doctors, do many things for them, and can do some things for you they do not. I cannot compare my background and knowledge to a doctor's, but

I think I have something to offer the average person, as well as the athlete.

The finest of athletes—a Koufax, for example—cannot always avoid an ailment or injury that will curtail his career, but proper treatment of his problem permitted him to perform for several seasons that he otherwise might have missed, seasons that sent him on to sports immortality. The surgeon's scalpel and the physical therapist's treatments brought back from near-crippling injuries such immortals as Wilt Chamberlain, Jerry West, and Elgin Baylor. Conditioning created excellent careers for a Norm Van Brocklin, a Ron Fairly, a Gail Goodrich, and others not blessed with abundant natural ability.

As assistant trainer at the University of Southern California and for the Los Angeles Rams, and as head trainer for the Philadelphia Eagles' football team, the Los Angeles Lakers' basketball team, and, recently, the Los Angeles Aztecs' soccer team, I have worked with these superstars I have mentioned, as well as with the great jockey Bill Shoemaker, hockey goaltender Terry Sawchuk, international soccer star George Best, boxing champion Lionel Rose, Olympic decathlon champion Bill Toomey, Olympic diving queen Sue Gossick, and, during her recuperation to a useful life, the crippled but courageous skier Jill Kinmont.

In recent years, I also have been working in movies, training or tending behind the scenes to such producers and directors as Bob Evans and John Frankenheimer and actors and actresses such as Bruce Dern, Burt Reynolds, Robert Shaw, Kris Kristofferson, and Marthe Keller. Dern is a dedicated runner, by the way, and Reynolds was a fine football player in college. Basically, however, these are average adults—splendid actors, but not true athletes. Their profession requires them to stay trim and look good, but they are no different from many of us who want this. It is just a matter of how much we want it and what we are willing to give up for it.

I have a few entertaining stories to tell about life behind the cameras. And some interesting stories to tell about life off the playing field. I think I can tell you what it is like in the locker room and on the road with great teams, and what it is like to be a trainer dealing in day-to-day routines as well as on those special days when you may hold a great competitor's career in your hands. But, far beyond that, I want to take what I have learned and try to teach you the secrets of how the superstars take care of their bodies.

I want to tell you how they train so you can condition yourself in the most professional way possible. I want to relate their routines to those you may wish to set up for yourself or your children so whatever level of physical fitness you may wish may be within your reach. I want to explain how they prepare themselves for activities so as to avoid many injuries and how they treat and deal with those injuries that do occur.

I am interested in you, whether or not you are an athlete, whether you are young or old, male or female. And I am interested in your children. I am interested in you, whether or not you wish to be an active athlete or merely someone who wishes to be in a little better shape and feel a little better. I am interested in your future, a future in which being in shape may be the most important thing you do with your life.

More than half the deaths in this country stem from heart attacks of one kind or another. Many of these can be avoided and most of them can be postponed by improved physical fitness. But I am not going to preach to you. I'll lay out the facts and let you take it from there. Four out of five men and women in this country are considered to be out of shape. How close you want to come to ideal conditioning is completely up to you.

I know what the superstars of sports do. I know what I and other trainers do to help them get in shape and stay in shape. I will pass it on to you and you will take from it what you want. You may be interested only in that section of the book that details conditioning and exercise routines. Or that part that discusses the pros and cons of walking, jogging, and running. Or those parts that discuss various sports in details. Or those parts that detail how to treat various injuries.

There are a lot of how-to books on the market today that deal with forms of physical fitness. Many of them are devoted to diet or exercises or jogging or running. Ours is intended to be more complete and deals also in areas others do not, such as the treatment of injuries. It is a general guide to good health that will be helpful to you in any of a hundred different ways, whether you just want a little information, whether you want to devote 10 minutes a day to activities or 365 days a year to sports. I am here to help, however you want to be helped.

Is there a time when a person should start physical activity and a time he should stop? Preschoolers and school-agers are naturally active, but should they be put on programs of planned activities? Should the young athlete be active beyond his sports? Should youngsters play tackle football? Or throw curve balls? Should an older person run? Should a person who has not been physically active plunge into heavy activity? Should a person past middle age jog? Or run? Should women be as active as men? Should young girls be as active as boys? Beyond the obvious, are there differences between the sexes that must be considered in planning programs of physical conditioning? As far as that goes, is sex a sport? And, aside from the obvious, how much does it help you keep physically fit?

Is work as valuable to physical conditioning as athletics? And how do the various sports we pursue compare to each other as concerns conditioning? Does a mailman or a salesman who walks door to door all day do as well physically as a golfer or a bowler? Is gardening as good as golf? Is golf as good as tennis? Is skiing as good as hiking? Should we walk, jog, or run? How far, how fast, and for how long? Is swimming as good as running? Is dancing a sport? Does dancing help our fitness?

What do we do for tennis elbow? Or golf elbow? Or bowling elbow? Or a bad back? Or shin splints? Or sore feet? Or aching muscles? What do we do for pulled muscles, jammed fingers, sprained ankles, and twisted knees? How do we treat cuts and bruises, bloody noses and black eyes? When do we use pressure bandages and when do we tape ankles? How do we tape ankles and apply bandages? When do we use heat and when do we use cold? What about massage? How can we avoid many injuries? How can we recognize serious injuries? When do we go to the doctor?

How does one warm up before physical activity and how much does one warm up? What calisthenics and exercises are best? What about those exercise aids you see advertised and can buy in stores? What about the gyms you can join and the physical culture classes you can attend? What about Jacuzzis and sauna baths?

How much sleep do we need? And do our children need? What

should we eat and drink before, after, and during activity? And at other times? What about vitamins? And other pills and supplements? How can we combine activity and diet to take off weight? Or put on weight? What about all of the things that go into an active life? How active should we be, anyway?

You decide how active you want to be. I will help you decide. And help you, whatever you decide. I am going to try to make this a simple, straightforward, and, I hope, informative and entertaining guide to athletic activity of all kinds, competitive or recreational, for the guy or gal who is interested on any level and at any age.

I am not going to get into a lot of mumbo jumbo, using scientific terms that could confuse you (I will leave that to the doctors). I am not going to tell you how to operate on yourself to correct a hernia, but I will help you *avoid* hernias. I want to stress right here and now that if you have any history of physical problems or are at the middle years, you should see your doctor for a full physical checkup before proceeding. I also want to stress that doctors do not so much prevent problems as treat those that have come up and doctors tend to discourage the sort of physical activity we encourage.

I have tried to write this book so you can take from it the information that will meet your own specific needs.

In this Foreword I have raised some questions to suggest some of the ground we will cover. I will try to answer all of these questions, and raise and answer many more. Along the way, I will tell tales of the high and the mighty that I have dealt with, and show how many of the experiences of these superstars relate to yours. They, however more gifted athletically, are really not that different from you personally. Much of what they do, you can do. Many of the problems they face, you face. What hurts them, hurts you. What helps them, helps you.

This is aimed at you, whoever you are. I hope it helps you. And entertains you.

Frank O'Neill
Los Angeles, 1979

ACKNOWLEDGMENTS

For their help in many ways, the authors wish to thank Doctors Robert Kerlan, Toby Freedman, and William Klein, as well as Jack Geyer of the Rams, Shep Goldberg, John Wolf, Mike Hope, Pete Newell, Chick Hearn, Mary Ann Carr, Mary Lou Liebick, and Joan Combs. Also, Jackie Sommers, who transcribed the tapes. And Wen Roberts and Johnny Johnson of Photography, Inc., of Inglewood, photographer Jim Walbert of Encino, along with Bob McAlindon, Bob Rigby, Doug Piper, Bob Jensen, Mike Jensen, Rich Jensen, Diane Breton, Janine Eisette, Jo Smith, Kendy Anno, Betty Liang, Jennifer Liang, Allyson Liang, Lee Ann Paris, Sharon Libby, Laurie Libby, Allyson Adler, Kelly Doran, Bridget Doran, Andrea Frankiewicz, Beverly Frankiewicz, Kelly Frankiewicz, Jerry Reynolds, and David Longino for their help with the photos. Also, photographers Robert L. Smith, Gary Ambrose, Lee Payne, sketch artist Judy Markham, and Melinda Mullin and Stan Brosette of United Artists, who provided pictures. Finally, the authors wish to thank Matt Merola of Mattgo, Inc., New York City, and Jim Menick and Harold Kuebler of Doubleday, who made the book a reality, as well as all the athletes and coaches, trainers and doctors who contributed so much over the seasons.

CONTENTS

SPORTS
CONDITIONING

1. CONDITIONING

The pursuit of physical fitness is desirable for several reasons. Most important, perhaps, we will live longer—short of being hit by a truck, of course. And we will feel better and enjoy life more for as long as we live. Even if hit by a truck, we will have a better chance of surviving. We will also have a better chance of fighting off disease.

The major causes of death in our middle years are from failures of the heart, lungs, and liver. More than half the deaths in this country come from failures of our cardiovascular system, which supplies blood to the heart, brain, and other parts of the body. Coronary heart disease is the No. 1 killer.

Seventy-five years ago, heart disease accounted for less than 15 per cent of the deaths in the United States. Today it is more than 50 per cent, partly because of better treatment of other diseases, but partly because of our softer way of life.

Of course, life isn't easy anywhere, but we have one of the softest lifestyles in the world. For all of our good life, American women rank only tenth and men only seventeenth in longevity among people of the world. By comparison with many other peoples, we are primarily spectators, and not participant athletes. We pay a price for this.

I am not trying to scare you; I'm merely laying out some odds for you. Up to the age of thirty, the odds are pretty good that you will not have a heart attack. For the next ten years, the odds drop to about thirty to one. For the ten years after that, they are cut about in half, to less than fifteen to one. For the ten years after that, they fall by about half, to eight to one.

The odds are short that you will have a heart attack after the age of sixty. But those odds are beaten all the time. If you do not have a family history of heart attacks and have had no heart problems, if you do not smoke or eat too much, or eat unwisely or take drugs, if you do not have high blood pressure or a high cholesterol count, or are not overweight and are physically fit, you lengthen all these odds. Otherwise, you shorten them.

I promised not to preach to you and I will live up to this promise. I have given you the odds; you play the game of your own life. How big a gamble you take is up to you. You have to give of yourself to get fitness. How much you give is up to you. You have to make some sacrifices. How much you are willing to give up is up to you. Anything bad you give up, anything you give to gain good, is all to the good.

You may or may not be an athlete. If you are, you can become a better one. If you are not, you can find something to do you can enjoy. Whatever you do, you can enjoy it more whether it is a game you want to play or work you want to do.

As an athletic trainer my job was to get the guys into the games. I drew lines, but I'd be lying if I said I didn't take chances with the health of my players. They *wanted* to take chances: this was their work and they were well paid to perform. Perhaps they were part of a team and owed their teammates anything they could give.

The owners, managers, and coaches always wanted them to take chances. They wanted to win. You win when your players are playing.

I never will forget when Wilt Chamberlain tore up his knee. Dr. Kerlan said he'd be ready in six months. Owner Cooke said he'd be ready in twelve weeks. Being a doctor, Kerlan was cautious. Being an owner, Cooke was anxious. Wilt was back in twelve or thirteen weeks. Being a player, he wanted to play.

Wilt was a physically conditioned athlete, in the prime of his life and stronger and more determined than two average men. Even the finest of athletes sit out games to recuperate properly and recover their conditioning. I do not expect you to push yourself past points of pain or run risks with your health. With the average person, I practice caution.

If you have any history of heart trouble or any other cardiovascular or physical problem, see your doctor before embarking on any of the programs proposed in this book. If you are past thirty or overweight, see your doctor. If you have any concern about your conditioning, I say, one last time, see your doctor.

Have your heart and blood pressure and lungs checked. Take an electrocardiagram test and a wind test. Take a treadmill test. These measure the capacity of your heart and lungs. One out of eight who had no notion of having a problem is found to have a problem.

Heed your doctor's advice. But heed this advice, too. Doctors tend to be cautious. Few practice preventive medicine. Most treat problems after they develop. Few will encourage excesses of exercise. Fear of malpractice suits stops most. They can tell you where you are and what to fear. Armed with this knowledge, you will have to decide for yourself what you want to do with yourself.

I am going to give you exercises you can do to loosen you up and build up your strength. I will deal with exercises in the next chapter. I am going to give you games to play that will improve your quickness, speed, and stamina. I will measure the value of one game against another, of one form of physical activity against another, all in later chapters. I will discuss diet in detail in a later chapter.

I will discuss different approaches to athletics and conditioning dependent on age in later chapters. Whether you are young or old, even if you are the worst athlete or the most poorly conditioned person in the world, you may still have an interest in getting into good shape. Good health is a desirable goal in itself, however you use it.

Basically, what I want to do is improve your flexibility, strength, and endurance. Along the way you can better your agility and balance, coordination and timing, quickness and speed. The end result should be not merely better performances in sports, but, using sport as a means to an end, better health and a greater feeling of well-being.

Perhaps a better understanding of the human body will be helpful.

There are more than five hundred muscles and more than two hundred bones in the human body. The bones are the basic framework of the body. Some, such as the skull, which encases the brain, and the chest and ribs, which encase the inner organs, serve primarily a protective function. Others, such as the vertebral column, which encases the spinal cord and supports the back, are both protective and supportive. Others are concerned mainly with our movements, and we are concerned mainly with these, except where in those later chapters we discuss treatment of injuries, including broken bones.

Muscles are attached to bones, connected by tendons. Muscle tissue is elastic and will lengthen and shorten. Tendons are not elastic, so are more easily torn, often away from the bone. The bones fit together at joints, bound by muscles. Muscle movement can be voluntary or involuntary, but muscles never relax completely because they are binding the body and joints together. Muscles can be built up, of course, but bones cannot. Bones do mend when cracked or broken.

The heart is a muscle, but the lungs are not. The lungs depend upon the contraction and retraction of the muscles of the rib cage and diaphragm for the capacity of air they can take in. The air we breathe contains about one fifth oxygen and about four fifths nitrogen. It is the oxygen we need. It burns up the foodstuffs we have eaten to provide fuel for the body in the form of energy.

As we inhale air into our lungs, the oxygen is removed, forced into tiny, balloonlike red blood cells, and sent through our blood stream to the heart, where it is pumped throughout our entire system to the muscles, nerves, and other tissues that feed upon it. The oxygen having been exchanged for carbon dioxide wastes, the red blood cells return through the system to the lungs, where the carbon dioxide is exhaled, and the emptied cells are ready to receive fresh supplies of oxygen to be carried back throughout the body.

This is a simplified look at a complicated process, of course, but it is as much as the average person needs to know.

One objective of exercise is to strengthen the muscles and improve their tone, but the main objective of any conditioning program is to increase the capacity of the lungs and the heart so oxygen can be fed more freely and easily throughout our system. In itself, this will improve our muscular network so we can perform physical acts more freely and easily, and such involuntary systems as our digestive system will function better.

If we do not have the proper proportion of oxygen to foodstuffs, we provoke problems. Either our body is not getting enough food and we are too thin, or it is getting too much and we are fat. Either it is not getting enough fuel and we are weak, or it is storing too much and we are lethargic.

Some foodstuffs are burned up more easily than others. Excess food fat will linger in the bloodstream, impairing its flow. That animal fat known as cholesterol will harden on the interior walls of our arteries, narrowing them so the blood flow is reduced, or blocking them so the flow is stopped. We may get that hardening of the arteries known as arteriosclerosis or that impaired flow of blood that cheats the heart and brain and develops coronary attacks or strokes.

The brain is dependent on oxygen to perform properly. The brain can be permanently damaged if deprived of oxygen for only four or five minutes. Bypass operations are done to provide an alternative to vessels to carry blood and oxygen in place of those that are blocked. It may not be true, as has been claimed in the heat of the jogging and running vogue, that new vessels are developed, but with proper diet and exercise we can make the most of those we have.

With conditioning, we can increase the capacities of our heart and lungs, of our entire vascular system. More blood can be carried to the heart and brain and throughout the body to the tissues and muscles of the body, and, with it, more oxygen to do the necessary work. Additionally, more blood can be carried on the outgoing route back to the lungs, and, with it, the carbon dioxide we do not want lingering within us, poisoning our system.

Even in well-conditioned athletes, the lungs do only about three fourths of the work they are capable of doing. In a well-conditioned athlete, the walls of the arteries are strong, the arteries are clear, and blood pressure is low. The average person has a heart rate of seventy to seventy-two. In the well-conditioned athlete it is lower. In the poorly conditioned person it is higher. A marathon runner may have reduced his to thirty-five or so. An inactive or overweight person may have permitted his to rise to one hundred or more.

There are tests you can take privately to determine how in or out of shape you are. For one thing, you can put a finger on your inner wrist and take your own pulse rate. If it is much over eighty, you need to lower it. Run in place at a pace of thirty steps to the minute and stop when it becomes a strain. Time not only the length of your run, but also check the time it takes your pulse to return to its regular rate. If you could comfortably run for less than three minutes and it took you more than half your running time to return to regularity, you have a problem.

We'll leave the charts and forms for other books. You don't have to follow a rigid schedule and keep score day after day. You know if you grow short of breath with any exertion, if your heart swiftly starts to pound when you do something strenuous. You know if you can walk briskly for a block or two without your legs starting to ache or can even run comfortably to the corner. You know if you can lift fifty pounds without straining. You know if you need exercise and you know how much you are willing to put into it and how far you are anxious to go.

Part of physical conditioning is psychosomatic. If you don't feel good, you don't think straight. It is no secret that the mental part of us plays a part in the performance of the physical part. For example, if we become nervous or frightened, our heartbeat increases and we start to sweat. A tense, worrying person can do damage to his body, developing ulcers. A relaxed person's body performs best. Exercise can be relaxing. You can develop programs of exercise that are no great strain on you.

All our muscles can be made more limber, larger, stronger. The heart is a muscle and can be built up to do more work with less effort, saving itself thousands of beats per year. The heart can wear out, although it is said we do not so much wear out as we rust out from inactivity. It is said you can't hurt a healthy heart, although you can hurt an unhealthy heart. However, the heart repairs itself. Half of those persons stricken die from the first heart attack, but those that survive often build their hearts back up to beat for twenty, thirty, forty or more years.

It is said we do not die so much as we kill ourselves. We age not only from the years, but from neglect. Some people twenty years older than we are chronologically are twenty years younger physically. We all are different, and in general age is not the critical factor in figuring out how much we want to condition ourselves. It is the years of inactivity we have behind us that are more appropriate measures of our need.

It is incorrect to assume that a youngster does not need conditioning. Merely because a boy or girl is young and healthy and active does not mean he cannot benefit from a proper program of exercise. For one, the games the youngster may be playing may not be the ones that best build up his lungs, heart, and body. For another thing, it is in the younger years that a proper program can best be established that can be continued on into adult life. Gym classes simply do not do this. Also, even with the increased emphasis on the participation of young girls in athletics, most simply are not active enough.

If you run, why not have your youngsters run with you? We know now that the capacity of youngsters for exercise is far greater than previously believed. Some youngsters of twelve and fourteen run twenty-six-mile marathons easily and swiftly.

It is incorrect to assume that because a person in his or her twenties is healthy and active that he or she does not need to establish some kind of consistent program of exercise. Again, the person may not be involved in the best activities. Again, the sooner a proper program is established, the better off the person will be in later life. Also, it is in these years and also the thirties that we are most involved in furthering our careers and more inclined to be erratic about exercise.

Physical-conditioning experts say they know when the weekend athlete will die; he will die on a weekend. It is dangerous to be underactive five days of the week and overactive two days.

Finally, it is incorrect to assume that because a person is in his forties and fifties it is too late for him to start a conditioning program. Obviously, if he has been physically inactive for ten or twenty or thirty years, he must take it slowly, building up gradually, but he can benefit from any exercises he engages in. He can never regain the years that have gone by, but he can save himself from the loss of some of the years that lay ahead. Many a man of forty or fifty has started the search for physical fitness successfully.

At fifty or sixty or, obviously, seventy, caution is advised, but if a person has no major health problems, walking or certain physical calisthenics could be beneficial.

Incidentally, when I refer to a "man" or say "he," it is for the sake of simplicity. I don't want to have to say "a man or a woman" or "he or she" every time. Almost anything I say refers to a woman as well as a man, to she as well as he. When I say, "you," I mean you, whether man or woman, he or she. We all are aware what is different about a man or a woman, a boy or a girl, about the physiological differences between the sexes, but these differences are not as drastic as had been believed, and most do not matter much as far as physical conditioning goes.

Studies show that women have a higher natural amount of fat in their body chemistry and a lower potential for muscle. Presumably, then, the male will be faster, stronger, and more agile than the female. This, however, does not apply to all males and all females.

Women have, on the average, about 25 per cent fat in their body weight, while men have only about 15 per cent. Thus women need to take off fat and build up muscle. However, the hormone testosterone, which males have and females do not, gives the male a great capacity for creating muscle. Many women athletes have taken testosterone to increase strength and performance, but have had to suffer an increase of other masculine traits as well.

The excess body fat does sometimes give women more endurance in the more grueling events such as long-distance running. Only enough energy can be stored in muscle tissue for about two hours of strenuous activity, after which we must draw on that stored in fatty tissue.

Generally, weight training is even more important to women than to men. Most women would not even think of taking up weight training, but it would be beneficial to them. There is at least a psychological difference between "weight training" and "weight lifting." In "weight training" you are interested in developing strength, while in "weight lifting" you want muscles.

You must lift enough weight to test you, but, in general, it is the rapid, repetitious lifting of this weight in the many ways you can lift weight, with your legs as well as your arms, for example, that matters more than the lifting of more and more weight each time. Women will find it tends to build long, smooth, strong muscles, rather than bulging biceps. Women will find it also tightens and slims stomach, hips, and buttocks, and does not add pounds.

To a great extent, females trail males in physical conditioning because females have had a lesser background of athletic activities. Most boys grow up playing games more than girls. This carries on to adulthood. As the recent trend toward increased emphasis on sports for girls and women accelerate, these differences will decrease, although human nature suggests that women will never be as athletically active as men. Some women will be, but not most.

However, it no longer is considered unladylike for a female to participate in sports, so many more will take part. Women not only will be playing golf and tennis, but also basketball and volleyball, for example. More and more women are running and jogging. The more they do, the better they will become.

In car racing, many women have shown they have the timing, coordination, and reflexes to compete successfully with men. Women such as Kitty O'Neill have set speed records, while Shirley Muldowney has won championships in "pure dragsters," the fastest of the specially constructed cars that compete in drag racing. Shirley, in fact, is the only woman who consistently beats the men in even open competition. She is one of the two or three best drag racers in the world, maybe the best. Janet Guthrie beats some men in car racing, but she does not beat the best or win many races against men.

The more body speed and strength enter into it, the less well women do against men. The best women golfers may be able to beat the best men on given days, but normally have to hit off the short tees even to be competitive. Bobby Riggs did not prove everything he set out to do, but I think he did prove that even a much older man can beat or play close tennis against younger women. Even lower-level male tennis pros can beat the best of the women. The women who practice with these men will tell you this themselves.

Like a man, the harder a woman goes at a game, the better she's going to be at it. The more her training is like a man's, the closer to his kind of condition she's going to reach. And if she trains harder and plays harder she's apt to be better. Maybe she can't take on a big guy at tackle football, but she might beat him at tennis or finish a long race that he does not finish.

Unless you're a pro or a highly competitive player, winning isn't where it's at, anyway. Getting in shape *is.* And having a good time.

To a great extent, health is beauty. I'm not a plastic surgeon and I can't do much about your face, but I can help your body. And if you don't have a trim, supple, strong body, other things might not matter. The times are changing, and there is nothing unladylike about walking, jogging, running, getting into weight training or calisthenics, skipping rope or swimming, golfing or playing tennis, hiking or riding a bike.

It is simply a fallacy that women can't take it or run risks with it. Although a woman's breasts need the protection of a good-fitting brassiere during running or other strenuous activities, a woman's reproductive organs are very well protected. Studies show strenuous activity does not inhibit any woman from becoming pregnant, and that well-conditioned women have fewer problems during pregnancy and childbirth, and bounce back better from both.

According to studies of the situation it also is a fallacy that women need to slow down during menopause. Active women should continue to be active, and inactive women should start to become active insofar as their age and health permit. It *is* believed that something to do with the menstrual cycle inhibits women from some heart problems because their susceptibility to these problems do increase with menopause.

We all know that on the average, women outlive men by about two years, which shows that women's basic body chemistry isn't too bad even if, in general, they do not suffer as much stress as men at work. Before the age of forty, men are twenty-five times as likely to have a heart attack, but, after forty, only five times as likely. So it is obvious that women would be wise to condition themselves for their later years.

American women have a higher rate of death from heart disease than those from any other country. Presumably this is because American women do not work as hard, but they can make up for it by playing harder.

Where exercise is concerned, women may go in for gimmicks more than men and are more apt to enroll in the neighborhood health club or gym as plugged on television. Actually, I have no objection to these, or "Y's." Most commercially manufactured strength-tension exercise devices are helpful in that they are set up so you use your energy economically instead of struggling with dead weight and they do get you to do something, preferably on a regular basis. If you do not demand miracles and limit yourself to these things, they should be beneficial to you. And, if you choose to avail yourself of such devices in the clean comfort of some fancy health facility, fine, but don't complain if your contract turns out to tie you to the place for a lot of money for a long time.

Many of these gyms may have facilities you could not otherwise use, such as a swimming pool or running track, weight-training equipment or whirlpool. I have always felt that with four basic pieces of equipment I could run efficiently any training room on an otherwise reduced budget. These are a whirlpool bath, an ultrasound unit, a hot-pack tank, and my hands.

The whirlpool bath provides a sort of warm massage with its swirling, hot waters. It works well to reduce aches and pains and promote healing.

Ultrasound provides dry heat in the manner of a massage. It is an electrical unit that looks a little like a hammer, and you rotate the head on a sore area.

Hot packs provide damp heat to a sore area. I prefer damp heat because it has superior penetration and so is more soothing, but some injuries call for dry heat.

For the most part, these pieces of equipment are useful for the treatment of injuries, as we will get into in a later chapter, but they also are helpful to ease aches and pains, especially when you are first starting a program of workouts.

A modality is a method, and we used it to describe those pieces of equipment with which we treat athletic distresses. Your hands may be the main modality of all. You have to use them well to use any of your equipment properly. And if you have nothing else, you can do a lot with your hands. In many cases, the laying on of hands can heal.

Rubdowns can be beneficial. If done right. If any of your muscles are sore, you might rub alcohol or analgesics on the affected area before going into action. Alcohol evaporates rapidly, yet is cooling and is an antiseptic and an anesthetic. Analgesics such as camphor, ethyl chloride, methol, methyl salicylate, and Ichthyol work in similar ways. All work well as a lubricant for massage. And massage will work well to relieve soreness and loosen up muscles in advance of action as well as afterward.

Never massage a recent injury. Never massage where there may be infection. Limit massage to the periphery of an injured area and wait a day or two after an injury to allow it to heal before rubbing the affected area to loosen it up. When massaging a specific area, limit it to five to ten minutes. Always use a powder or oil as a lubricant on the skin under your hands so you will not irritate the skin.

As much as possible, work in the direction of the heart. Start at one point from an injury or ache and progress to a point directly opposite the start. Do not dig deep, but use the fingers to gently lift and gather and work with the muscles. Use a pushing-pulling stroke, rather than a circular, rubbing motion. Joints should be rotated gently.

Essentially, what you want to do is stretch, loosen, and warm the muscles, and increase circulation, which does not mean you want to maul, bruise, strangle, or irritate them. Strong hands and fingers help you to do the job easier, but you do not want to show off your strength at the expense of your subject—or victim. Practice it until a partner starts to feel the benefits that stem from it. You will improve.

If you want a professional massage, go only to recognized health facilities. If you want something else, you can go to your local massage parlor. That's another book altogether.

Massage is one way of loosening up prior to athletic activity of any kind. But it should not be the only way. In the next chapter, I will describe exercises that will adequately loosen you up. Before beginning any strenuous activity, even gardening, it is wise to loosen up. Most people know this, but don't do it. Professional athletes do it, but not enough of it.

Youngsters don't do it, unless directed to. They are impatient to start their sport. They don't think they need it. They are wrong. They are inviting injury. And the older you get, the more you need it. The less active you are, the more you need it. However active you are, you need it.

Jerry West did few stretching exercises before games, refused to be taped, and suffered from more pulled muscles than any athlete I've ever known. The Laker coach and former Laker star hated to be called injury-prone, but he didn't do anything to prevent injuries and wouldn't take care of them when they happened until late in his career. He never had the time to be treated. He was perhaps the toughest patient to treat I ever had.

Del Tanner, who was the trainer of the Lakers awhile after I left, had his players go through a series of stretching movements before every game, designed to make the body more flexible and the muscles stronger and more durable. It was a strange sight to see the Lakers stretched out on the court in various contortions before every practice and game, but the players didn't suffer from thigh, hamstring, or groin pulls, except in exceptional cases, afterwards.

I wanted to introduce such sequences as a regular pregame ritual, but it is difficult to convince coaches and players that it is worthwhile to take the time and suffer the distraction. More power to Tanner, a former high-school phys-ed instructor, that he swung it. He believed correctly that it is hard to injure a flexible muscle, and he had the players hold various stretched positions for thirty seconds or more at a time. Perhaps West sees now that he could have extended his career with such routines, and he gave the go-ahead to Del. Still, few teams follow suit.

I was at Bill Shoemaker's home once when the great jockey went to play tennis with a pal. Before Shoe even took his racquet out of its cover, he spent ten minutes at calisthenics. He's a superbly conditioned athlete, but he recognized the need to loosen up prior to playing a game. On the other hand, I don't think Jerry West has touched his toes since he was a boy. And it certainly is ridiculous for the average golfer to tee off fiercely, for the average tennis player to serve strongly, for the average bowler to pick up that heavy ball and let fly without having loosened his muscles.

What does it take—three or four minutes? Six to eight minutes would be better. Take your time. Do the basic exercises I will describe. Before running, jog. Before swinging a bat or a golf club or a tennis racquet hard, swing your arms across your body and swing your weapon softly. Slowly increase the speed of your swing. Enter the tennis serve and golf swing gradually. Before throwing a ball hard, throw some soft. Start close to the catcher and gradually increase the distance. Dr. Kerlan recommends that golfers who want to avoid Monday-morning aches and pains do about ten toe-touches first. Also, rotate your body from the hips.

It is almost as important to cool down after athletic activity.

Just as a racehorse is cooled down with walking after running, you too should cool down by walking after running. After any running activity, your blood will largely have settled in your legs, and it is good to get your circulation going through your entire body again. Some even believe in doing light exercise as a way of slowing down and relaxing. Let your muscles slowly relax. Don't collapse from weariness and allow your muscles to tighten up. Force yourself to some slowed-down activity to allow your body time to adjust to reduced activity.

You should expect to feel tired after any athletic activity. If not, you haven't put much into it. But, unless you're running a distance race in the Olympics, you shouldn't go so far as to collapse at the wire. The average person should put out, but pace himself to prevent an overexertion he is not conditioned to handle. If possible, rest when tired. Many aches and pains are warnings that we are overextending muscles and are in danger of doing damage to them. We should heed these signs of danger. You should be able to build up to the point where you can go as far and hard as you want, but until then don't push yourself past points of pain. And if you don't have a fairly rapid recovery, take it as a sign that you have overdone. Roughly fifteen minutes' rest for every hour's exertion would be a reasonable recovery rate.

Seek gentle massage of sore muscles if possible. Hopefully, most of us will have husband or wife, boyfriend or girlfriend who can help us in this way. Ice any bruises, sore arms, sore elbows, sore feet, and so forth. I'm a great believer in ice after activity, and to a limited extent. I pioneered its use in athletics. Ice is immediate first aid to stop internal bleeding and reduce swelling. Today, there almost isn't a baseball pitcher who doesn't soak his arm in a tub of ice after working a game, and it helps his recovery from the exertion. I think tennis players and bowlers could benefit similarly. And although it may look like an old cartoon, runners should not be too shy to soak their feet or legs in a tub of ice after runnings. All you need is a tub or container of some kind and ice or even cold water.

Afterward, a warm shower is soothing, but it is best to keep it cool to warm, rather than hot. Sometimes it does do good to soak in a hot tub, but this is better between activities than immediately afterward. Athletes like whirlpools. This is water heated higher than one hundred degrees and circulating strongly in a tub. A Jacuzzi is a device to create strong water circulation in your own tub, developed by a man named Jacuzzi. A sauna is a steam room, similar to the old "Turkish baths" popular some years back. In some, you move between an icy bath and a hot room.

The heat in saunas or whirlpools sometimes is soothing, but sometimes too much for the skin and body to bear. In any event, don't jump right from a hot game into a hot tub or hot room. In exercise, you already have sent an increased flow of blood, rich with oxygen, pumping through your body, expanded your blood vessels, and built up your heartbeat. Unless you give your cardiovascular system time to cool off and return to normal you may be asking more of it than it can take. Wait awhile until you have cooled off to warm up in a relaxing way in a whirlpool or sauna. Do not, in any event, linger too long.

It does soothe sore muscles and aching joints and it does help rehabilitate an ailing athlete. Late in his career, the old Laker, old "aches and pains," Elgin Baylor, spent so much time in our whirlpool, soaking his sore knees, legs, and feet, that we nicknamed our tub the S.S. *Baylor*.

Which reminds me of the time when Baylor roomed with Jim "Bad News" Barnes. One afternoon, before a game, Baylor walked into his hotel bathroom to find it full of steam. He searched through the steam until he found News deep in a tub of hot water. Asked what the hell he was doing, News said, "I got to get loose for the game." Elgin said, "You'll weaken yourself, dummy. You'll get so loose you'll come apart on court." He walked out to the other room and heard the tub draining. Then he heard water filling it up again. Walking back in, he found News sitting in a tub of cold water. Asked what the hell he was doing now, News said, "I felt too loose. I got to tighten myself up."

When you shower, wash and dry yourself thoroughly and throw your athletic togs in the hamper to be washed. We sweat not only to cool our bodies but also to get rid of poisons. Cleanliness is not only next to godliness, it is a good way to avoid infections. Frequently we may suffer small cuts or breaks in the skin in our athletic battles. We may blister. We'll deal with all this in the later chapter on the care of injuries, but it is clear that cleanliness is the first step toward avoiding sores of different sorts.

In professional and top-level collegiate sports, each player usually is provided four sets of uniforms—home and away, game and practice uniforms—each season. The equipment man or trainer has to see that these uniforms are washed and dried between sessions and mended or repaired as needed. You do not have an equipment man or trainer, so it is up to you. It is not a small matter. Take, for example, the Little League or Bobby Sox team your son or daughter may play on, or the high school team that may not have the help or facilities it needs. Someone has to see that the uniforms, underwear, athletic supporters, etc., are kept clean and in good shape, and that someone may be you.

Protective pads have to be provided and fit to the players, of course. Where youngsters' athletics are concerned, it may be up to you to see that your child's gear is right. A poorly fit pad may not provide the protection desired and may do more harm than good. Football players use by far the most specialized protective gear, but hockey players use a lot, too, and baseball players use some, such as sliding pads. A basketball player may use elbow or knee pads, but that is nothing compared to the shoulder pads, hip pads, leg pads, and so forth the football player uses. The average recreational athlete may not need much in the way of protective padding, but some do.

Helmets have to be fitted to those who use them. Football players use them, of course. More and more hockey players are using them; almost all hockey players on the youth level are using them. Baseball players use helmets, when batting or running the bases. Baseball catchers use masks, and a new and handy device that has been developed is a sort of flap that hangs along the neckline and provides protection to the neck and Adam's apple. Goaltenders in hockey use masks, and many use this device now, too.

If a sport calls for pads, helmet, mask, use them. Many youngsters will avoid some of these because they may be uncomfortable, so it is up to you to see that they use them.

Take the time and trouble to find the equipment that is right for you. Get a bicycle with a seat and handlebars that fit you. Get a tennis racquet with the right balance and weight for your swing and strength. Get the golf clubs that feel right to you. Don't blame bad scores on the clubs, regularly replacing them in search of some magic wands. I have had golf-shop pros tell me that some players have traded in so many old sets for new ones, and picked up so many used sets, that they eventually have had their original sets sold back to them without their knowing it. Get good clubs in the first place. Get a bowling ball that is the right weight for you, drilled for your hands and your fingers. Get booted skis fit to you. Get good equipment.

Hockey and baseball players pick out their own gloves, generally. Hockey players pick out their own sticks and baseball players their own bats, and as a rule they work on these themselves. Trainers do most of the sharpening of ice skates, and it is important that these are sharpened properly and have protective cups at the ends to prevent the injuring of others. You're allowed to do quite a bit to a hockey stick as far as taping the handle and shaping the blade goes. You can't do too much to a bat, which is not to say that players don't try. In basketball, you only have to be sure that the balls are pumped up and round. In baseball, you throw the balls out there and the pitchers throw them back to you. Every ball seems to feel different. In hockey, you have to freeze the pucks or they won't slide right.

Details, details, details, from athletic supporters to sunglasses.

Wilt Chamberlain liked sweat bands, not only on his wrists but also on his head, as tennis players wear them. I had some designed for him in stretchy, towel-like material. They did the job, a lot of players copied them, and the Lakers made some money selling them to fans who wanted to wear them. Sometimes you can provide a player with some special piece of equipment that fills a need for him. A sponge used in a catcher's glove may take the sting out of the pitcher's pitches, for example. Jerry West broke his nose nine or ten times, and I devised a face guard he could wear while continuing to play. Kareem Abdul-Jabbar has been poked in the eyes so often he wears goggles when he plays.

In general, wear clothes appropriate to your sport, not too many clothes and not too few. Wear loose and comfortable clothing of a porous material that "breathes" and permits the flow of air. Do not wear rubber or plastic clothing, even to try to sweat off weight. These slow the evaporation of sweat, which you need to maintain a proper body temperature. And they can increase body heat to a dangerous extreme. Wear cotton underclothes, which breathe and absorb sweat. Do not wear synthetic fabrics, which may irritate your skin and sexual organs. Women sometimes suffer irritations of their vaginas from such fabrics. Women should wear cotton bras to prevent irritation of and provide support for their breasts. Men and boys should wear supporters and, if needed, protective cups, and care should be taken that the cups can be fit properly into the supporters. The proper size often is not provided for youngsters, and sometimes these supporters must be altered to carry the cups properly.

The single most important part of your clothing is your shoes. Different types of shoes now are provided for different types of activities, and you should take advantage of this. The day of making do with any old shoe or the good old "tenny" is done. While you do not need to pay a lot of attention to the advertising claims of commercial manufacturers, you can take advantage of the competitive situation that has developed and that resulted in specially designed footwear for your sports. Do not let your child make do with old, out-of-shape shoes. New shoes are not cheap, but the benefits are well worth the expense. Spend less on fancy uniforms and more on proper footwear.

Do not pay a lot of attention to the top of the shoe other than to see that it fits the top of your foot properly. It doesn't matter how fancy it is. All it is there for is to keep the shoe on your foot. The sole is the important part. Be sure it is cushioned throughout. The cushion should be soft, but not too soft; thick, but not too thick. If the sole is too soft or too thick it will not absorb the shock properly and will cause your foot to twist and wobble.

A shoe should have a good arch support that is not too far forward. If you normally wear inner soles, the size of your shoes should permit the insertion of these. The heels should be built up a bit. Broken-down arch supports and run-down heels create trouble for your legs and feet. Women who wear high heels commonly have problems adjusting to flatter sports shoes and must expect some soreness in their legs from them. High heels or clogs of any kind are unhealthy for feet and legs.

Don't hesitate to twist, bend, or squeeze an athletic shoe you are examining to make sure it is well built and flexible. You are going to give it punishment and it has to be sturdy enough and sewn well enough to take it. The front portion should be especially flexible to accommodate the bend of your foot when you run. The back part can be a bit stiffer.

Adidas makes more than a hundred different types of sports shoes. Puma also makes a great many. These are popular imports, but there are others. Many American manufacturers are making similar shoes. In many cases they are made to look like the more popular imports. Be selective. You have a wide variety of types from which to choose.

The single most important factor in the selection of shoes is that they should fit properly. This must be done by each person for himself. The shoe should feel comfortable. Normally, the lighter the shoe, the more comfortable it will feel. Most sports shoes are built light. And remember that you have to move around in them. If they are heavy they will help wear you out. However, also remember that heavier shoes often stand up to punishment better and last longer. Also, they often provide superior protection for your foot. The shoe should fit the sport and provide the protection needed in that sport. Hikers, for example, want shoes heavy enough to protect them from the rough ground on which they are worn. In any event, you don't want to play golf in tennis shoes, or tennis in golf shoes. You wouldn't run in basketball shoes or play basketball in running shoes. Or you shouldn't, anyway. If you want a high shoe that provides protection to your ankles when playing basketball, for example, by all means buy that kind. You wouldn't ski in low-cut boots, would you? And definitely do not let your youngster use hand-me-down basketball or baseball or football shoes. If the team does not provide for them, you should provide new ones.

Pay less attention to the listed size of the shoe than to the actual fit. Shoe sizes sometimes vary from manufacturer to manufacturer, especially in the foreign makes. The shoe must fit *your* foot. Or, rather, the shoes must fit *your feet.* Try both shoes on. One foot is always larger than the other. And try them on with sweat or other cotton socks. Everyone does not wear socks, especially runners, but they should. Your feet should feel neither cramped nor loose. And feel for ridges or seams that could cause irritation. Wearing them, lace them snug, bottom to top.

Don't go with the "in" shoe, but the shoe your feet fit. And as the shoes wear out or stretch and lose their effectiveness, go to the expense of replacing them. Jerry West and Elgin Baylor wore out ten to fifteen pairs of basketball shoes a season.

Your legs in general and your feet in particular are the bases of your effectiveness in any sport or athletic activity. Part of the purpose of calisthenics is to make your legs limber and strong. There really are few sports that do not require running of some sort and, of course, walking or running is the basic sport. If your legs or feet get tired or start to ache, get off them. You have to build up to the point to where you can continue without undue weariness or any pain. But if such problems persist, try checking your shoes to be sure they fit properly and provide the proper support.

I have said that you should not be too proud to rest if possible during strenuous activity so as to regain your strength and energy. Some people benefit from naps during the day. If you're one, fine. Normally, they're not necessary, but some people prefer to nap more and sleep less. Although studies show eight hours really is a good average amount of sleep for an adult, some do well with less and some feel the need for more, and there are no rules. We all are different. The key is whether or not you fall asleep fast, sleep soundly, and wake up refreshed. If you have trouble falling asleep or wake up feeling groggy or sluggish, you either are not getting enough sleep or good enough sleep. The quality of your sleep is more important than the quantity. If you sleep restlessly or suffer from some form of insomnia, if you have the kind of dreams that destroy sleep, you may have psychological problems that call for the advice of a psychiatrist, not a trainer.

Studies show that active people tend to sleep better, and benefit more from the sleep they get. If you get into a program of exercise, you will find you sleep better and are more alert all day. It is important to groove your body into a routine if possible so you sleep at the same time every day or, preferably, night. It is helpful if you wear such sleep clothing as is comfortable for you, but are not overdressed for bed and do not have too many heavy blankets or too-hot blankets, in the case of electrical blankets, over you. You should be warm enough to be comfortable, but not so hot as to sweat. You should be cooled by fresh air from a window if possible, but not so cold as to be inviting trouble from wintry winds blowing into your bedroom.

A lot of professional athletes can sleep anywhere. They have to travel a lot, often at odd hours, and catch their rest where they can, which may be in airport waiting rooms or airplanes. Wilt Chamberlain always insisted on having the front aisle seat on airplanes. He'd stick out his long legs and go to sleep. Since this seat often was in front of the rest room, he often blocked others from using these facilities. Since he was as big as he was, players and other passengers sometimes hesitated to awaken him. Often I was asked to awaken him. Usually, I told the poor person he simply had to suffer. Wilt did not like to be awakened, although fans frequently did so in search of autographs they'd never get. The rudeness of fans sometimes is unbelievable. And the anger of a Wilt sometimes is startling.

One of my problems in basketball was making sure the hotels in which we stayed had big enough beds for these guys. One time at the Marriott Essex House in New York, a manager gave me such a palatial suite I was suddenly suspicious. It turned out he wanted me to talk Wilt into taking some publicity pictures in a specially constructed ten-foot bed they had installed. I warned him that Wilt didn't go for such gimmicks, especially for free, but he prevailed on me to ask. I went to Wilt and said, "Hey, big fella, you got a big bed, right?" He said that was so, suspiciously. He asked why I asked. I said the hotel wanted to take some publicity pictures of him with the bed. He asked how much they'd pay. I said nothing, so far as I knew. He said that then he wouldn't do it, so far as he knew.

Five minutes after we returned to the hotel, my phone rang and Wilt was howling. He told me he had walked into a room full of floodlights and photographers. He said he was furious with me for giving permission. I said I hadn't and would take care of it. He said he already had. "I threw them out of here," he said. And he went to sleep in his ten-foot bed.

Speaking of bed, by the way, I do not believe, as some do, especially in boxing, that sex spoils your athletic ability. It can be tiring, so I do not recommend it an hour before pursuing other sports, but I have known athletes who handled this well. It is at worst an entertaining exercise of sorts all by itself. Even heart patients are seldom forbidden it. The fact is that a fit person probably performs better in bed than one who is not. He has the energy and enthusiasm for it. Wilt, for one, will tell you this.

I often have wondered why basketball and hockey players did not practice at night since they play at night. It probably would be beneficial to them to groove their routines in this way, but they do not want to surrender their free nights. However, most of us can groove our routines in this way, and it is beneficial to the body to do the same things at the same times each day and night as much as possible. If, for example, you run every morning at seven or every evening at seven, the body is ready to run at these times. If you run or do whatever you want to do only when you feel like it, you'll find a variety of excuses for skipping it.

It is easy to say it's too hot or too cold. The weather shouldn't matter that much. There may be times when it *is* too hot or too cold to do your thing comfortably, but these will be rare. There is some danger in strenuous exercise during a heat wave, for example, but the key is in doing less, not in doing without. Do not perform to points of exhaustion, but you must push yourself to extents that will benefit you, especially when you are beginning a program of activities that are bound to produce aches and pains. Dress to suit the weather. If it is freezing out, bundle up a bit. You have adapted the rest of your life to the area and climate in which you live; adapt your activities, too. If you have to seek indoor activities through northern winters, do so. But be consistent for months at a time.

I have found it is helpful to have a partner if possible. In most sports you cannot compete without one or more, of course. You can run alone, and if you don't mind the loneliness, this is good because you are not dependent on another person's whims or abilities. But if you can find someone who is at your level and has your interests in exercise, it is beneficial to have a buddy to share the experience. You can encourage one another. But whether on your own or with others, it is of value to you to do something with your body that will benefit it. You will do that if you develop a regular program that you can stick to and not duck out on.

It is important to develop a program that gets you into some activities every day or every other day, not just once a week or on weekends. Remember! The weekend athlete dies on the weekend. The body suffers from stresses imposed on it by five or six days of inactivity and one or two days of activity. Perhaps you can't play tennis every day, but you can do calisthenics, walk, jog, or run at least every other day.

You can put as much time to it as you want. Up to a point, the more the better, but any amount will help. The day has 24 hours in it, the week 168 hours. Hopefully you can afford 30 minutes or more a day, 4 to 8 hours a week to making fit this container we live in and carry around with us.

2. EXERCISES

The closest we come to weightlessness, short of being an astronaut on a flight into outer space, is to lie face down and dangle in a pool of water. Even then, as relaxed as we may seem to be, some of our muscles are at some level of tension. As I have said, the muscles bind the body together and never are relaxed completely. Lying down, sitting down, or standing up, our muscles are at various levels of tension. They are not working the way they would be if we were active. Working them through activity stretches and strengthens them. The more limber we are, the stronger our muscles, the better we are able to perform those actions we want to perform. We even improve our posture.

Physical fitness is a lot of things. It is the ability of our body to perform as close to its peak as possible. It is not only inner performance but outer performance as well, our appearance as well as our real condition. It is the health that helps us to resist or overcome injury, infection, and disease. It is the lack of excess weight, and the presence of flexibility, agility, speed, strength, and endurance that helps us do well our daily tasks. The present trend tends to favor running over all other forms of physical activity because it benefits our heart and lungs and lessens our susceptibility to cardiovascular problems. This is as it should be, the first consideration in conditioning our bodies. But other activities benefit us in other ways and should be considered in any conditioning program.

The trend away from calisthenics is regrettable, not only because some of these, too, contribute to a better cardiovascular performance, but also because they loosen us up and enable us to function more freely and avoid active or athletic injuries, strengthen our muscles, and build up our endurance. And it is not a minor consideration that calisthenics are more easily and quickly done than other activities, can be better fit into our daily lives, and thus can be more regularly followed. I think they have an important place in any physical fitness program. They will not only help to condition you, but also they will help keep you in condition.

Whatever running does, and it does a great deal for us, it does little for our upper bodies. Calisthenics can be aimed not only at toning up the body in general, but also specific parts of the body in particular, such as the arms and legs, shoulders and groin, breasts and buttocks. And a weight-training program can be aimed at not only upper and lower body strength, but also our physical speed and endurance. All of which will help us play our games easier and better. And enjoy them more.

Everyone should do some walking or running, but everyone won't. Climbing stairs, gardening, even dancing is exercise. Some prefer to play tennis or bowl or ski. There is running in most games, which the pure runners refuse to recognize. Although a lot of people are running these days, there is more companionship and socializing in other sports, which many people like, and which is apt to keep them active. And a greater element of competition, which some people need. Few runners race, but tennis players play one another, for example. A score is kept. Sure, runners can time themselves, but an end result is more readily recognized in other sports, and some people need this. They are not satisfied with running longer, faster than last week or last month, even if it is a truer index of their performance.

Anything that gets people active and keeps their interest up is all to the good.

There are a few organizations around the country, such as the National Athletic Health Institute in Inglewood, California, at which a person can be tested for his personal physical fitness and put on a specific program. He is given an electrocardiograph test of his heart and a blood-pressure test, plus a cardiopulmonary examination of his vital organs in the area of his heart and lungs. He is subjected to a series of exercises that test his lung capacity, body strength, and flexibility. He is subjected to walking a treadmill test that determines the speed, degree of grade, and distance he can handle. And finally, he takes a tub test that determines the proportion of fat on his frame. He is graded, and from this a program of diet and exercise can be laid out for him. Dr. Robert Kerlan, a prime mover in the organization, says, "It is more specific and complete than the average medical exam." However, it costs $330.

It is safe to assume that most of you need exercise to improve your fitness, and your reaction to exercise will reveal how much you need it. Gus Hoefling, a training specialist who worked with the Eagles and now works with the Phillies, has devised an interesting program that stresses stretching exercises and calisthenics. He says, "What we're aiming for is a full range of body motion. Strength creates motion, flexibility permits it." He puts Steve Carlton through a series of exercises that takes his heart to 210 beats a minute and holds it there for 10 minutes. He says, "With the average person, that would be hyperventilation, but with a Carlton, that is his capacity. I love to see the human body perform to its maximum." Carlton says, "I have regained suppleness I was losing. I can now bend my hand twice as far backward as before. It stands to reason the more limber your wrist, the more snap to your pitch. It used to be that in the late innings my legs would get shaky and I'd be gasping for breath and wondering where I'd get the strength for the next pitch. Now I feel I can pitch a game and a half easily. It has improved my performance and prolonged my career."

Bob Boone, the catcher, is another who swears by the trainer's teaching. "Crouching 9 innings a game, 150 games a year, 10 years or so has to take a lot out of you and your legs," Boone observes, "but with Hoefling's exercises I can handle it and have a lot left over to give." Hoefling points out proudly that Boone recently did 1,100 situps in 37 minutes. Hoefling's program stresses stretching and calisthenics. He is not a believer in weight training. Doc Eberhardt of the Cardinals is another who stresses stretching and calisthenics, conducted in conjunction with a running program. He believes that by getting the great Stan Musial into a gym 5 days a week near the end of his career he stretched

Stan's career 4 years, and feels he has cut Cardinal muscle pulls 30 per cent over the years.

Others believe also in weight training. The Vikings are the only big-time pro or college football team without a weight-training room. More and more baseball teams are turning to it, too. Dr. Ellington Darden, director of research of Nautilus Sports and Medical Industries in Chicago, put third-baseman Eric Soderholm on the Nautilus machine to develop his neck, torso, legs, and arms, and he developed from a mediocrity into a star, maybe the strongest man in the majors. "Weight training turned the trick," says Soderholm. "And instead of making me musclebound, it gave me a full range of motion." Tennis star Dianne Fromholtz says, "One of the reasons we lady players hit the ball harder than we used to is weight training, and instead of slowing us down it's speeded us up. I have a barbell with a twenty-pound weight on it and I use it to strengthen my arms, back, stomach, and legs. Lots of ladies are doing it. It's a trend in tennis."

And it isn't just for the athletes. Illinois Governor James Thompson, a hefty man in his forties, works out three times a week at the Nautilus health club in Springfield. He says, "My job is a man-killer. You can absorb only so many budget-meetings and job-seekers without saying, 'I've got to do something where I don't have to think.' After an hour in the gym, I'm not only stronger, refreshed, and more limber, but I can go back to work in the evening and tackle three more hours of budgets with a clear head." If it will work for professional athletes, politicians, and more busy businessmen than I can name, it will help you, whether salesman, desk jockey, or housewife.

Here, in this chapter, we are concerned with the specific exercises of calisthenics and weight training, those conditioning programs that are of value all by themselves and contribute so much to our ability to handle other activities. Some of the exercises are designed to improve flexibility so we can move our joints through their normal range of motion. Others are designed to increase our speed and strength and endurance. Although few will burn up many calories, all will work in conjunction with a proper diet to slim us down if we are fat and build us up if we are skinny.

Some do not require a lot of effort, but all require some degree, and some are strenuous. You can select from them those you want to do, but the more you do, the better off you will be. You can give it no more than five minutes a day, but ten to twenty minutes would be better, and thirty minutes better yet. Five minutes will be plenty for those that are designed to loosen you up for some other activity.

If you do not do any other activities from day to day, these exercises should be done every day. Research shows that it takes only about seventy-two hours to lose what we have gained when we are inactive after activity, which makes for a lot of wasted effort. And you do have to put effort into it. You have to subject your body to stress or it will not improve to where it can handle this stress comfortably. You then have to subject it to increased stress. If you are too comfortable, your body isn't being built up.

The exercises are not hard to do. You don't have to be a gymnast to do them. You probably won't be able to do them well or fully at first, but you will be after a while. You just have to do them, whether you are tired or not. They are not tiring. They are designed so if you do them you will not feel tired all the time. After doing them a few days you will begin to feel better. After a few weeks you should find them refreshing. Runners speak a great deal about the joy of running. There is joy in anything we enjoy doing. I doubt that doing these exercises will be a joyous experience for you, but if they make you feel better and make you better able to get through your workday there will be joy in that.

Most of these exercises are designed to be done slowly. Don't race through them just to be through with them. Do them at a slow, level pace. Don't see how many you can do. Do the amounts suggested and increase the number as suggested. Do them before breakfast or at midday or before dinner or at day's end, but don't do them less than an hour after eating a major meal so you can complete basic digestion. Do them at home or at the office. Do them with friends or alone. Do them in front of the television set, if that makes it more enjoyable for you. But do them.

I will divide them into slow and fast exercises and into the up and the down positions. I give them the names by which I know them. You may know them by other names. It is the exercise, not the name, that matters.

THE SLOW EXERCISES

The Up Position.

1. The shakes: Simply stretch your arms horizontally and shake them to loosen the muscles and promote circulation. Wind them in small and then large circular motions. Shake and wind your hands, wrists, arms. This is an especially good loosening-up routine prior to playing golf, tennis, or such games. In fact, it is a good idea to swing your arms as you will in your golf stroke, or forehand and backhand as you will in your tennis stroke, both with and without your racquet or club.

2. The stretch: Stand on the tips of your toes and reach for the sky, stretching upward with every muscle as far as you can, aware of the stretching of your fingers, hands, wrists, arms, torso, and legs. Again, a good warmup for tennis or golf. You can prepare for tennis by reaching up into the peak of the serving stroke, stretching those back and shoulder muscles that will be involved. Then repeat the original stretch, leaning slightly backward, stretching your back and neck muscles. Do each about three times and hold each about five seconds.

3. The twist: Stand with feet slightly apart, and your hands at your side. Drop your chin to your chest and hold it there. Keeping your chin down, twist to the right shoulder and hold, then to the left shoulder and hold. Lean your head back as far as you can and hold, then twist to the right shoulder and hold and to the left shoulder and hold. Then, raising and bending your arms so your fingers are touching in front of you, twist from the waist as far as you can to the right, then to the left, holding each briefly, stretching the spine and side muscles. Then, hands locked behind your head, rotate as far as you can from the waist forward, right side, back, left side, returning to the front. Finally, repeat with hands on hips. These are basic stretching exercises designed to increase your spinal power and muscle flexibility for golf and tennis strokes, as well as for baseball, softball, etc.

4. The forward bends: Standing with feet slightly apart and knees locked, lean forward, hands and head dangling down, as far as you can comfortably. Hang there for ten seconds, but do not force yourself farther than comfortable, and beware of dizziness as your blood settles in your head. Then, standing erect with feet at shoulder width, knees slightly bent, reach down with your right hand and try to touch your left toes twice, then with your left hand try to touch your right toes twice, then alternate in rhythm —left, right, left, right. Return to original position, spread legs, and bend over trying to touch the floor between your feet with the palms of both hands. These exercises loosen the muscles of your lower back and the backs of your legs.

5. Leg pull: Spreading your legs as far as you can comfortably, bend your right leg and put your weight to the right over that leg, stretching the left thigh muscles. Repeat the left, stretching the right muscles. Repeat each twice.

6. Knee pull: Feet comfortably close, bend and raise your right leg, lock your arms around it, and pull it as close as possible to your chest. Repeat with the left leg. This flexes the knee, but not as severely as in deep knee bends or duck walking, which I consider dangerously traumatic to a delicate joint.

7. Achilles stretch: Stand with your right leg a long step and directly in front of your left leg, both pointed directly ahead, and, without raising your left heel, lean forward by bending your right knee, stretching the muscles and Achilles tendon of your left leg. Repeat with left leg in front.

8. Achilles walk: Barefooted or, possibly, in stocking feet, curl your toes over a pencil and walk while retaining the pencil, strengthening the muscles of your feet and also the Achilles tendon. Also walk around on your heels, without a pencil.

9. Pullups: If there is a sturdy, secure bar available, wrap your hands around it at shoulder width, palms up, and try to pull up your body weight until your chin is higher than the bar. Try to do it slowly, but do not hang there. If possible, a partner with his hands at your waist can prevent you from dropping down too hard. Do only what you can do, but as your strength increases, your ability to perform this exercise will increase.

The Down Position

10. Raises: Lying down, place your hands to your side, elbows bent, palms down, and slowly raise yourself until you are executing a half circle. Hold briefly, then repeat. Lying down, knees bent up to a "V," arms at side, palms down, raise your hips as high as possible, bringing your lower back up, but keeping your shoulders down. Lower and raise, lower and raise, slowly. This strengthens your abdomen, back, buttocks, and thighs.

11. Shoulder stands: Lying on your back, arms at your side, hands under your hips, legs straight, raise your legs from the waist, helping with your hands under your hips, until your legs are directly overhead and you are, in a sense, standing on your shoulders. Then bring your legs back over your face as far as possible until your toes are pointed in the opposite direction. Eventually, you may be able to touch your toes to the floor behind your back.

Returning to the legs-up position, supporting yourself with your hands under your hips, begin to pedal with your feet as though on a bicycle, but upside down. Pedal slowly but steadily. Continue for about thirty seconds.

All of this will add to the flexibility of your torso and legs.

12. Leg lifts: From flat on your back, arms and hands flat to the floor, legs together, raise first your right, then your left leg to eighteen inches off the floor, return, raise again, one-two, as many times as you can without undue exertion. Keep your legs straight, toes pointed upward. Then raise both legs together—one, two. Then, holding your legs up, alternate kicking them, as though swimming. Then turn on your right side, left leg lying on your right leg, and lift your left leg one foot to eighteen inches, return, and raise again. Repeat lying on your left side, lifting your right leg.

Roll over onto your stomach, hands down and tight to your side, and raise your legs, then your head and upper torso, then both at the same time, holding, almost in a rocking position. Then raise your legs and kick them alternately in a swimming motion. Return to your back and lift your legs straight overhead, bend at the knees, and draw your bent legs back over your chest and face, and hold. Do these "holds" about five seconds each. This strengthens leg, groin, and torso muscles.

13. Hip roll: Lying on your back, bring your knees up to the "V" position. Spread your arms wide, at right angles to your body. From the waist, roll your hips until the points touch the floor to the right, then to the left, and continue in slow, rhythmic motion about five times to each side.

14. Situps: From flat on your back, raise yourself from the hips until you are sitting straight up. Do it first with the knees up, bent into a "V," then with your legs straight. Keep your feet flat on the floor. It may help to hook your feet under some sturdy piece of furniture or to have someone hold down your ankles. Do these with your hands clasped behind your head. Do these as many times as you can without undue strain. While in the up position you also can bend forward from the waist and twist, touching your left elbow to your right knee, then your right elbow to your left knee. This stretches and strengthens groin, back, and leg muscles.

15. Sit stretch: Sit with your knees bent and extended in opposite "Vs" and press the soles of your feet together. Lean forward, grasping your ankles with your hands, resting your elbows on the insides of your knees. With your elbows try to push your knees down to the floor, but do not exert excess pressure. Hold the position for about ten seconds. This stretches your leg muscles.

16. Sit reach: Sitting with your legs about a foot apart and stretched straight in front of you, knees locked, lean forward and reach as far as you can alongside your legs, striving to grasp your ankles or even the soles of your feet with your hands, bending your head between your legs. Go as far as you can and hold about ten seconds. This can also be done with a partner, facing one another, soles of your feet pressed together, holding hands, and pulling with reasonable exertion to stretch each other's back and leg muscles.

17. Hurdler's stretch: Bending your right leg at the knee as far behind you as you can, lean and reach as far to the left as you can, striving to grasp your left leg at the ankle or foot. Go as far as you can and hold for about ten seconds. Then repeat to the other side, holding another ten seconds. This stretches back, shoulder, and leg muscles.

18. Sprinter's stretch: Assume the starting position of a sprinter, leaning forward onto the fingers of your hands with your hands at shoulder width and alongside each other, with one leg pulled forward and bent under you and the other stretched straight back, toes down. Stretch forward with your upper body as far as you can. Do it with the right leg in front, then the left leg. In each position, also first push the rear heel down as far as you can to increase tension on your hamstring muscles, then turn your rear foot face down and push your ankle down as far as you can to increase tension on your shin muscles. These maneuvers stretch and strengthen the muscles all along your legs, ankles, and feet.

19. Pushups: From a face-down, prone position, bend your arms at the elbows and place palms down on the floor at your shoulders and try to push your upper body up until your arms are straight. Your upper body must be kept straight. But you can start with a knees-bent position, rising beyond your knees, before progressing to a knees-locked, leg-straight position. Do as many as you can. Many cannot do any. It is not easy. But it builds up arm, shoulder, and chest muscles.

THE FAST EXERCISES

20. Straddle hop: From an erect position, feet together, jump to a position in which your legs are wide apart, swinging your arms overhead to clap your hands with each spread, returning your hands to your side as you bring your feet back together again. Repeat ten times at a brisk pace. Loosens and builds.

21. Running in place: From an erect position, arms bent and held loosely at your sides, start to walk, then pick up the pace until you are running in place, bringing your knees high at a brisk but steady tempo, sixty steps to the minute for about two to three minutes. This will do for you much of what regular running will do, but it is jarring to the joints, monotonous, and does not make the demands on your body that running over irregular surfaces makes.

22. Stepups: There is no better running exercise than running up and down flights of stairs, although the downward run can be dangerous if done too swiftly over too steep a set of stairs. For

years, football coaches have conditioned their athletes by having them run up and down stadium steps. This can be approximated at home by running up and down a stairway. It also can be done virtually in place by standing in front of a stairway and stepping up and down the first and second stair, first with the right foot, then with the left foot as you come down with the right foot, then with the right foot as come back down with the left foot, and so forth. It can also be done with a strong, stationary stool or bench about twelve to eighteen inches high, but this must be fixed in place so you will not shove it out from under you.

23. Skipping rope: This is not only a good general exercise, which gets the blood circulating strongly throughout the body, but it is also terrific for your timing and coordination. You may not have done it for a while. If you are male, you may not have done it ever. It will take time to get good at it. Give it time. When you can get that rope slapping ground about thirty beats to the minute for about three minutes, you've got something.

As with running in place, this can be jarring to the joints, so jump up and down on the balls of your feet with your knees slightly bent to absorb some of the shock.

Currently, jumping rope seems to be coming into popularity. Sporting goods stores are selling fancy ropes for from five dollars to fifteen dollars, and selling out. Two out of three customers are women. Most of the women are aged twenty-eight to forty. But there is no reason we all cannot benefit from it.

Bobby Hinds, a former athlete, dropped the insurance business to sell jump ropes after he successfully recovered from a leg injury by skipping. "The beauty of it," he says, "is you can do it anywhere, indoors or out, and it is especially handy in the North and East during winter weather that tends to keep you indoors. In only ten minutes, you can have the same cardiovascular effect as if you jogged thirty minutes. And, done properly, it is less stressful than running. You move your feet only about a quarter inch off the ground."

Dr. Fred Kasch of the San Diego exercise laboratory disagrees to some extent. He says it is an aerobic or oxygen-demanding exercise and his studies showed the amount of energy expended by a person jumping rope is no more nor less than by a jogger. He claims that the energy needed to effectively twirl a rope any length of time may be more than some have to give.

He also suggests that anyone who may have joint, bone, or back problems should beware because of the shock to which jumping subjects the individual. Gary Scherer, director of the National Athletic Health Institute, says, "All weight-bearing exercises done in place produce some shock and trauma. By adding forward movement, you minimize stress. Thus, jogging or running is less stressful than skipping rope or running in place."

However, ropes are an inexpensive item that can be carried on your travels and used anywhere, and, if used with soft shoes on a soft surface, can give you excellent exercise.

24. Stationary bicycling: If you can get to some sort of stationary bike apparatus, this is splendid indoor exercise. Many who can afford it buy a unit, place it in front of a television set, and mix the business of fitness with pleasure. Others use a gym unit. In any event, pedal briskly, extending yourself ten to fifteen minutes at a time.

25. Stationary rowing: Again, if you can get to a stationary apparatus, this is splendid exercise, especially for the back, but it is not recommended to anyone with a back problem. It is strenuous, so limit yourself to five minutes, at first, anyway.

GYMNASTICS

Gymnastics is something the average person does not pursue, although it has great value as a general conditioner.

More and more young people are getting into gymnastics, especially young girls, following the widely televised and publicized Olympic success of such attractive teen-agers as first Olga Korbut and then Nadia Comaneci. When a young man bursts similarly into superstardom (and a few, such as the American Kurt Thomas, may be on the verge of doing this), more boys no doubt will get into the act.

Gymnastics is superb exercise for young and old alike. Many of its routines are similar to calisthenics and develop the flexibility of the body to a great extent. Others, such as front and back walkovers and the work on the uneven bars and rings, require great timing and exceptional strength. Most routines require balance. If you just do some of the tumbles and cartwheels, headstands and handstands, you will be helping yourself a great deal. We all know how to do these. Doing them is something else. All of these should be performed on a firm but not hard mat.

The front tumble is basic. You place your hands flat in front of you, lower your head, and roll. However, it will take time to execute this in good form—legs tight together and tucked in neatly—and finish on your feet.

The backward roll is more difficult. You start from a seated position, legs straight in front of you. Bend forward, pressing the palms of your hands flat by your hips, push down hard to provide force, and roll backward, providing added impetus by bringing your knees up to your chest, replacing your hands—bent backward—at your neck and pushing down hard again. It will take time to roll all the way over, to roll over straight and tight, and to come to a formal finish, moving from a crouch to an erect position.

To do a cartwheel to the right, stand with your right side to the mat and execute a sideways roll on the palms of your hands, pushing off on your right foot as you kick up with and swing your left leg directly over your head, and as you place first your right palm, then your left firmly on the mat. Formfully, you will perform a tight maneuver in which you describe a perfect circle with straight legs and come to a standing position directly opposite the takeoff spot. To do one to the left, simply reverse these directions.

The secret to many maneuvers such as this one is courage. It takes courage to throw yourself into these with sufficient force to execute them in one continuous motion. If you hesitate, you will flop into failure halfway through. With practice you will begin to build the confidence that will bring you the courage to continue successfully. As with diving, once you do it right you will realize it is not as difficult or as frightening as it seemed at first.

It will be helpful to practice headstands against a wall. Facing the wall about a foot from it, place your palms on the mat alongside your shoulders at shoulder width and push up with your feet and kick over until your feet are against the wall. It will be helpful to have a partner to help you practice, helping to raise your feet up to the wall, then bringing them away from it as you seek to find the balance needed to hold them directly overhead. A partner will insure that you do not hit too hard as you lose your balance and your feet fall back, bringing your body back over. If you are not facing a wall, your feet may fall forward, bringing your body forward. Bending your knees and going into a rolling position as you fall will ease the impact.

It will take time to find the right width of your hands that provides you the stability you need to maintain your balance in a headstand, but most of us should be able to execute this simple maneuver. Eventually you will be able to bring your legs up slowly to full extension, finding your balance comfortably.

A handstand is much harder. Most of us will not be able to do this well. As you place your hands flat in front of you, you must bring your legs up in one continuous motion until they are held straight overhead. Most of us either do not push off hard enough and simply fall back, or we push off too hard and continue over into a hard fall. It takes courage to begin with, and a lot of balance to finish properly. Again, a partner who can serve as a "catcher" can be a big help.

Front and back walkovers are even harder. In these, a handstand to the front or the back is the halfway point of one continuous maneuver in which you go from a standing position facing one way to a standing position facing the other way. It takes considerable courage to execute this manuever properly, as it will not be completed if you do not throw yourself into it with enough force to continue over. Beginning gymnasts have helpers who catch them halfway and provide the push to send them over the rest of the way. Accomplished gymnasts can do these slowly in perfect form and also can do a fast series of them.

Most other gymnastics events require equipment that you may find at a gym or "Y." A long flat block of wood can serve as a balance beam on which you walk up and back, executing turns in tight circles, and perform slow rolls and cartwheels. The official beam is sixteen feet, four inches long, four inches wide, and mounted almost four feet high. However, beginners would do well to work on one laid on the floor because of continuous risk of falls off this narrow surface.

The average person probably will not want to go deeper into gymnastics, but the rings can be used for pullups to build strength even if you do not go into the swinging maneuvers experienced performers execute on these. The uneven parallel bars and the vaulting horse are really for those enthusiasts who join a gymnastics class and are taught to execute intricate maneuvers properly, skillfully, and safely. The same is true of the trampoline. Youngsters find it fun to bounce around on these, but if you try to execute high, fast turns and twists you run the risk of neck injuries, which, unfortunately, are not uncommon on this apparatus.

Gymnastics builds balance, agility, and strength. If you are so inclined, by all means join a gymnastics class. If not, you can put together a limited program that will be helpful.

ISOMETRICS

Isometrics have fallen into disfavor because they do not build up the heart and lungs or stretch your muscles, but they do strengthen your muscles, which is a desirable goal in itself. The beauty of isometrics is that they are conveniently done in inconvenient places at inconvenient times. You need no equipment to do most isometric exercises. You use your own muscles to strengthen themselves. You can do it sitting in an easy chair watching television, sitting in a theater seat seeing a movie, sitting at a desk, even while at work.

1. Carry a tennis ball or firm rubber ball around with you and simply keep squeezing it in each hand. It must be a ball with some give, but not too much. Squeezing it will strengthen your fingers, hands, wrists, and forearms.

2. Standing in a doorway, place your palms on the sides and press outward as hard as you can, five to ten times, three to five seconds at a time. Lying on your back in front of a doorway, feet in the opening of the doorway, spread your feet to the two sides and press outward as hard as you can in the same series. Leaning against a wall or desk, legs straight and well behind you, you do pushups. These exercises build the arms or legs.

3. Seated in a chair, put your palms on the seat, alongside your thighs, and press downward as hard as you can, five to ten times, three to five seconds at a time. Repeat with your hands hooked

first to the front, then to the sides of the chair, pulling up as hard as you can. Placing your hands, palms up, under a desk or table, lift up as hard as you can. This is good for your finger, hand, wrist, arm, and shoulder muscles.

4. Seated in a chair at a table or desk, hook your feet under the frame of the desk, a drawer, a chair, anything with a lip close to the floor, and pull upward as hard as you can. Wrap your feet around a chair, a wastebasket, anything sturdy, and squeeze your legs together as hard as you can. Press your feet flat to the floor and press down as hard as you can. All of these strengthen your leg muscles.

5. Standing or seated, place your palms together and press them against each other as hard as you can, five to ten times, three to five seconds at a time. Repeat with one fist covered by the other hand, pushing up and down as hard as you can, first with one fist, then the other. Cross one palm across the other, wrapping the fingers of each around the back of each, and push and pull, side to side and up and down. Hook your fingers and try to pull your hands apart, again five to ten times, three to five seconds at a time. Repeat some of these with your arms behind your back.

6. Take your tennis racquet, golf club, baseball or softball bat, or whatever, assume the stance of various strokes at the point of impact with the ball, and, placing your racquet, club, or bat against an unyielding surface, apply pressure. This builds up body and arms strength where it will be needed most in your pursuit of these sports. Use a weighted racquet, club, or bat to practice swings to loosen up. Many stores have weighted "sleeves" that slip over your equipment. You will build up your arm strength, and your real weapon will feel lighter when you return to it.

WEIGHT TRAINING

It was not so long ago that weight lifting was frowned on for all but weight lifters and body builders because it was supposed to build large and heavy muscles that supposedly put you out of proportion, slowed you down, and tended you to fat if you stopped. Now, weight training is enjoying popularity with both serious and recreational athletes and the physical-fitness set because it has been found that by stressing repetition rather than weight, one can lengthen as well as strengthen muscles that make for an attractive body and increase speed and endurance.

Also, studies show that all athletes must make adjustments, primarily in diet, if they do not want to have muscle turn to fat when they discontinue an exercise program and become inactive. Those on exercise programs tend to eat more because they need more fuel to burn off. As you go off such a program, you have to eat less because you are burning less. The balance is critical, in any case.

Weight-training programs are attractive because they can build up specific areas of the body you want built up. They are not as good as the running games in improving your lungs and heart and general health, but they are better than many activities. You will benefit if your only exercise is weight training, but it is better if other exercise goes along with weight training.

Weight training can aggravate problems such as sore shoulders, tennis elbows, and bad lower backs, so caution must be taken in this respect. It is especially important to warm up and loosen up before entering weight training, as you will be subjecting your muscles and joints to unusual stress, so you have to do some of the previously described warming, loosening exercises before beginning with the weights. And because weight training tends to heat up the muscles and centralize blood circulation, it is unwise to go into other athletic activities sooner than two hours afterward.

Preferably, isolate your weight-training program from other athletic programs. Do your weight training early in the morning, well before going into some game, or late in the evening, long after. You should never lift two days in a row, nor let more than two days go between lifting. Ideally, then, something like a Monday-Wednesday-Friday program is desirable.

Preferably, lift from one-half hour to one and one-half hours, never much more. Rest at least one minute between "sets," which are any series of, say, eight lifts, and at least five minutes each half hour. Give your muscles an opportunity to recover from the exertions. Breathe any way that is comfortable for you, but one way is inhale as you raise a lift, exhale as you lower it.

People lift at all ages, but the ideal would be between sixteen and thirty-two. Thus, anyone younger than sixteen or older than thirty-two must take caution. Anyone much less than sixteen who is still well into skeletal growth shouldn't do it. Otherwise, start slower and lift less. The more inactive you have been, the more slowly you start, the less you lift. You can build up as you go along, but unless you are going into weight lifting as a serious sport there is no point to building up beyond your body weight.

As a general rule, you can do well lifting about half your body weight. One good test is to try eight repetitions of a given lift. If you can only do four, say, then you are lifting too much for your present development. If you can do twelve, say, then you are not lifting enough. That is as a starter. The lift to be of value must stress your muscles, and if you reach the point where you can do twelve or sixteen repetitions while still stressing yourself, fine. Do them faster. But speed is not the ultimate goal.

One serious problem with weight training is the expense. Once you purchase the equipment you have no added expense, but the equipment is expensive, and the expense is wasted if you do not go on with it. Also, you probably don't have the safest setup for weight training at home and may not have a partner or partners to work out with you to help keep conditions safe. For example, a common lift is the squat lift, which is done with the weight on your shoulders, across your back, and behind your neck. Alone, this is difficult to do, and dangerous, except in a gym that has a squat rack, which contains the weight as you are raising it and lowering it. Thus, if you can afford it, membership in a gym or a "Y" that has suitable weight-training equipment is desirable.

If you are buying the equipment, the recreational athlete planning serious weight training might wish to purchase a 5-pound pair and a 10-pound pair of dumbbells, two 5-pound discs, four 10-pound discs, and two 25-pound discs, and a bar with the sort of sleeves that will hold the weights safely on the bar. Used in combinations, you then can attach from 10 to 90 pounds of discs on your bar.

If you wish to buy full sets, these frequently come in 90-, 120-, or 150-pound combinations. Doing it this way may be cheaper, but will give you less flexibility. Any large sporting goods store sells weights separately or in sets. The cast-iron weights are more durable, but the vinyl-covered weights will do less damage to your floor.

Many athletes, including Reggie Jackson, Carl Yastrzemski, Mike Marshall, David Thompson, Gary Player, and Valeriy Borozov are ardent weight trainers. They have found that it builds strength and endurance, increases speed and jumping ability, and helps them avoid muscular injuries.

Weight training in itself can cause injuries and must be practiced with care. You can make exciting gains in a short time. You can increase your strength 50 to 100 per cent in six to twelve weeks. But do not overextend yourself.

Read the instructions for each lift carefully, and if you feel you are not doing them properly, seek additional instruction elsewhere. If you do each lift properly and start with light weights, you should be able to build up to a desirable level swiftly and safely.

Do each lift to its full range of muscular motions or you will not benefit from it as you should. Do each slowly.

Start with dumbbells. They are underrated and useful. If you used only dumbbells you would be doing something useful. Even if you go on to barbells, retain some dumbbell work in your program.

Again, as with any of the exercises we have explained, use those you find most useful to you.

DUMBBELLS

Up Position

1. Wrist curl: Holding one bell in each hand, arms down and in front of you, hands on top of the bell, facing downward, roll wrists back as far as you can. Repeat five times. Then repeat five times with hands below bell, facing upward, rolling wrist up toward you. Start with five-pounders. After three or four weeks, go to ten-pounders. Develop wrists, hands, forearms.

2. Forearm curl: Holding one bell in each hand, arms down and in front of you, hands on top of bell, facing downward, bring

arms up, bending at the elbow and tight to your chest, as though making a muscle, rolling wrists back as far as you can. Repeat five times. Then repeat five times with hands below bell, facing upward, rolling wrist up toward you. Start with five-pounders. After four to six weeks, go to ten-pounders. Develops wrists, hands, forearms.

3. Wrist roll: Get a sturdy wooden or metal rod and tie a strong rope to the center of it and to the center of the bell, about three feet apart. Some stores carry such wrist rollers. Hold rod at each end, palms down, bell dangling. Pull up bell by rolling in your palms, using only your wrists. Repeat three times. Start with five-pounders. After six to eight weeks, go to ten-pounders. This is an especially good development exercise for wrists, hands, and forearms.

4. Forearm twist: Stand with feet spread comfortably, elbows tight to your sides, forearms pointed straight out, a bell in each hand, hands on top of bells, bells facing each other. Roll arms outward as far as you can to palms-up position, then bring back. Then reverse, rolling arms inward as far as you can to palms-down position. Repeat each three times. Start with five-pounders. After four to six weeks go to ten-pounders.

5. Arms out: holding bell in each hand, palm down on top of bell, arms at sides, feet to shoulder width, bring arms up to horizontal level, then bring arms down. Repeat five times. Start with five-pounders. After three to four weeks turn to ten-pounders. Develops arm and shoulder muscles.

6. Arms forward: Same exercise, except arms are brought up and in front of you, pointing straight ahead.

7. Arms back: Same exercise, except arms are brought down as far behind you as possible, pointing up and behind you.

8. Arms up and back: Holding one bell in both hands in front of you, bring arms up and over head and down until top of bell is resting on back of your head, bottom on back of your neck. Builds arm muscles, especially those in back and back of upper arms. This can also be done with a broomstick. See how close you can hold your hands and how far you can lower stick, twisting wrists.

9. Bending row: Bending from the waist, a bell in each hand, feet at shoulder width, bring one arm up at a time, elbow bent and

pointing upward, before returning to original position. Alternate arms at a slow tempo. Do each five times. Start with five-pounders, and after three to four weeks increase to ten-pounders. Builds arm muscles, especially front of arms, and develops back and chest muscles.

10. Upright row: Same exercise, only done from upright position, bringing hands from hips to chest, elbows pointed outward.

11. Upright swing: Standing erect, feet at shoulder width, one bell held in two hands directly overhead, swing it slowly down until it passes between your legs and goes back as far as you can push it and you come to a bent position, bent at knees and hips. Repeat five times with ten-pound weight.

12. Side bend: Standing erect, holding one ten-pound bell in one hand and at side, slide free hand as far as possible down free side, drawing other side and arm with bell upward, bending sideways at waist. After returning, slide hand with bell as far down as possible, drawing free arm upward. Then repeat, switching bell to other hand. Do each three times. Develops muscles at the sides of your body.

13. Hip bend: Standing erect, feet at shoulder width, holding one ten-pound bell in both hands, resting on shoulders directly behind neck, bend forward from the hips until your upper torso is horizontal to floor, then swing erect again. Repeat five times. Develops back muscles.

14. Trunk stretch: Standing with feet at shoulder width, one about one foot in front of the other, holding a barbell in each hand, lean forward to stretch first one arm, then the other as far as possible toward the forward foot. Repeat three times. Then repeat with other foot in front. Stretches torso muscles.

Down Position

15. Seated curls: Seated, with elbows resting on thighs, repeat wrist and forearm curls.

16. Seated lifts: Seated, arms dangling at sides, a bell in each hand, raise arms forward until horizontal to floor, then raise directly overhead, pointed up, then bring down to sides, holding horizontal to floor before returning to dangling position. Start with

five-pounders, then, after four to six weeks, increase to ten-pounders. Strengthens arm and shoulder muscles.

17. Prone raises: Lying on back, a bell in each hand, hands at side, raise arms until hands and bells are aimed directly overhead, then return. Repeat five times. Then stretch arms until pointed outward and repeat raises. Start with five-pound bells. After four to six weeks, increase to ten-pounders. Builds upper body and arm muscles.

18. Arm curls: From prone position, arms stretched to sides, a bell in each hand, brings bells to shoulders by bending arms at elbows. Repeat five times. Start with five-pounders. After four to six weeks, increase to ten-pounders. Builds upper body and arm muscles.

19. Situps: From prone position, but with legs drawn up and bent at knees, one ten-pound bell in two hands held over neck, do customary situp, made harder by the weight. Do as many as you can. Builds muscles along front of body.

20. Stretches: From seated position, one leg hooked behind you in hurdler's stretch, hold five-pound bell in opposite hand and stretch it as far as you can to opposite foot. Then reverse. Repeat three times. Stretches torso muscles.

Repetitions

Start with repetitions suggested. After four to six weeks with each weight, double repetitions. After another four to six weeks, you may, if you wish, double them again. But it would be best not to go past twenty repetitions, even with the easiest exercises. It would be better to do other exercises.

BARBELLS

Up Position

Always grip bar at shoulder width or wider, palms up or down. Grip bar firmly. Use weight that applies stress to you, but weight you can handle. If you drop the barbells, they can hurt you. It is more important to increase repetitions than it is to increase weight.

Up Position

1. Curls: Stand erect, hands holding barbell down at about your thigh, palms down. Hold your elbows at your side and raise bar by bending elbow and curling forearm upward, until bar is held at chest. Bring down, then back up. Keep body and back as straight as possible. Start with weight you can use easily—say, twenty pounds. Increase slowly as strength increases. This is the basic biceps builder, but will do well by your hands, wrists, chest, and shoulders, also.

2. Dead lift: With barbell on floor, stand directly behind it, centered to it, close to it. Bending over bar, head down and beyond bar, knees bent, legs at shoulder width, place hands palms down on top of bar, and bring your body to erect position, bringing bar up with it. Bending down at knees, lower bar back again. Repeat three times. Can also be done with legs held straight. Start with weight you can use easily—say, thirty pounds. Increase slowly as strength increases. When done improperly and with excess weight, this can cause back or groin problems. Done correctly, it builds strength in back, groin, and entire body.

3. The squat: Holding barbell, palms up, across shoulders and behind head, drop into squatting position. Repeat, holding barbell palms up, across chest, in front of your chin. Keep head erect and back straight. A squat rack in which weight is locked on rollers into rack is ideal. Without one, you may need a partner or partners to help you put barbell in proper position. Also, you will have to start with a low weight of, say, thirty pounds, and build up slowly to higher weights, for the sake of safety. Repeat each three times. This is an ideal lower-body exercise, especially good for strengthening those hamstring and other muscles of the lower legs that are easily pulled. It also increases speed and jumping power. But do not drop below a seated position for fear of doing damage to your knee joint. In fact, you may use a chair or bench and start from a seated position, rising erect, and returning to a seated position while doing this exercise.

4. The lunge: This is not done as dramatically as it sounds.

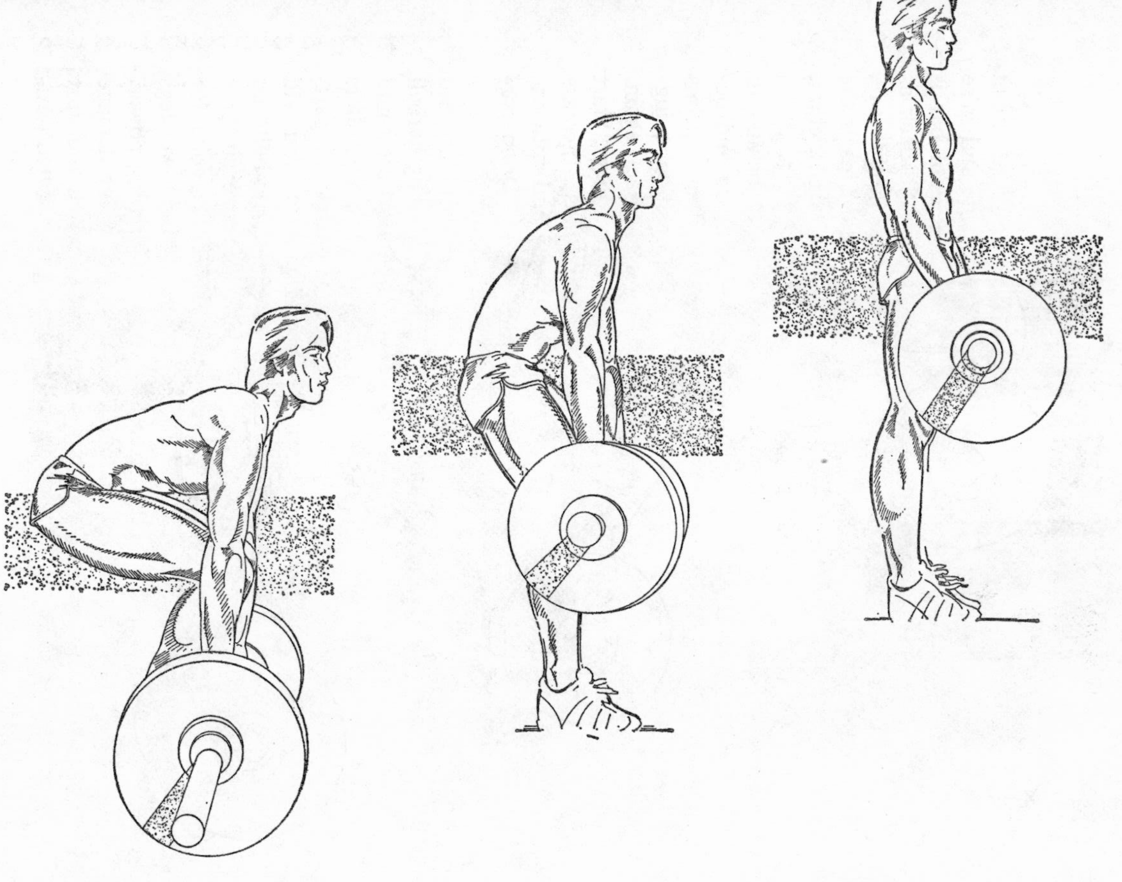

THE DEAD LIFT.

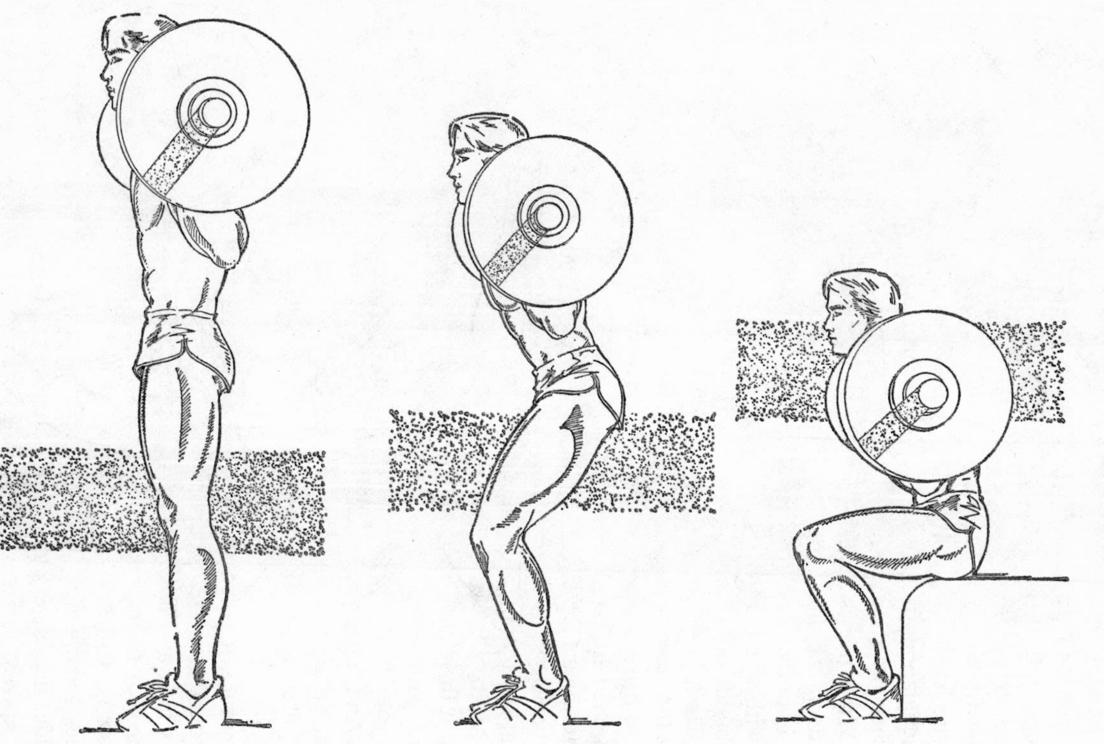

THE SQUAT.
(Seat saves excess stress on knees.)

With barbell behind back and at the neck, palms up, stride forward with one leg while lowering yourself halfway between your two legs, both bent at the knees, the one thrust forward, the knee pointed straight ahead, the other lagging behind, the knee pointed downward. Stand erect, bringing legs together again. Repeat to opposite leg. Repeat each three times. Use weight you are using for squats, starting low and increasing slowly. This exercise stretches and strengthens your leg muscles.

5. Waist bend: Holding barbell palms up, behind head, across shoulders, standing erect, feet together, bend forward until upper body is horizontal to the floor, then come back up again. Again, start with squatlike weights and increase slowly. Repeat five times. This builds the muscles along your back from head to toe.

6. Chest press: A continuation of the dead lift. With same technique that has brought the barbell up, arms down, curl arms upward to bring bar to chest. You must keep your back straight and not arched to avoid lower-back injury. Accordingly, start with a weight you can handle, which, because you are raising it higher, may be less than in the dead lift, and increase slowly. Do not start at more than three repetitions, and increase these slowly.

7. Military press: A continuation of the dead lift and the chest lift, you then push the bar upward until you are holding it at the end of your extended arms directly overhead. Again, you must keep your back straight and not arched to avoid lower-back injury. And, again, you must start with a weight you can handle, which, because you are raising it higher, may be less than in the other lifts. And start at three repetitions or less and increase slowly.

However, if you start light and do it slowly, this is an excellent all-around exercise to build your body all around.

8. Clean and jerk: This is a competitor's lift and is not recommended for the beginner or recreational athlete. So you may know what it is, you bring the barbell up as in a dead lift, and, as it reaches waist height, you bend at the knees under it, raising it to shoulder height, which is the "clean" portion, then stand up, pushing it upward to an arms-upraised position over your head, which is the "jerk."

9. The snatch: Again, this is a competitor's lift, not recommended for beginners or recreational athletes. It is similar to the

THE MILITARY PRESS

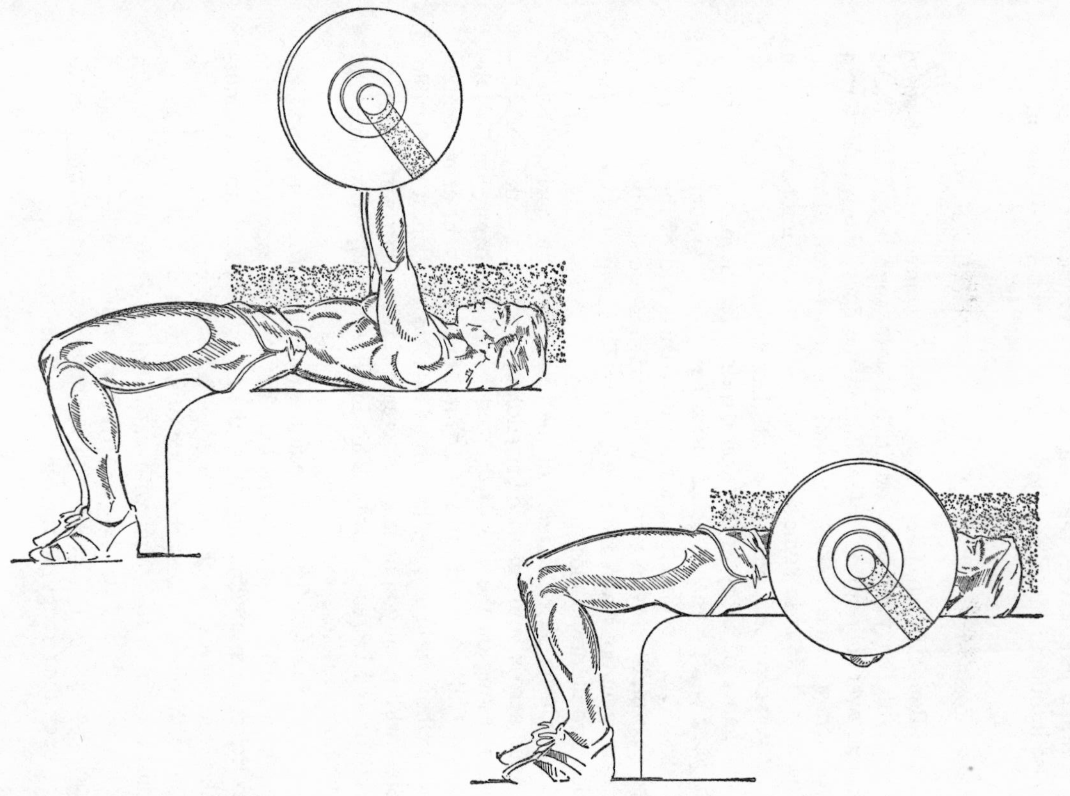

THE BENCH PRESS.

clean and jerk, except that you do not bend under the bar as you raise it, but pull it up, purely with arm and upper-body power.

Down Position

10. Bench press: Use a long, sturdy, secured bench of some sort, lying on your back on it, but with your legs, bent at the knees, over the end of it, feet flat on the floor, the weight across your chest, arms cocked under it. Raise it to full extension, then lower it. This is in some ways preferable to the military press in that you can use more weight with less chance of injury, but there is a chance of injury in that you dare not let the bar drop sharply to your chest or neck. Bench-press equipment, available in gyms, is desirable. Beyond that, a friend on each end of the bar would be helpful. Start with forty pounds and increase slowly. Start with three repetitions and increase slowly. This improves arm, shoulder, and chest muscles.

11. Curls: Sit on the end of the bench with the barbell in both hands across your knees or straddling the bench with your forearms resting on the end of the bench and the bar resting on the bench. Curl your wrist to full closure, then curl your arm, bending your elbow, bringing the bar up as close to your chest as possible. Start with twenty pounds and increase slowly. Start with four repetitions and increase slowly. This improves hand, wrist, arm, and shoulder muscles.

12. Leg raises: This will require either the proper gym apparatus or a partner to steady the bar, but it is an especially effective exercise for strengthening all of the leg, groin, and stomach muscles. Lie on your back on the floor, a bench, or in the apparatus, and with weight across the ankle of one foot or both feet. Do leg raises about a foot high with each foot or both feet. Start with thirty pounds and increase slowly. Start with three repetitions and increase slowly. Athletes use this exercise extensively when building back the strength in their legs after knee surgery.

Other Equipment

Many gyms have the Universal Gym, or Nautilus, or other commercial sets of equipment that provide weights in racks or tension pulleys that will enable you to lift and lower, pull and push with your arms and legs in many ways that will do wonders for you, and do them in safety. If such is available to you, by all means use it.

Repetitions and Weights

For the purposes of weight training and not weight lifting, for the purposes of the recreational athlete or the competitive athlete who wishes to improve performance in some area, it is, as I have stressed, the repetitions that matter more than the weight.

I have started with low weights that might seem much too low to the average weight lifter or experienced weight trainer, but for safety's sake I do not want you to strain yourself as you build up to weights that will stress your body but not endanger it.

If you keep at it regularly, you can build up to half your body weight or more, but it is doubtful the average woman will want to go beyond fifty to sixty pounds at the top, the average man beyond ninety to one hundred pounds. Some exercises call for top weight, some for less.

Ideally, you will start with a low level of repetitions, but build up to twelve to twenty of each exercise, and do each twice—in two "sets"—with a brief recuperative break in between. If it takes you forty minutes to do the series of exercises you have selected, you should be able to cut the time in half to twenty minutes, eventually.

However, speed is not the goal at which you are aiming, and it is important to do each exercise slowly enough to sustain stress on your muscles for reasonable periods. Do not hesitate to take reasonable rest breaks. Muscles under constant stress require rest, and in weight training muscles are being subjected to constant stress.

Many athletes have found pure wrestling—as found, for example, in amateur wrestling as opposed to the phony histrionics of the professional shows—to be more exhausting than contact sports such as football, active sports such as two-man basketball or handball, or pure running, simply because you get into holds of constant tension in which there are no breaks for recovery.

The idea of calisthenics is to loosen the body and stretch and strengthen its muscles for general fitness and for warming-up and cooling-down purposes. The idea of isometrics is to strengthen. Weight training lengthens and strengthens your muscles for general fitness and for more speed and endurance in your athletic activities.

The stronger and more limber you are, the better you will feel, the better you will be able to conduct your daily life, and the better you will be able to play the games you like to play. So now, let us get on to the games people play.

3. GAMES PEOPLE PLAY

The games people play are countless, and all can do good for you if you are conditioned to them. How fit you are, and how many ailments you have, have to be determining factors in the games you choose to play. Some are more strenuous than others. And how much you like playing a given game has to be a factor. If you don't enjoy it, you are not apt to stick to it.

If you can, find some things you like to do that you can do with others, which will help you stay at it. Companionship encourages competition, which is why golf clubs, tennis clubs, and bowling leagues, for example, flourish. We all know of the loneliness of the long-distance runner. But so many are running today, there's little need to run alone.

Unless you are a loner by nature, find some people who enjoy playing the games you enjoy playing at your level. You can golf alone, but even if you go out alone, you probably will have to fit into a foursome. You can practice tennis against a backboard, but you can't play the game alone. You can bowl alone, but it is more fun with someone who bowls about as you do.

As a general rule, it is best to play a competitive game against someone on your level. You will improve faster by playing someone a level above you, but it is no fun for him to play someone a level below him, so he may not always be available to you.

Walking, swimming, skating, skiing, cycling, and so forth are among those things you can do very well alone, but probably will enjoy more when done with others. Handball, racquetball, basketball, baseball, and so forth all require someone else to play with.

Jack Wilmore, executive director of the National Athletic Health Institute, and a Ph.D. in physical education, favors walking, hiking, jogging, running, skating, cycling, and swimming as sound basic activities for those who have not been active. He considers tennis, skiing, handball, squash, badminton, and basketball as excellent activities for those who have been active, as long as they go at them with vigor. He considers golf, bowling, baseball, and softball as less useful, especially in building up your cardiovascular system. Like most experts, he considers running the single best activity of all. It certainly builds up your cardiovascular system and your legs, though it does little for your upper torso.

The good doctor understands that a lot of us are not good at games, describing some of us, rather cruelly, as "motor morons." He stresses, as I do, the fact that exercise is good even for those who are not good at it. He recommends that we find that thing or those things that we do best and find companions who like to do those things so we will enjoy them and be encouraged to continue with them.

Maybe you were one of those who was not picked when your childhood companions were choosing sides. Left out of games then, you have left games out of your life since. Perhaps, then, it is time to get back into the game, realizing that living a long time is better than the alternative.

A lot of games may be beyond your reach. You're not going to ride racehorses or drive race cars. Unless you're young, you're not apt to play football or soccer or hockey or baseball, though a few do. Some ride horses recreationally. Some play softball. A lot of us skate.

Many walk, jog, or run. Few run marathons. Many hike or bike. Many skate or swim. A great many play tennis or golf or bowl. Many ski, though few go in for the cross-country variety. There are games and there are games.

Some time back, the National Athletic Health Institute tested about twenty jockeys at Hollywood Park and found them to be in better overall condition than some four hundred other professionals tested in baseball, football, and hockey, plus pros and amateurs in track and field. Wilmore said the jockeys were found to be extraordinarily fit. He admitted the researchers were surprised with the jockeys' cardiovascular endurance, upper and lower body strength, and flexibility. They took to the treadmill routine better than any athletes except distance runners.

Based on this, jockeys can be considered the best-conditioned of all athletes. Certainly they need the variety of vision, the eye-to-hand coordination, the quick reflexes, and the great strength and endurance of the most able of athletes. Little men (and women), they must guide those large animals through tight traffic. The prolonged pull of horse against reins subjects their hands, wrists, and arms to constant stress. They must make split-second decisions and remain cool under thunderous circumstances.

Curiously, however, the tests did reveal a higher content of body fat among jockeys than among the average athletes tested. The researchers were at a loss to figure out why, and began to wonder about the equation they used. Considering the constant battle these little guys wage against weight, this finding was startling. Possibly they do not require the overall body fitness of other athletes. Although the great ones like Bill Shoemaker go on well into their forties and an occasional Johnny Longden lasts into his fifties, the average jock lasts only about six years and is through at thirty, possibly from the fight with weight. A teen-ager such as Steve Cauthen can come along and dominate this sport even before his body is fully developed. This suggests that age is as important as physical fitness.

Boxers also are finished fast. An occasional Ali lasts until he is close to forty, but even then the loss of his speed and skills is startlingly evident with each year. Fighting ten to fifteen three-minute rounds on a given night is exhausting. Try holding your hands and arms up and out three minutes at a time with one-minute rest breaks for forty to sixty minutes sometimes, even without moving them or being hit on them.

The physical punishment absorbed by a boxer being hit on the arms, body, and head for thirty to forty-five minutes is staggering and has to sap his swiftness, strength, and endurance, if, indeed, it does not do serious or even fatal harm.

The successful fighter probably trains harder than most athletes, though it must be admitted that many get by without doing as much as they should do. Most run, skip rope, hit the light and heavy bags, do all sorts of calisthenics, and box for as much as four hours a day of exercise before a big bout.

Swimmers and skaters also appear to be finished fast, but this probably is because of the extensive training required for success in their sports. Swimmers, speed skaters, and figure skaters often train four to six hours a day and often at odd times because they cannot get pools or rinks to use except early in the morning or late at night. Their enthusiasm seems to fade fast and they tend to retire young. There really is no reason to believe that these athletes could not continue to do better if they continued to compete through their twenties and thirties, provided they continued to train as they do in the beginning.

It may not be coincidence that there is little money to be made in these sports. A figure skater may make a lot of money, but must turn pro to do so, and there is little pro competition. So he or she skates in ice shows.

Similarly, while they can enjoy a good gypsylike life, the lack of professional opportunities stops most track-and-field performers from continuing in competition into their thirties. Those who do, tend to improve. Sprinters tend to do worse, but long-distance runners tend to do better up to the early thirties. Conditioning can improve speed a lot less than it can endurance. An athlete tends to get slower but stronger as his body develops. Throwers and jumpers seem to hit their peaks later than sprinters, but sooner than distance runners.

There are those who believe that the great track athlete is the best-conditioned athlete in the world because he is pushing himself to extend his limits. There probably is some validity to this. However, just because his performances are measurable in seconds or inches does not mean he is pushing himself harder than an athlete in another sport.

The great runner, especially at middle and long distances, is not going to have excess fat on his frame and is apt to have an exceptional cardiovascular system. His lung and heart capacity and his blood pressure should measure marvelously well. However, he may not have great timing or rapid reflexes. Similarly, the great jumper or thrower may not have great speed or endurance.

The great swimmer, especially at middle and long distances, is also apt to be slim and have a well-working cardiovascular system, but he may not have leg strength or running speed or great timing or reflexes.

We tend to condition ourselves to the demands of what we do, not what we might do.

From my experience, professional basketball players seem to be among the best-conditioned athletes anywhere. It is a running game played on hard wooden floors, so demanding that the NBA plays a forty-eight-minute game compared to the sixty-minute games of football and hockey and the ninety-minute games of soccer, to say nothing of the two to three hours of baseball.

Basketball players benefit from the brief breaks of free throws and time-outs, but they run and jump hard and have more bruising contact than was supposed to be in this sport. You don't see a fat pro and you don't see many old ones. Their careers run far shorter than those in football, hockey, soccer, and baseball.

Hockey is a hard game, full of contact, but skating, while good exercise in itself, simply is easier on the legs than running and jumping. Hockey players seem to last the longest of any athletes in any other team sport. Players play well into their thirties, often into their forties.

Soccer has less contact, though it is a fast, rugged game, and a long one, and there are not time-outs. Soccer players play the whole game; however, most soccer players are not involved in most plays.

Although the cardiovascular system benefits more from pure running, to my mind the most demanding games are two-man basketball, handball, and possibly squash and racquetball. You are on the go all the time, going hard, and making quick starts and stops. These are exhausting sports.

Volleyball demands quickness, and there is a lot of jumping and diving, but the sport does not demand the strength and endurance of others.

Skating and skiing are good for the legs, lungs, and heart, comparable to running, but not as demanding. However, in skiing consider only the time on skis—climbing up the slope or zooming down it. The ride in the lift cannot count any more than can a ride in a golf cart.

Cross-country skiing is comparable to hiking, though fewer individuals pursue cross-country skiing. Both are demanding activities, good for the legs, lungs, and heart. Hiking up and down over uneven ground for long periods is similar to walking only in the basic movement. Walking over level territory does not ask as much of your body.

Walking can be considered the basic sport. If a person can do nothing else, brisk walking for a mile or more will do a great deal for him. Recuperating cardiac patients are asked to walk to build themselves back up. But it exerts you less than jogging, which exerts you less than running.

The walking you do in golf will do a lot for you, but it can't be compared to the running you do in tennis, say. It is good as far as it goes. But if you use a golf cart, forget it. And if you play a lot of doubles in tennis it is possible to play a long time without exerting yourself much.

A tennis player playing singles, going for every ball hard under a hot sun, perhaps for hours at a time, is stressing himself a great deal. Whatever the game, it is all in how you play. The harder you play, the more you run, the more you are asking of your body.

Done vigorously, bowling is exercise, but it simply cannot be compared favorably to tennis, handball, or pure running, say, for the demands it makes on your conditioning. Out-of-shape men and women bowl three or more games through a long night without wearing themselves out. Bowlers often are fat.

The fattest professional athletes are the football players, which is not to say they are the worst-conditioned of athletes. Linemen often find excess weight helpful to them in blocking and tackling, and there are more linemen than any other players by position on a football team. Sheer size is an asset. However, many of these men cannot run a mile in five minutes. Many All-Pros cannot. In fact, they dread the running routines of training camp. Running backs and receivers usually have good speed, though not necessarily endurance. They are timed at forty yards, for example, not even a hundred yards, to say nothing of a mile. However, you seldom see a fat running back or receiver.

Baseball players probably are the worst-conditioned of athletes in major-league team sports. They play more games than anyone else, but they stand around a lot. They are asked to make short sprints in the field and on the bases. Many cannot run from first to third without getting winded. Many are fat.

The same applies to softball players, which is why it is a popular recreational sport. For the most part, it does not demand a great deal of you, which is not to say that many baseball and softball players are not fine and fit. It is just that it is not necessary to be so to compete with some success.

It is not easy to get your bat squarely on a hard-thrown ball, nor is it easy to field a fast-moving ball. The good baseball player does have to have good eyes, fast reflexes, and good timing.

The good golfer needs good timing. The ball is not moving, but it is not easy to hit correctly, especially if there is something at stake, eyes on you, pressure on you. Those who say a golfer is not an athlete have not tried to perform this sport under the pressure the pros face. Getting your muscles to work well under pressure is an important part of an athlete's performance and conditioning. As he tires, the shooter may lose his touch and start to miss his shots in basketball, for example.

Those who say race drivers are not athletes have not tried to perform this sport under its pressures. It is not just a four-foot putt a race driver may lose if he makes a mistake, it is his life.

Clearly, there are aging and fat race drivers. You do not start driving race cars until ten or more years after boys have begun in baseball or basketball, and experience means a lot. Maybe you don't have to have a lean body, but driving a heavy, hot car in tight traffic for three hours under a hot sun, cramped in a cockpit, demands endurance.

The race driver may not need speed of foot, but he has to have great timing and reflexes, strength and eyesight. He has to have most of the abilities of any athlete, and he has to use these under the dreadful pressure of possible death or injury.

Each sport makes its own demands on you, and each offers its own rewards.

As a general rule, the stop-and-go sports such as baseball, basketball, football, tennis, soccer, and volleyball do not provide the nonstop performance that builds endurance such as pure running, hard hiking, or cross-country skiing.

One way to rate sports is by calories burned per hour. Accordingly, here are some averages:

CALORIES BURNED PER HOUR

1.	Running (at 10 mph)	900
2.	Cycling (at 20 mph)	660
3.	Rowing (at 5 mph)	660
4.	Two-man basketball	650
5.	Handball	600
6.	Racquetball or squash	600
7.	Cross-country skiing (10 mph)	600
8.	Stationary cycling (10 mph)	500
9.	Stationary running (5 mph)	500
10.	Tennis singles	420
11.	Hockey	400
12.	Football	360
13.	Downhill skiing	350
14.	Soccer	320
15.	Calisthenics	300
16.	Basketball (Five-man) or volleyball	285
17.	Baseball or softball	270
18.	Weight training	250
19.	Walking (1 mph)	210
20.	Isometrics	160

However, other factors than the burning of calories enter into the effectiveness of a sport as a conditioner. Considering the muscles stressed and so forth, the all-around value of various sports can be ranked as follows:

SPORTS AS CONDITIONERS

1. Cross-country running
2. Cross-country skiing
3. Long-distance running
4. Long-distance skiing
5. Long-distance skating (ice or roller)
6. Long-distance cycling (bicycle)
7. Long-distance swimming

8. Middle-distance running
9. Middle-distance skating
10. Middle-distance cycling
11. Middle-distance swimming
12. Two-man basketball
13. Handball
14. Squash or racquetball
15. Hiking or rowing
16. Tennis singles
17. Speed running
18. Speed skating
19. Speed cycling
20. Speed swimming
21. Basketball
22. Hockey
23. Football
24. Soccer and volleyball
25. Baseball and softball
26. Walking
27. Slow cycling or skating
28. Tennis doubles
29. Golfing (walking)
30. Bowling

We have charted some sports—not including distance events or running—to show how many minutes you would have to put into each to get comparative value from them.

However, this is based on the average rate of performance. Clearly, the more you put into each minute, the harder you pursue your sport, the faster you walk or run, swim, or pedal, the more you are asking of your body and getting from it.

Studies show we get more from five miles than from one mile if we walk or run at the same pace. A mile run at a really slow pace isn't worth much more than a mile walked at a slow pace. A mile run fairly fast is worth as much as a mile walked at a furious pace. Two miles run fast is worth more than three miles walked fast. A mile swam fast is worth more than two miles run at a jogging gait. To equal two miles of swift, steady swimming, you'd have to pedal eight times as far.

COMPARATIVE VALUE
MINUTES PER SPORT

Golf or bowling	120	240	360	720
Baseball or softball	40	80	120	240
Tennis doubles	35	70	105	210
Weight training	30	60	90	180
Brisk cycling or skating	30	60	90	180
Brisk walking	25	50	75	150
Volleyball	25	50	75	160
Soccer or football	20	40	60	120
Five-man basketball, hockey	20	40	60	120
Tennis singles	15	30	45	90
Speed cycling, swimming or skating	15	30	45	90
Hiking or rowing	12	24	36	72
Two-man basketball or handball	10	20	30	60

Many different experts in the field of conditioning have developed point systems of the various values of the different sports as a guide to the individual planning a program of conditioning.

For your convenience, here is a guide you may wish to follow:

RUNNING

Distance	*Time*	*Pts.*	*Distance*	*Time*	*Pts.*
1 mile	15 min.	1	2 miles	30 min.	4
	12 min.	2		25 min.	5
	10 min.	3		20 min.	6
	8 min.	4		16 min.	8
	6 min.	5		12 min.	10
4 miles	60 min.	8	8 miles	120 min.	16
	50 min.	10		90 min.	20

Distance	*Time*	*Pts.*	*Distance*	*Time*	*Pts.*
	40 min.	12		70 min.	24
	30 min.	14		60 min.	28
	25 min.	16		50 min.	32

10 miles	150 min.	28
	125 min.	32
	100 min.	36
	80 min.	40
	70 min.	50

WALKING

Distance	*Time*	*Pts.*	*Distance*	*Time*	*Pts.*
1 mile	25 min.	1	2 miles	50 min.	3
	20 min.	2		40 min.	4
	15 min.	3		30 min.	5
	12 min.	4		20 min.	6
3 miles	75 min.	5	5 miles	150 min.	9
	65 min.	7		125 min.	12
	50 min.	9		90 min.	15
	40 min.	11		75 min.	18

10 miles	300 min.	18
	250 min.	22
	180 min.	26
	150 min.	30

SWIMMING / CYCLING

Distance	*Time*	*Pts.*	*Distance*	*Time*	*Pts.*
200 yards	8 min.	1	1 mile	8 min.	1
	7 min.	2		6 min.	2
	6 min.	3		4 min.	3
	5 min.	4		2 min.	4
400 yards	15 min.	3	2 miles	15 min.	3
	12 min.	5		10 min.	5
	10 min.	7		8 min.	7
	8 min.	8		6 min.	8
800 yards	30 min.	7	4 miles	30 min.	7
	25 min.	9		25 min.	9

Distance	*Time*	*Pts.*	*Distance*	*Time*	*Pts.*
	20 min.	11		20 min.	11
	15 min.	15		15 min.	15
1 mile	60 min.	12	8 miles	60 min.	12
	50 min.	15		50 min.	15
	40 min.	18		40 min.	18
	30 min.	22		30 min.	22
	25 min.	25		25 min.	25
2 miles	120 min.	20	16 miles	120 min.	20
	100 min.	25		100 min.	25
	80 min.	30		80 min.	30
	60 min.	35		60 min.	35
	50 min.	40		50 min.	40

If you can accumulate 50 points a week, you will be doing well. However, if you can run 10 miles in 70 minutes, you should do more, for your 50 points should be spread over at least 3 days of workouts a week. Most of us will settle for 25 points, but you should strive for 50.

However, many of us will pick up part of our conditioning in games such as tennis or bowling. If you played two or three sets of tennis a day, five days a week, you would not need much more work, though some running would always be helpful. If you played golf five days a week, it still would not be enough. Or if you bowled five days a week.

However, if you do bowl or play golf once or twice a week, count that as conditioning. Just add something more strenuous to it, such as playing tennis once or twice a week, and running, cycling, skating, or hiking once or twice a week. Try to be doing something at least three or four days a week, even if only for a half hour at a time.

And if you can add calisthenics for a few minutes every day, the chances are you will get in good shape. Weight training, too, will help, but most will not turn to this.

Much depends on your daily activities. For example, if you walk stairs instead of taking elevators, so much to the good. If you walk to work or to the store as often as possible, so much to the good. A good, brisk walk will burn off about 200 calories an hour. Stair climbing might claim 300 calories an hour. General gardening about 350, digging ditches or shoveling snow about 450.

A day's housework might take its toll on 180 calories, driving an automobile around town about 120, sitting at a desk all day about 80. So when you get home you might want to mow the lawn, which will burn off about 250 calories.

I mentioned dancing. The great dancer is a great athlete. Astaire, Kelly, Baryshnikov, and the rest have speed, timing, grace, leaping ability, and endurance far beyond most of the great athletes. Have you ever seen Baryshnikov leap? Dwight Stones should have his spring.

Dr. Kerlan is an *aficionado* of the dance. He recently said, "Ballet performers are the ultimate athletes in a noncontact environment. Taking everything into consideration, and including the O. J. Simpsons and all the basketball players, the epitome of athletic function, discipline, endurance, and artistic performance is the ballet dancer." He concluded, "Rudolf Nureyev may be the greatest athlete in the world."

Others consider Nadia Comaneci the best. All great gymnasts are among the best. The late sportswriter Jimmy Cannon once wrote that the great trapeze and high-wire artists were the greatest athletes in the world.

So, each to his own taste.

There are many ways to group sports. In order to discuss them specifically in the following chapters, I will group them roughly into leg, arm, and body sports. I realize that there is a lot of overlapping—for instance, the legs are almost as important as the arm in tennis—but basically you play tennis with your arms.

Thus I group running, jogging, walking, skating, skiing, and cycling with the leg sports; tennis, golf, bowling, rowing, swimming, handball, racquetball, and squash with the arm sports, and softball, baseball, basketball, football, volleyball, and hockey with the body sports.

You make your own choices.

4. WALKING, JOGGING, RUNNING

The most natural athletic activities are walking, jogging, and running. They require no special equipment other than the right shoes, so they are inexpensive. They require no special place, so they are easy to do. And they do more for you than any other exercise.

Up to a point, the more you do, the more these will do for you, but you should not overdo. For example, you should not try to run a four-minute mile unless you are young, healthy, and aiming at the Olympics. In general, walk, or run farther rather than faster.

But you do have to move fast enough to get the blood moving briskly through your body. I have explained to you how hard exercise benefits the cardiovascular system by bringing more air into the lungs and expanding the blood vessels' ability to carry oxygen through the stream to the heart and throughout the body. It expands the heart and enables it to do more work with less effort.

Here is something to think about: Running is tiring. At first. But the more running you do, the less tiring it becomes. And the less tired you will be as you go about your other activities. If you do not walk or run much, you cannot even walk much without getting tired and feeling pain in your feet and legs.

When we are sitting, we are supposed to be resting. But the businessman who sits at his desk all day may feel exhausted by the end of the day. He does not work his muscles enough. He does not take in enough air. He does not supply enough oxygen to his body. He develops oxygen debt by doing too little as surely as a runner does by doing too much.

If, through exercise, you can reduce your resting heartbeat from seventy to fifty beats per minute, your heart will beat six million fewer times per year. Over a period of five to ten years, you will have saved your heart a lot of wear and tear. It is bound to be better off. Most medical men who have gone into running believe it will prevent heart attacks. There are no guarantees, but it is superb preventive medicine.

Dr. Art Mollen, a doctor of osteopathy at Biltmore Medical Center in Phoenix and the author of *Run for Your Life,* says he prescribes running for his patients because it slows the heartbeat and increases lung capacity, as well as lowering weight and cholesterol levels. "It is the best medicine of all," he says.

Dr. George Sheehan, a New Jersey cardiologist and author of *Running,* says, "I can't think of anyone who shouldn't run. It is not only good for you physically, but psychologically. The adult desperately needs to rediscover the child in him. We all need to find time to play games every day. And running is the best of all games."

Running is the "in" thing these days. It is popular with celebrities from Senator William Proxmire to Jacqueline Kennedy Onassis, from Erich Segal to Bruce Dern. But you should not do it because others do it. You should do it because you want to do it.

The actor, Dern, says, "I praise running whenever I'm asked about it because I believe in it, but I don't try to sell it. I've learned that if you want to run, you will, and if you don't, you won't. You can lead a horse to water. . . . I turned Bob Redford and Jack Nicholson on to it, but they wanted it because they're athletic, competitive people, and because they could see it was good for them. But I haven't turned my own wife on to it. She won't run a step. She just doesn't want it.

"But for those who want it," he concludes, "it is by far the best exercise in the world."

As I said, you do not require extensive equipment. Most walkers or runners wear sweatsuits. You can get fancy ones these days. I think we think these make us look like athletes. Maybe they do, but they do not make us athletes. Heavy clothing, which flops around, is not good for runners or walkers. It is good for warming up when you want to start sweating. After that, you want to be able to sweat freely. Your sweating skin will benefit from fresh air.

If possible, wear lightweight shirts and shorts. Nylon is excellent. Unlike cotton or wool, it will not retain the sweat and get heavier. It is not only good in warm weather, but also you will find you will not need much more in cold weather—at least until you reach freezing temperatures. At that point, you must dress warmly, especially as soon as you stop your running. Start by adding clothes at the top. Add a sweatshirt or jacket before you add anything on your legs. When it's cold, always wear a cap of some kind. A wool cap that pulls down and fits snugly is good. About two fifths of our lost body heat is lost through our head. In cold weather it is important to retain as much body heat as possible. However, unless you lack hair on your head, you will not need a cap in warm weather. A hot sun on a bald head can be bad.

Women should wear brassieres when running. Their breasts swing, which is uncomfortable, and internal damage can be done. Similarly, men should wear athletic supporters.

Dern says when he sees runners with knee-high sweat socks he knows they don't know what they're doing because they are not allowing their ankles and calves to sweat freely. He prefers running with low-cut socks or without socks. I think low-cut cotton or wool socks are good for you because they help prevent blisters. Nylon socks create blisters. And if your socks slide around in your shoes or crease under your feet they will create blisters. Blisters are apt to develop, anyway, when you first begin to walk or run extensively. But as your feet toughen, blisters will not occur. Socks will keep your feet warm and dry in cold or wet weather and will protect your feet from hot surfaces in hot weather.

Shoes are critical. Each shoe hits the surface about eight hundred times a mile with all your weight on it. Our feet are asked to absorb tons of impact. Fortunately, they are well built. But they need help. These jolts also travel through our ankles, knees, and hips; they need help too. There are different shoes for different sports that are available today and you should take advantage of this. It is one place where I recommend you spend a little money.

It is important to purchase a good shoe that is right for your game. Don't throw your money away on a fancy manufacturer's name or a fancy shoe, but spend twenty-five to thirty-five dollars for good low-cut shoes. Good walking or running shoes are lightweight but sturdy. The weight is less important than the sturdiness. As your legs develop, a few extra ounces in weight will not bother you.

It is important to warm up before walking or running. In fact, walking is a good warmup for running. But you should do some loosening and stretching exercises before either. Do some of the exercises described earlier that stretch your legs and Achilles tendons. The more you are going to walk or run, the more exercise you should do. The older you are, the more you should do. You should do ten to twenty minutes' worth if possible. This will save you a lot of aches and pains and even injuries.

When you are starting a walking or running program you are going to get sore feet, ankles, calves, and shins. This is to be expected. As you continue, you will get past these problems. You will develop pain, known as "stitches," in your side. You can run past these. As you condition yourself, you will not get these anymore. These stem from gas in the colon, which is common and natural, but occurs most commonly to people who are not conditioned to running.

Walking is the first step to running. Walking, not strolling. Walking briskly (but even strolling is better than nothing). If you can, follow the old custom of window-shopping or lawn-gazing. Do not drive short distances. If possible, walk to the store or to work. Take a walk every morning or evening. Or at lunchtime. If it is not too far, walk up the stairs instead of taking the elevator or escalator. Walking up the stairs is excellent exercise.

At some point, most heart patients are advised to walk a mile or more daily. Maybe they start at a half mile and gradually advance to two miles. But they are asked to pick up their pace from a mile in a half hour, to a mile in twenty minutes, and finally in fifteen minutes, then two miles in a half hour. If walking is what you want, you can go on to four miles in an hour. The walking must be brisk. If you do not get your heart working hard you are not doing much for yourself. You will feel winded at first. Eventually you will be taking in more air more easily. Your legs will ache at first. Eventually they will not.

Less strenuous than running, walking should be done daily, whether or not you run. If walking is what you want, start with a mile in thirty minutes every day for two weeks. Than walk faster and cut your time to twenty minutes a day for four weeks. Then to fifteen minutes or less daily for four weeks. And go to a mile and a half. After ten weeks, you should be able to do two miles in thirty minutes every day. This will work wonders for you. Your legs will feel strong and you will not easily be winded. Within you, your heart will have strengthened.

If you haven't had heart trouble, why wait? Walk now to prevent it.

As in jogging or running, it may motivate you more to continue if you find companionship. Husbands and wives walk together a lot these days. There is no reason their children should not join them. No matter how active boys and girls may be, a regular routine of walking will build them up and build a good habit into them. Vary your routine. Walking or running around a track or around the same area every day can become monotonous. Walk around different areas of your neighborhood. See how your neighbors are doing with their lawns. Walk around a park. Enjoy nature while you walk.

A natural step from walking is hiking. As you walk over more rugged terrain, you will need more rugged shoes—hiking shoes. You will need high-tops to protect your ankles from twists. The more ups and downs of hiking will exert more stress on your legs and lungs. You will have to build added endurance. And there are dangers. You have to look out for holes in the ground. You have to look out for snakes, a very real threat to hikers and runners. Some snakebites are poisonous. If you want to walk or run in the woods or other rough terrain, never run alone and know what to do for snakebite. Despite a few minor drawbacks that can be overcome, hiking is a wonderful way to get back to nature.

A lot of people like to walk or run on the beach. I believe in it, but there is some controversy over it. There is a give to the sand that requires more effort and is good for your legs. I don't think I have known a lifeguard who was out of shape. Buzzy James, a twenty-five-year-veteran of the Los Angeles lifeguards, says this is as much because of running in the sand as it is because of swimming.

Lifeguards swim a lot. They also walk and run on the sand a lot. They are required to run at least a half mile a week on sand, but they regularly run much more than that. Buzzy runs several miles a week on the sand and he has strong legs and a strong body. He recalls having to run almost a mile on the sand, then swim more than two hundred yards through a heavy surf to effect one rescue. He says, "I never could have done it if I had not been conditioned for it."

However, it is best to walk or run on sand when the tide has just gone out, when the sand is damp but not deeply wet. Running in mud or hot, loose sand exerts a strain on your Achilles tendon that could be dangerous. If you can embark on a program where you begin on firm sand and progress slowly to soft sand, then I am all for it. It is beautiful to walk or run along the oceanfront with the waves breaking in and the fresh salt air around you. It encourages you to continue.

Walking or running in dirty air, in smoggy circumstances, is dangerous for your lungs and has to be limited. We do not always have a choice, but it is best to walk or run where the air is clear. If it is not, and if you feel pain in your lungs, stop. This is why it is best to run by the beach or in the country. Hiking and cross-country running are excellent because this usually is done where the air is clear and the terrain is interesting and attractive.

We do not always have a lot of choices as to where we will walk or run. We walk or run in dangerous places. Often on the highways, sometimes between cars parked on the shoulders of roads and cars coming by at fifty-five or sixty miles per hour. The roads are not for runners, and you have to practice considerable caution when running where cars have the right of way.

It is best to walk or run on a flat surface that has a bit of give. Dirt is best. Grass is good. A golf course is great. Cement and asphalt are not as good. The right kind of sand can be good. Really steep slopes that require sharp up-and-down walking or running are an excessive strain on your body, especially your Achilles tendon, but the sort of slopes that you will encounter in ordinary hiking or cross-country running can be beneficial because they do demand more of you. Never run hard down a steep slope because the jarring can damage the spinal column and supporting muscles.

Dr. Kenneth Cooper, whose book *Aerobics* contributed greatly to the running boom, admits, "The overwhelming advantage of walking is that it can be done by anyone, anytime, anyplace. It doesn't even look like exercise. For those who are timid about being conspicuous, this can be a deciding difference. But the best thing for you by far is running."

"Aerobics" means, roughly, "living in air." In running it has come to mean using running to build up our intake of air and thus, oxygen, and so building up our lungs, heart, and cardiovascular system. Dr. Cooper was the first to use a system of points to suggest the various values of different athletic activities. Others followed. I have one such system earlier in this book. His center for physical fitness in Dallas has become an important place for research in conditioning, and all his research has led him to believe running to be the best exercise of all.

Walking is only a step from running, but jogging is maybe a half step in between. A boom in jogging led to the boom in running. But jogging has come into controversy.

Many experts feel that the slow, pounding gait of jogging jars the feet, ankle, shin, knee, and hip past reason. In faster running, the feet come into contact with the surface less often and less directly, and the impact is spread better over the body. I think there is merit to this. But I consider jogging a preparation for running. It bridges the gap between walking and running. It gets you into running. It really is slow running, and the more you jog, the better you will be able to build up to faster running.

Dr. Kerlan says that it has the advantage of giving you maximum benefits in minimum time. He says, "It is, for most people, about the best general exercise to stay in shape, keep healthy, and remain active."

There is a difference between health and fitness. Health is the absense of physical ailments. Fitness is the ability to perform physically. The greater degree of fitness you achieve, the more you will be able to resist physical ailments.

Dr. David Adamovich, chief exercise physiologist of the Nassau County, New York, Medical Center coronary unit, is a jogger who says, "My feeling is that jogging fits into the context of total fitness, and is not just something for your heart."

One of his patients, 73-year-old Eric Lynn, suffered a heart attack running, recovered, and now warns that you have to cut down as you get older. Dr. Adamovich notes that while Eric had a heart attack, he did not die.

The good doctor adds that while jogging or running does not immunize you against attacks, they help you avoid them or recover from them. Anyone who does anything strenuous runs the risk of a heart attack, but the healthier the heart, the less the risk.

When you take a stress test under close supervision, a doctor is studying your internal responses to determine your limits, and he stops you when he feels you may be exceeding them. You will have signed a form acknowledging that you are running a risk, but he is there to provide immediate treatment if needed.

When you stress yourself without supervision, there is no doctor there to stop you if you overdo or to treat you if you suffer a coronary attack of some kind. Our hearts can handle only so much, and this differs from heart to heart. It is critical to know our limits and to stop short of them.

If in doubt, underdo.

If you know you have or have had a heart or other problem and doctors have determined how much exercise you can handle, fine. If you know you have no heart or other problem, you can probably handle a lot of exercise. The problem is that many of us do not know we have problems, and these may be exposed under stress.

You should be aware of the risks.

Karen Krantzcke, a 30-year-old tennis pro, died after jogging. John Holewinski, a 25-year-old, died during the 7½-mile Bay-to-Breakers Run in San Francisco. But Paul Spangler, a 78-year-old doctor, who went the distance in little more than an hour, noted, "People have died sleeping, too."

There are an estimated 10 million recreational runners in this country today, some 7 million of them joggers. Those who preach running as the way not only to physical fitness but also to good health and long life, believe you have to go beyond jogging to running to get the best benefits, and if you can go beyond to the marathon level, you are the best off of all.

A marathon is 26 miles, 385 yards. At 59, Dr. George Sheehan ran the famed Boston Marathon in 3 hours, 11 minutes, which averages out to about 7 minutes a mile. He says, "Once you build up to it, it's beautiful. But you have to build up to it. If you can, you will be in the best physical condition possible."

Dr. Jack Scaff, a 41-year-old cardiologist from Honolulu, says,

"You don't have to be in perfect health to be a runner, but the more you run, the better health you will be in. There are risks in any athletic activity, depending on the physical condition you bring to it, but once a runner reaches the marathon level, the possibility of heart disease is remote."

Dr. Thomas Bassler, a California pathologist, advises heart patients that if they stop smoking, run at least one marathon, then settle into a regime of three six-mile runs a week, their heart condition never will worsen.

There are those who disagree with this. I am one. "Never say never." But most medical men who have gotten into running believe the pluses far outweigh the minuses.

Lieutenant Colonel Victor Gorelicher, an M.D. in the U. S. Air Force School of Aerospace Medicine, runs 50 miles a week and says he wouldn't do without it, but concedes there are risk factors, especially if you get into it in bad health and rush it.

He says, "A smoker who quit cigarettes or an eater who cut out fats and sugars would be doing more for himself than he would do by running, but one of the benefits of becoming a runner is that you tend to cut down drinking, smoking, and bad diet, if not eliminate these entirely."

It is no secret that these things are bad for you. It also is no secret that they are hard to resist. Many of the great athletes I've known smoked and drank, and many ate junk foods. Possibly because they were yet young and healthy and had unusual physical makeups they could get away with this, whereas you could not.

Most athletes I've known have liked their beer after games. I know runners who drink a lot of beer the night before running. They believe this loads their bodies with carbohydrates they can use the next day when stressing themselves. There is something to this, but not enough. I don't believe a beer will hurt you, but overdoing anything won't help you.

It is said that most of us have done a lot of damage to our bodies before we reach the adult ages of 18 to 21, which is a good reason for turning our children onto exercise such as running early in life. Certainly most of us have done a lot of damage to our bodies by the ages of 30 or 40 or 50. We have to take this into account before we move from walking to jogging and on to running or advance into other rigorous games or exercises. We have to see where we are before we can decide how far we safely can go.

There are tests you can take to determine your fitness for running. You can determine your own resting heart rate. Placing the tips of two fingers on your radial artery—on the thumb side of your wrist—count your pulse for 10 seconds, and multiply by 6. Average men will have heartbeats of 70 to 80 per minute, women about 5 beats faster. If you do a lot of exercise it may be lower; if you do very little it may be higher.

There is no way to determine exactly your maximum heart rate on your own. A stress test, such as a treadmill test administered by a doctor, is the only way to find this. It may be more than twice your resting rate. It is important to know it because you should limit your rate of exercise to no more than 70 per cent of your maximum. In general, people up to the age of 30 should not exceed 190 to 200 beats per minute; to the age of 40, 175 to 185; to the age of 55, 160 to 170; and to the age of 65, 140 to 150. But if you have any kind of heart problem, this may be too much. If you have any doubts, you should see your doctor before embarking on an exercise program.

In general, a slow 5-minute walk will pick up your pulse to 50 per cent of your maximum; a brisk 5-minute walk to 60 per cent; and a 5-minute jog to 70 per cent. Dr. Leroy Getchell of Ball State University's adult physical fitness clinic in Muncie, Indiana, says, "If you can walk for a mile or two and do not feel discomfort or dizziness, and then alternately jog for 30 seconds and walk for a minute without problems, you're probably okay."

Take your pulse rate before, during, and after exercise. Even if you do not have discomfort, if your pulse rate remains above 100 10 minutes after exercise or remains above the resting level 1 to 2 hours after exertion, what you are doing is too strenuous for your condition.

The recovery rate is another valuable tool for you to use. If you return to your resting rate rapidly, say an hour to two after exercise depending on the extent of the exercise, you figure to be fit for what you are doing.

Stepping up and down a bench 16 to 20 inches high depending on your height, 30 times a minute for 4 minutes will give you a maximum heartbeat you can use, and if your recovery to a resting rate is completed within 8 to 10 minutes, you can figure to be fine, but this is not scientifically precise. A stress test and recovery rate made medically under strict supervision is surest and wisest.

If you have pain in your chest or left arm, a choking or burning sensation in your chest, throat, or lungs, stop what you are doing and go to a doctor. Many times stomach gas will create symptoms similar to a coronary attack, but it is better to be safe than sorry.

If your legs hurt or you find it hard to get your breath or you feel a stitch in your side, this simply is to be expected, especially at first. One of the risks in running is in attempting to break through the pain barrier. Many do run past pain, but you have to look out for the type of pain that is a warning.

Bruce Dern says, "I have run the equivalent of several times around the world and I think it has hurt every step of the way. When I had the time, I ran as much as 50 miles a day, and ran 10-mile runs and 15-mile runs and marathons and supermarathons, which were 50-mile and 75-mile runs. Now that I am going good and am busy in my career, I train less and I run shorter races faster—I run about 15 miles a week and race half miles and miles as I did in high school and college. I believe that everyone who wants to run should decide what he wants to get out of running and where he wants to go with it before deciding which of the many kinds of running programs to pursue.

"I don't believe there is such a thing as jogging. I think it's just slow running. When I see my 45-year-old agent running, it may look like jogging to me, but he has just started to run, and to him it is running, because he is running as hard as he can for as long as he can and it hurts him. He is into long, slow running, and he can build up to where it won't hurt him. But if you run short races as fast as you can it has to hurt. I never ran into oxygen debt in marathons as much as I did in half-mile races. Most people don't run races. They run for fitness.

"I have heard and read all about the joy of running, but I have to say it never has transported me to a super plane of consciousness in which my senses were sharpened and everything became beautiful for me. It is too much like work for that. But I do it because I believe it's good for me and because it's satisfying to me. It's something to pick a point and get from here to there on your own, and it doesn't matter if you do it faster than this guy or slower than that guy, only that you do it as well as you can.

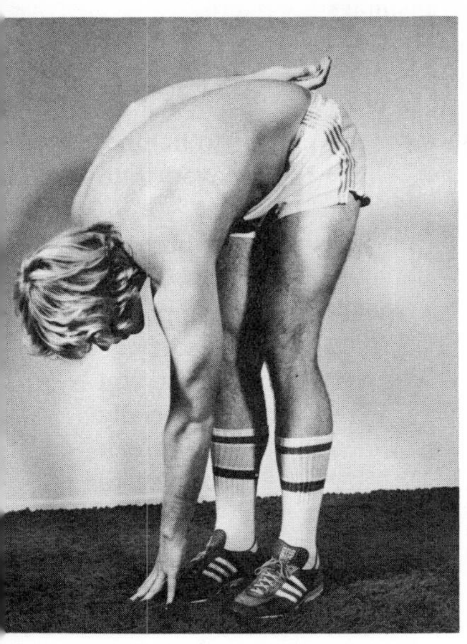

Toe touching: Legs kept straight, you reach down as far as you can, if possible touching the right toes with your left fingers, your left toes with your right fingers, loosening the muscles of your lower back and the backs of your legs. *(Photo by Lee Payne.)*

ıe leg hug: Legs straight, bend over as far you can, embracing the backs of your ;s. Most of you will not be as limber as ›lden West College soccer star Doug per, shown here. *(Photo by Lee Payne.)*

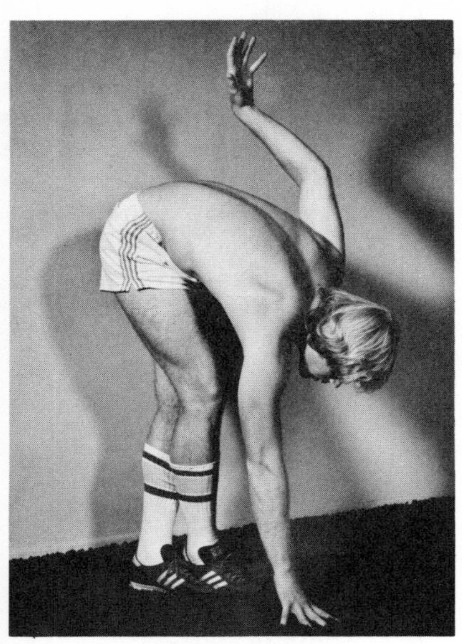

Floor touching: Legs crossed to increase stretch on the backs of the legs, lean forward, if possible, press the palm of first one hand, then the other, to the floor. *(Photo by Lee Payne.)*

Forward stretch: The subject leans forward from an extended sprinter's start to wrap hands around one shin and pulls to increase stretching action. *(Photo by Lee Payne.)*

AN ANKLE IS WRAPPED FOR PROTECTION.

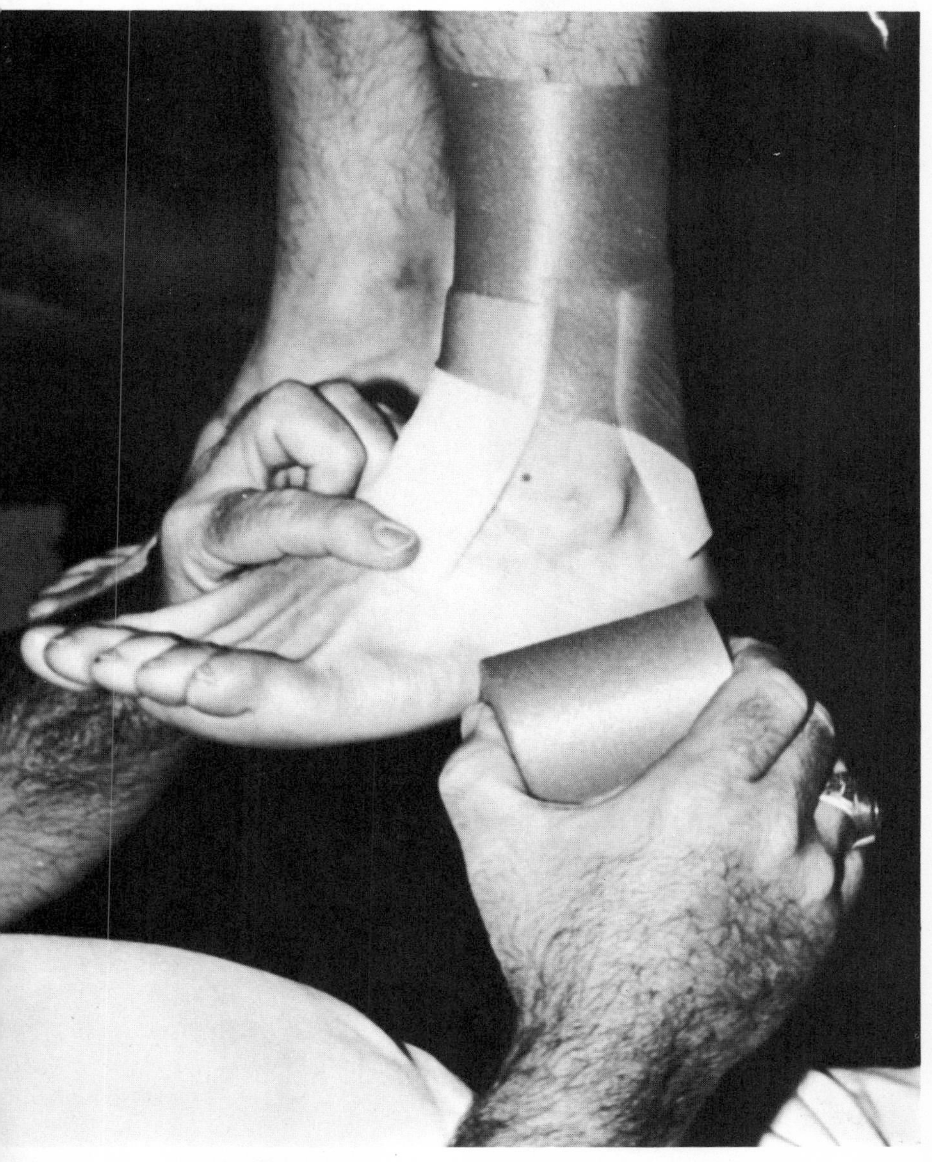

After a lubricant of grease is first applied to protect the skin, protective pads are placed at the front and back of the ankle, the points of most friction where the foot bends. *(Photo by Jim Walbert.)*

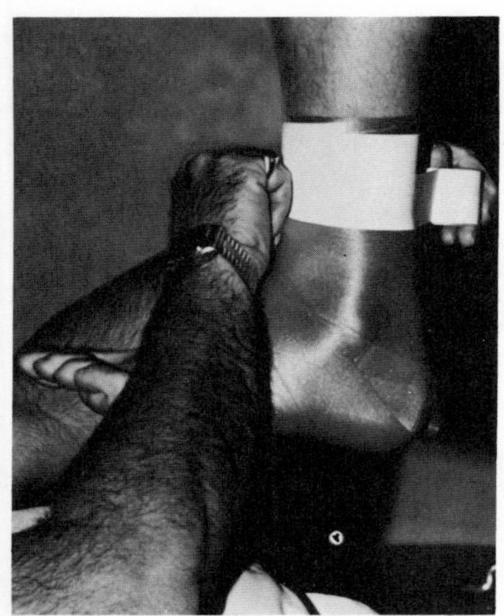

Pads are placed on ankle and held in plac by a polyurethane underwrap, which als protects the skin from the tape that wi then be applied. This underwrap is tissu thin. *(Photo by Jim Walbert.)*

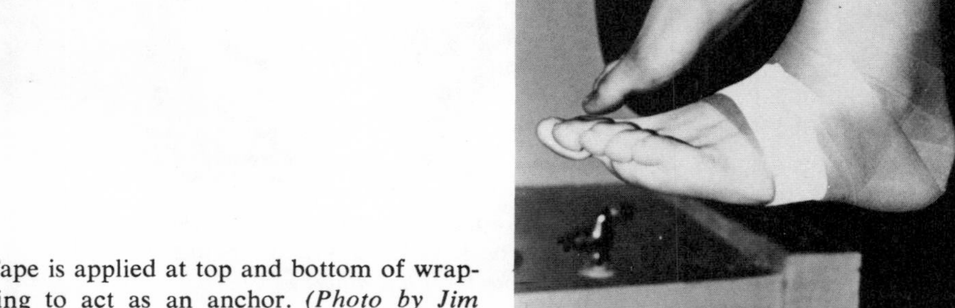

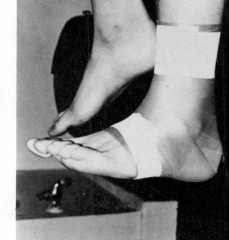

Tape is applied at top and bottom of wrapping to act as an anchor. *(Photo by Jim Walbert.)*

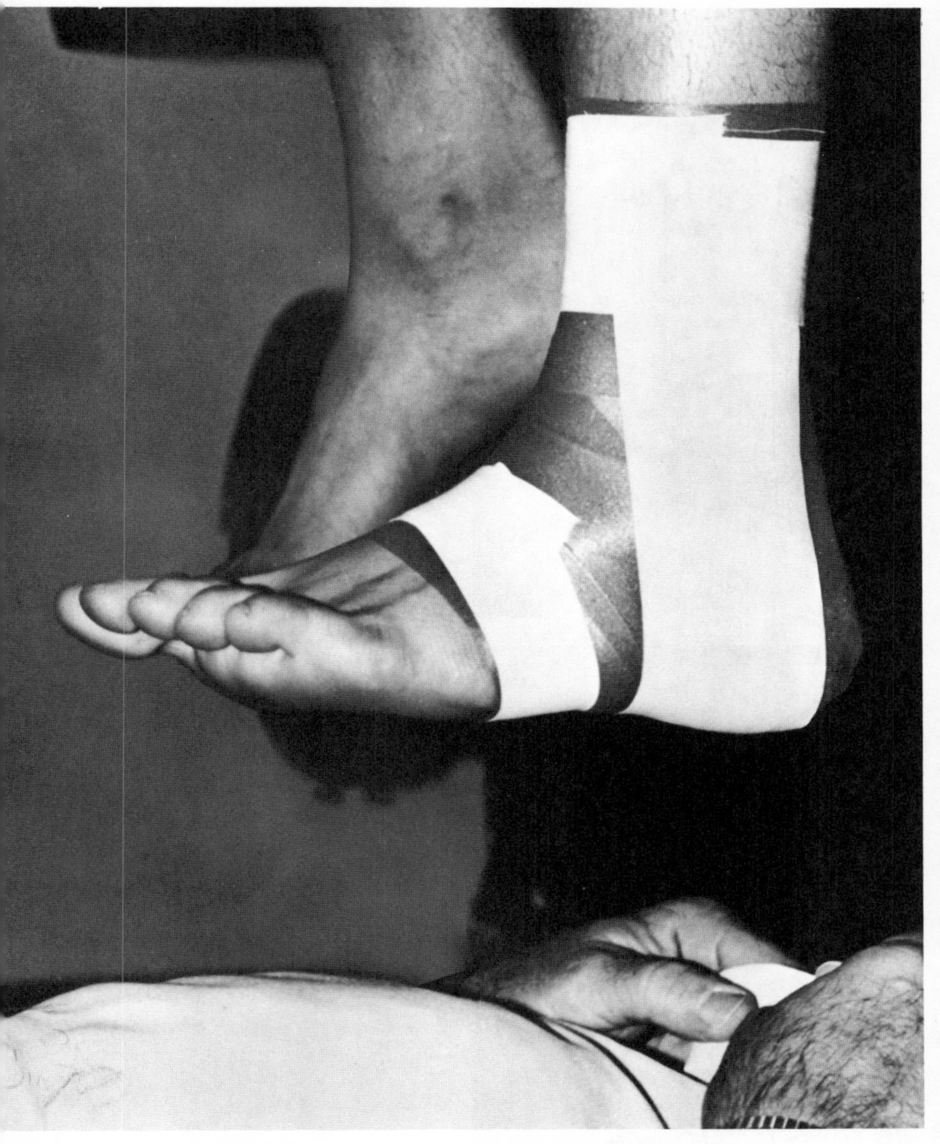

Tape is applied laterally in what are called "stirrups" to act as additional anchors for further taping. *(Photo by Jim Walbert.)*

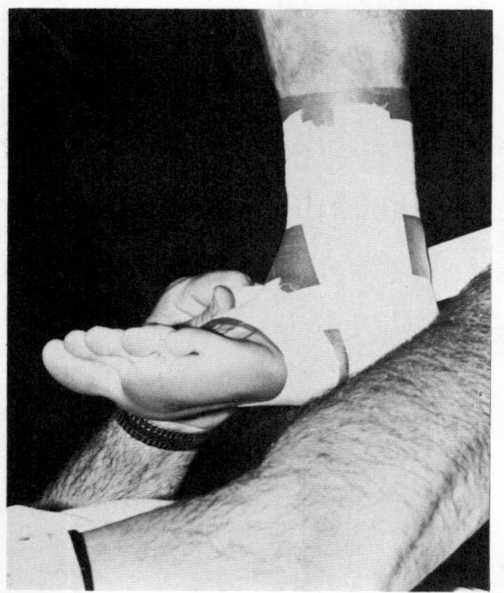

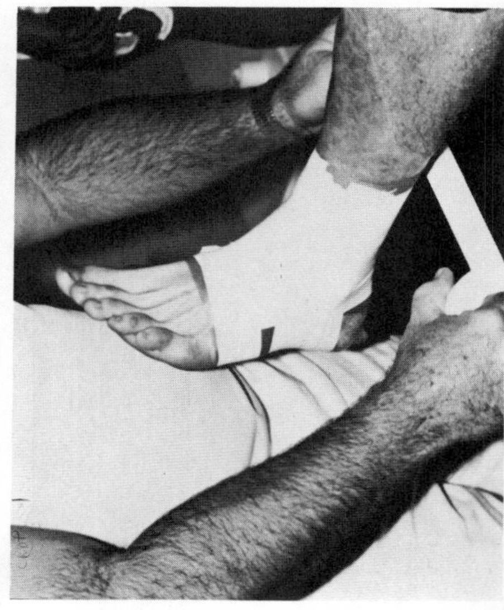

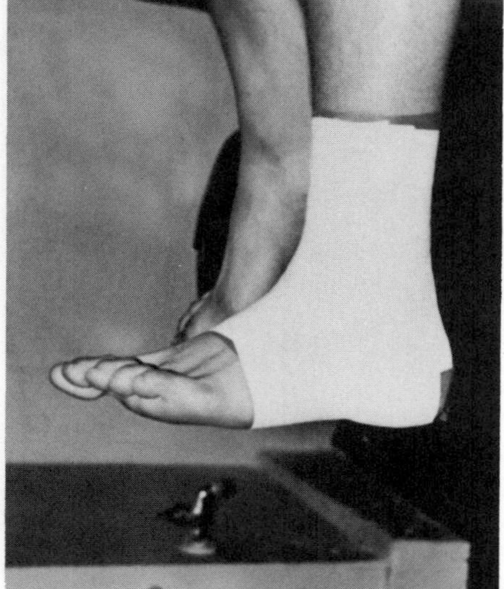

The ankle is then completely enclosed i
tape. *(Photos by Jim Walbert.)*

A KNEE IS WRAPPED FOR PROTECTION.

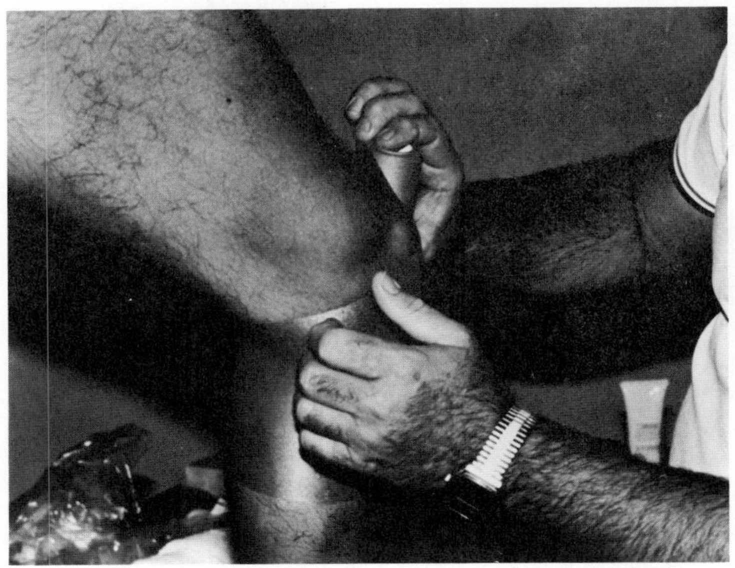

Following application of protective spray, a polyurethane underwrap is wound around the entire joint to further protect it from friction and taping. *(Photos by Jim Walbert.)*

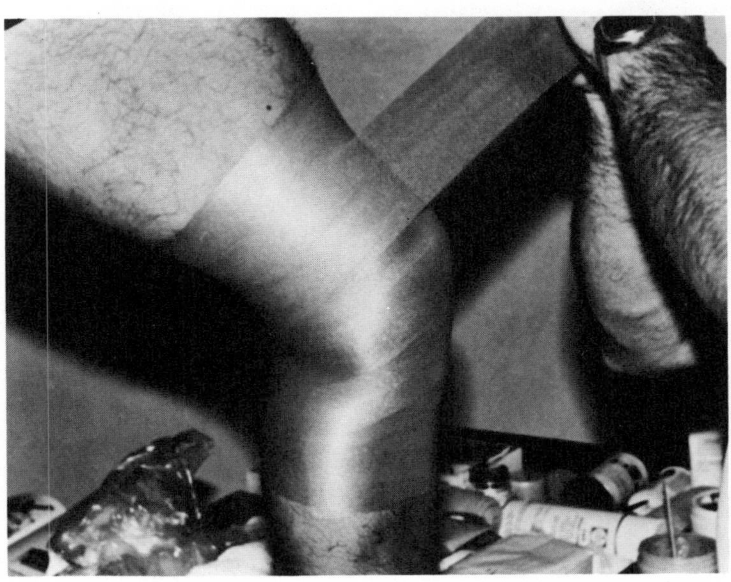

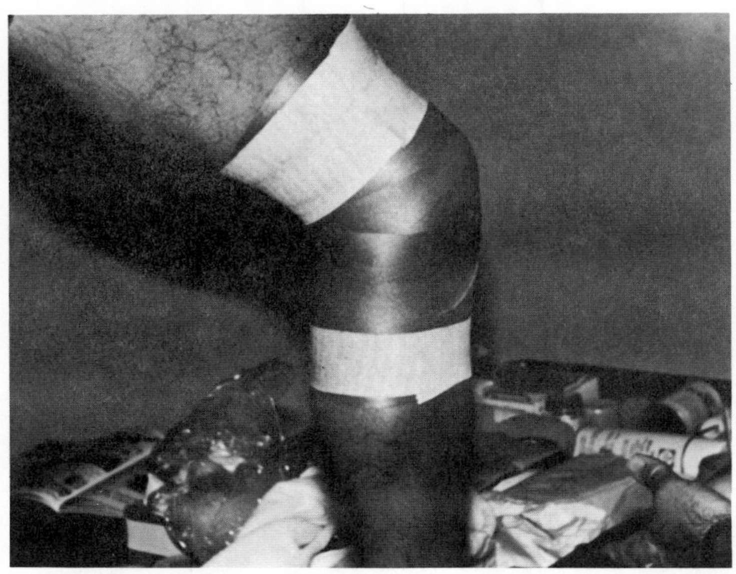

Horizontal taping top and bottom of knee provides anchors for supportive taping. Normal adhesive tape provides a joint the best protection, but elastic tape is lighter and permits more movement. In this case elastic tape is used as a base and then adhesive tape is applied for additional support. *(Photo by Jim Walbert.)*

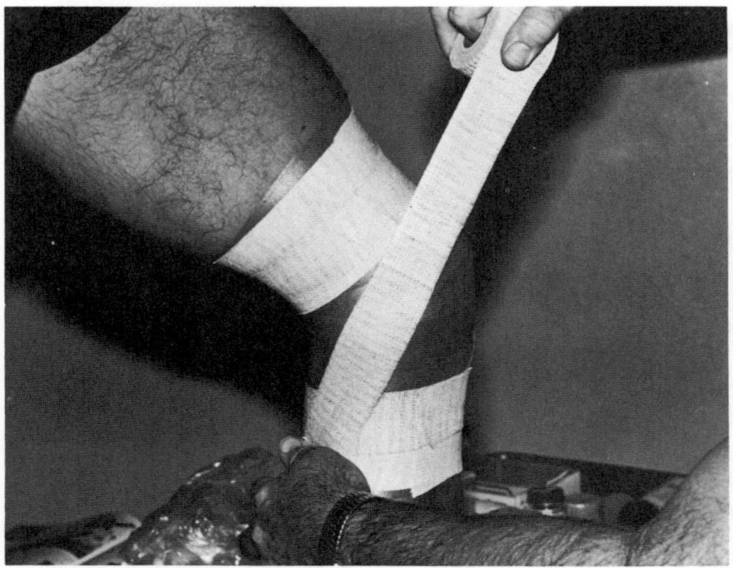

Elastic tape is applied vertically to inside of knee to provide "stirrups" of support for other taping. Outside of knee must be similarly taped. *(Photo by Jim Walbert.)*

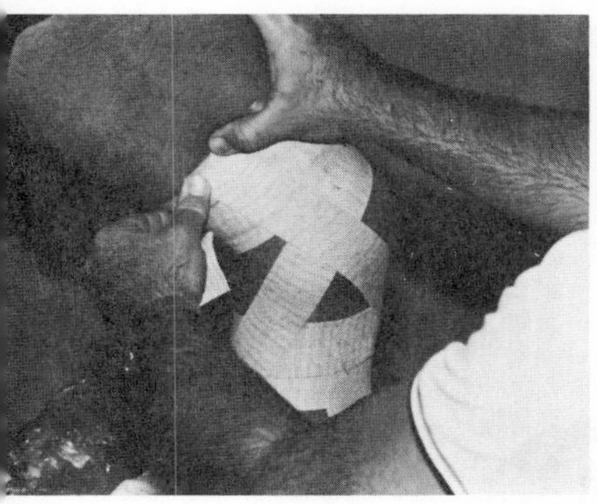

pe is applied in an overlapping manner ng natural pattern of ligaments to fit t and smooth. *(Photo by Jim Walbert.)*

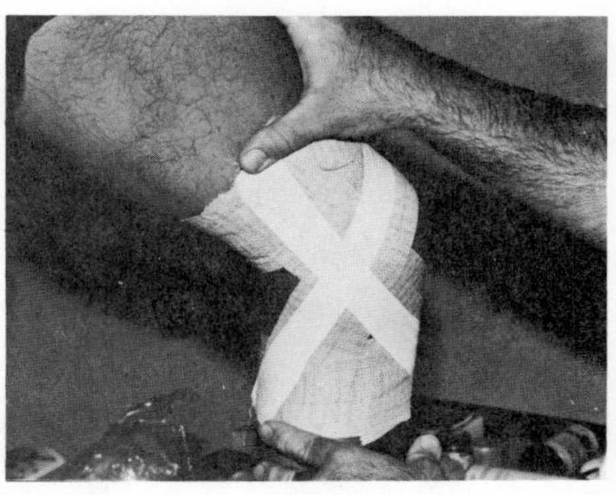

Adhesive tape is applied in an overlapping manner over elastic tape to add support to knee. *(Photo by Jim Walbert.)*

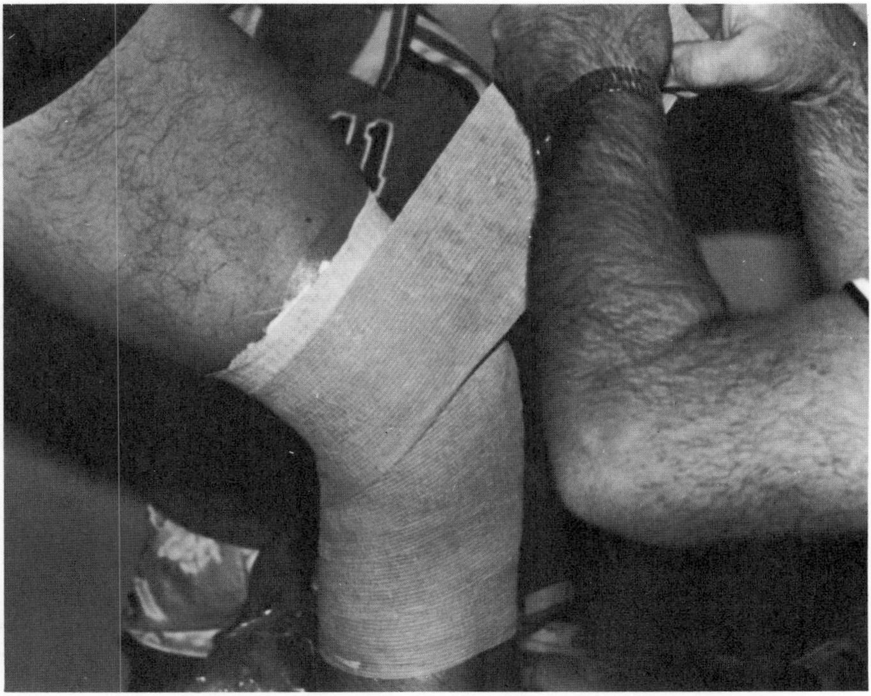

Completing supportive taping of knee, a final covering of elastic tape is applied in an overlapping, crossing pattern to provide greatest support. Elastic tape can be applied to a joint in a figure-eight pattern without anchors or stirrups. *(Photo by Jim Walbert.)*

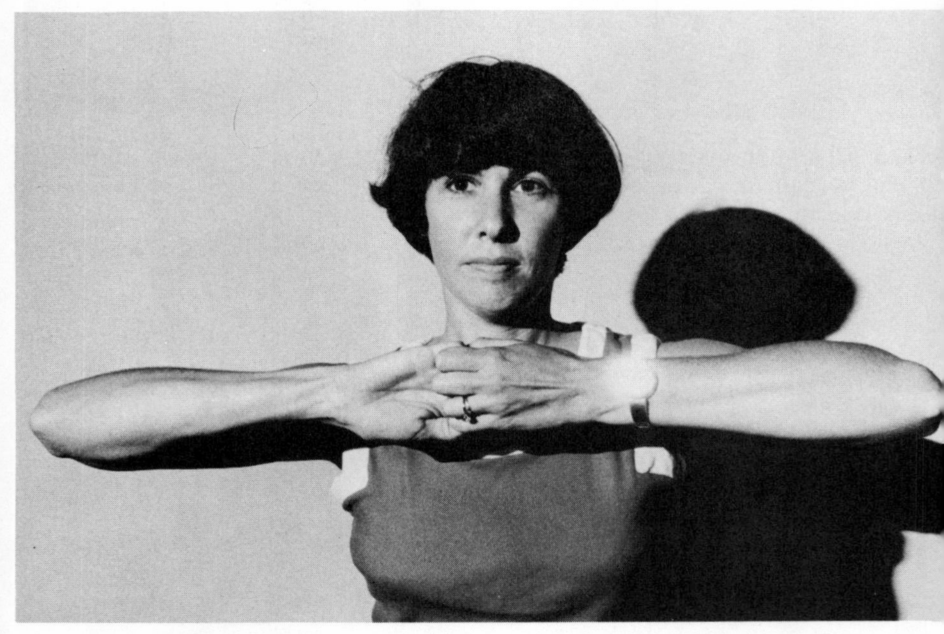

The finger pull, a standard isometric exercise. In isometrics, you use your muscles working on themselves, mainly, to increase strength. *(Photo by Gary Ambrose.)*

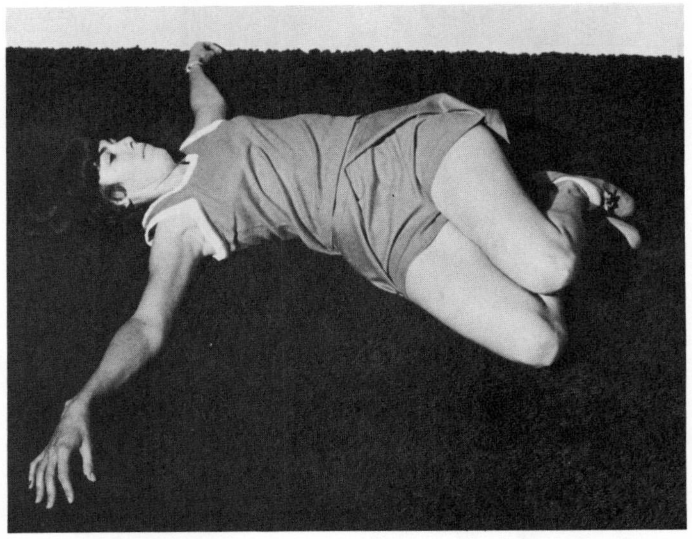

The hip roll, a calisthenic designed to stretch and loosen leg, hip, and side muscles, is demonstrated. *(Photo by Gary Ambrose.)*

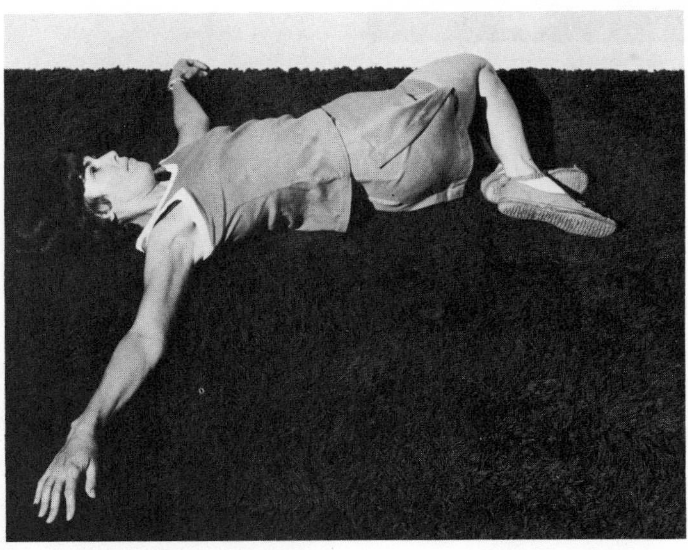

In doing the hip roll, you roll first from one side, then to the other, back and forth, ten or more times. *(Photo by Gary Ambrose.)*

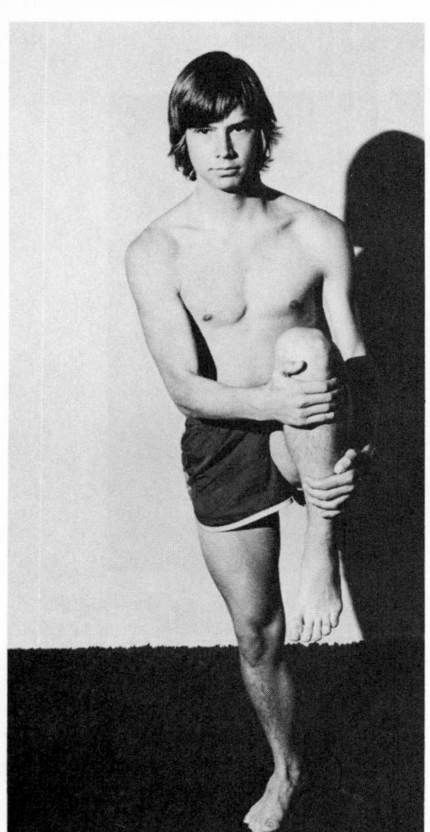

The knee pull, a standard calisthenic. N
only the leg muscles, but also arm and ba
muscles are stretched. However, the kn
should not be doubled too hard, as the joi
is a sensitive one. *(Photo by Gary Ambros*

Bicycling, from a shoulder stand, is a good exercise, stressing stomach, back, and leg muscles and increasing intake of oxygen. It is an "active" calisthenic. *(Photo by Gary Ambrose.)*

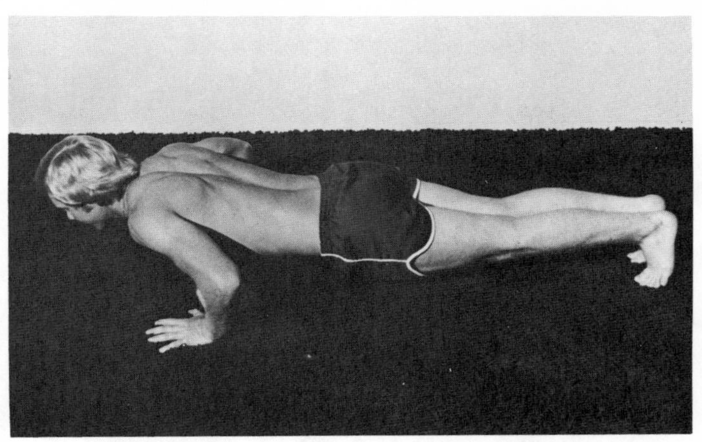

Pushups start with the knees straight. *(Photo by Gary Ambrose.)*

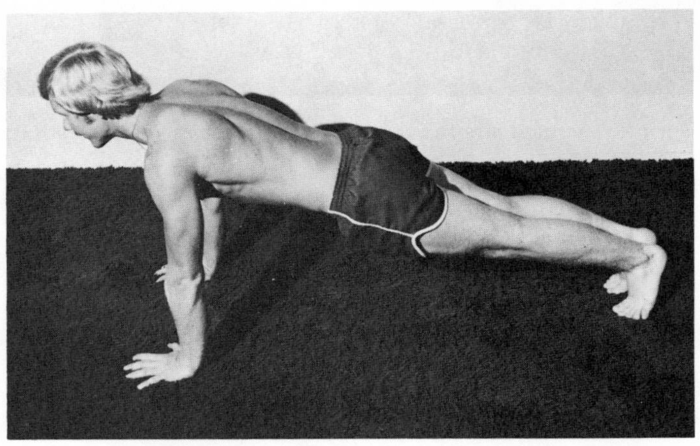

Knees are kept straight as subject does pushups. *(Photo by Gary Ambrose.)*

The sprinter's stretch stresses the hamstring muscles of the leg. *(Photo by Gary Ambrose.)*

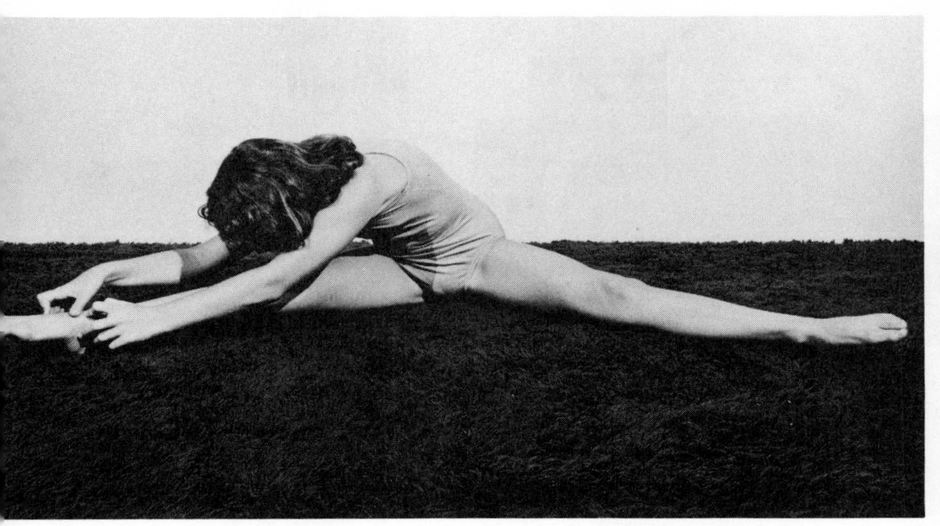

The sit stretch stresses back and leg muscles. *(Photo by Gary Ambrose.)*

The sit stretch is done first to each foot, then to both at once. *(Photo by Gary Ambrose.)*

Gymnast Lee Ann Paris builds a back arch. *(Photo by Gary Ambrose.)*

Gymnast Lee Ann Paris starts a back wal
over. *(Photo by Gary Ambrose.)*

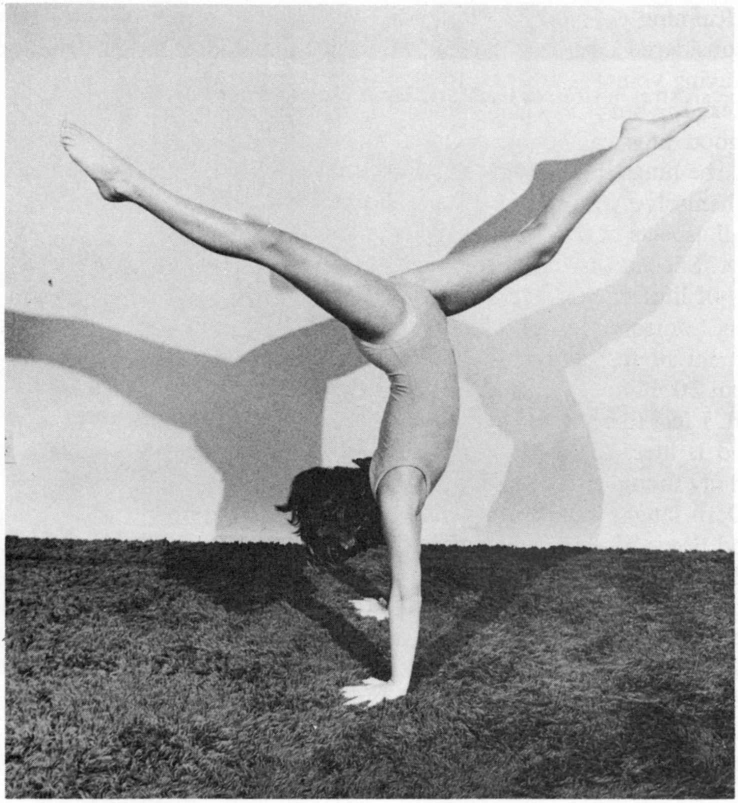

Completing a back walkover. *(Photo by Gary Ambrose.)*

"Running is a narcotic and I'm hooked on it. I don't miss a day, and haven't for years. I even run when I'm not feeling well. Redford and I talk about 'leaving it on the mountain.' When we've got the flu or something, we bundle up and go into the woods and run and get that stuff moving around inside of us and it helps us. Because I run there aren't many times when I didn't feel well. I run until it hurts and that makes me feel good."

James Fixx, author of *The Complete Book of Running,* says he has a friend who runs when he is not well and who says, "Running is my doctor." Fixx himself says, "There is a growing number of physicians who practice preventive medicine by prescribing running. Running helps your entire body feel better. And it qualifies as what the American Medical Association calls a lifetime sport—one that can be participated in long after contact sports have become too hazardous.

"Running does some startling things. We live in an age when it is considered desirable to be young and unfortunate to be old, so if staying young is what you want, running can help. The pleasure of sex, for both men and women, is invariably heightened. Being in good physical condition involves not just muscles, the heart, and the lungs, but all the senses as well. Runners are more aware of themselves and of others, and are able to participate more fully in all aspects of life, including the sexual."

Dr. Sheehan is one who believes in the beauty of running as a way of life: "Sex is supposed to be equal to only about a 70-yard dash. Someone figured it out. That won't keep you in shape. But that initial thrust toward body awareness is important. It takes about 30 minutes, but after 30 minutes you begin to feel it in your soul. I feel like I could run forever. I am a peace with myself. My mind is alert to all that is around me. My senses are sharpened and my thoughts are sharper. Movement makes one think better."

Dern laughs and says, "Movement makes you tired. But it is a good tired. When my career was going bad, my marriage had gone bad, and my life was lousy, I used to run all the frustrations right out of me, and it calmed me. It was a psychological outlet I needed at that time. Now it is the physical thing that I need. Running does fill needs. Even if I don't feel what some others say they feel I think we agree that running is the greatest exercise going."

I agree. Running is *the* basic exercise. It is a good basis for any game you may want to play or a satisfactory substitute for any game. It does not build up your upper body, but it does build up your legs, which support your body, and it builds up your inner body, which is the most important part of all.

Do not run every day. Once you get going on your running program, it will take too much out of you. Walk and run on alternate days if you wish, but do not run more than every other day. Play tennis or golf or go do whatever games you like on "off days," but give your body time to recover from every run.

Experiment with different types of running to decide which you prefer and which will do what you want for yourself. Speak to experienced joggers and runners or join a jogging or running club so you can come to understand the different types of running and what each does, and set up a schedule that is right for you. Generally, middle-distance, slow runs are best for the average recreational runner. Sprints or other short, fast runs are less beneficial for your body, and long runs up to a marathon or more are too hard and take too much time to train for. However, to each his own.

In any event, start slowly. If speed and racing satisfy you best, start by alternately running and walking 100 yards two times each the first two days, three times each the next three days, and four times each the next four days. Then run and walk, first 220 yards, then 110 yards twice the next two days. Then run and walk two 220s and two 110s for three days. Then run and walk a 330, a 220, and two 110s for four days. Then run and walk a 330, two 220s, and three 110s for four days. Then run and walk a 440, a 330, a 220, and a 110 for four days. This is called interval running and is favored by most track coaches.

This basic schedule will carry you through twenty-six running days over fifty-two days or almost two months. It is a form of interval training and eventually you will peak at one 440, two 330s, three 220s, and four 110s, alternately run and walked on your heavy days, one 330 and one 110 on your light days. This will provide you basic conditioning for races from 100 to 440 yards. This can only be done on a measured track.

You should rarely run all-out. Once a month, or one week before a race if you run races, you may wish to time yourself so you can measure your capacity and improvement, but usually you should run at 70 per cent of capacity in any kind of running. On the days on which you run hard for time, do not run the other distances, except leisurely.

It is beneficial to keep records of your running, both distances run and occasional times, in any kind of running, so you can keep your program balanced and keep track of your progress. Expect plateaus at each level and do not expect improvement past certain points that may represent your reasonable limits.

My co-author has a friend, Bob Longood, who had never run, but believed he could run a four-minute mile. The fellow figured he would run the mile as fast as he could, then keep running it faster all the time, cutting off fractions of seconds steadily until eventually he got to the four-minute mark. It is an interesting theory, but it doesn't work in practice.

Like the person who carried a calf upstairs every day until the day came when the cow had grown too large to be lifted and had passed the person's peak of strength, this ambitious fellow embarked on a crash program, but when he stopped improving he got discouraged and quit.

Take your time and don't expect miracles. Like a dieter who gets discouraged when the pounds drop off slowly or stop entirely for a while, it is easy to give up. Often it is hard to go on. But if we don't demand four-minute miles of ourselves, we may make it.

Jim Bush, the UCLA track coach, is one who believes a relaxed run of a mile or so is better for your body than a fast, straining sprint of 440 yards or less or a slow, jarring jog of 2 miles or more. He says, "If you take eight to ten weeks or even more to learn to run right and build up to a mile or so at a reasonable speed, you will be the better for it." Bush has helped many athletes from other sports and many individuals out of sports. He may give a Gail Goodrich sprint work to increase his quickness, but Bush will more often give him fast middle-distance running to increase his leg strength and speed and overall body stamina.

Actually, Bush thinks a mile may be too much for most of us as a steady diet. Basically, Bush believes in running from 800 to 1,000 yards five days a week. Most believe in running farther less often, but you can find what suits you best. Bush believes you should eventually be running a mile in eight minutes or less five days a week and seek to cut your time to six or seven minutes. Most believe eight to ten minutes a mile, 2 miles a day, three or four days a week is better.

Dr. Kerlan believes in slow, long runs and feels any exercise pursued less than fifteen minutes at a time is unsatisfactory. You have to give it twenty minutes to a half hour a day doing something, even if you run only every other day. An hour a day, maybe an hour on alternate days, is better yet.

If you want to stop short of a mile, start with a half mile. Jog a quarter mile, then walk a quarter mile for four days. Then jog a 660 and walk a 440 for four days. Then run a 440 and walk a 440 for four days. Then run a 440 and jog a 440 for four days. Then run a 660 and jog a 440 for four days. Then jog an 880 and walk a 440 for four days. Then run an 880 and jog a 440 for four days. In about two months, you will have increased your running over about 30 days of sessions. Following this pattern, you will move up to jogging three-quarters mile and running one-quarter mile, then to jogging a mile and running a half mile, then to running a mile and jogging a half mile.

Always do the hardest or longest interval of running first, followed by the easiest, whether sprinting, jogging, or running, so the most tiring will be taken while you are fresh, the least tiring when you are tired.

If you want to limit your running to a mile or so, do so, but try to increase your speed as you go on. What might have taken you fifteen minutes at first almost certainly can be cut, half minute by half minute, to twelve minutes or ten minutes in time. Depending on your potential, you may be able to get down to seven or eight minutes, but take your time. It will get easier as you go along, but you have to run hard enough to get your heart working to 70 per cent of capacity.

If you want to run more than a mile, which most believe to be best—myself included—follow the same pattern of walking, jogging, and running at intervals, building up your distance before you build up speed. After you are comfortable at a 2-mile run on running days, you should get to the point where you can run a mile in ten minutes, 2 miles in twenty minutes. This averages out to only about an hour a week and is an excellent level of exercise.

If you want to put a little more into it, you can go up to 2½ or 3 miles in thirty minutes every other running day or every running day. You may want to build up to 5 miles once a week, say on Saturdays or Sunday, or even, eventually, 10 miles. If you want to run marathons, you will have to run 10 miles most running days and 20 to 30 miles some days. Dr. Sheehan, who runs marathons, runs 10 miles on Tuesdays, 10 miles on Thursdays, and races longer runs on weekends. Frank Shorter, an Olympic marathon medalist, runs 140 miles a week. Obviously, this is far beyond most of us. We do not have the energy, enthusiasm, or time to devote so much of ourselves to our running.

For members of certain professions, programs of exercise are encouraged. This includes policemen and firemen, whose work requires strenuous physical activity and who must continue to perform even as they advance in age. Many have found that distance running sustains fitness better than anything.

A friend of mine, Los Angeles policeman Sandy Hansen, works out every other day in one way or another, playing basketball or softball, lifting weights or running. He dotes on distance running. He tells a tale of chasing a suspect over walls and fences, down driveways and up alleys until cornering him at a dead end, only to discover the fellow was a former city cross-country champion. These days, the fellow ran only from the law. The law caught him because it ran regularly. Sandy says, "It was just like in the movies, but I never could have caught him if I didn't run and train regularly."

An amazing number of recreational runners are into long-distance running these days. Long-distance races draw fields of several thousand. But it is not for everyone. Everyone does not have an hour or two to devote daily to training. Or if they did, they would want to use it in other ways.

Interval training does increase speed, and sprinting is good for you. Running quarter miles and half miles are good for you. You can compete in races if you wish, perhaps at your age-group level.

Seniors' track is increasing in popularity, partly because more older men and women are into running today than they were yesterday, and partly because if they want to compete, they want to do so on their level. In seniors' meets, forty-year-olds race against forty-year-olds, and so forth.

By far the most popular race in seniors' competition today are distance races at from 3 miles to the marathon. Frankly, I am not in favor of a lot of competition for recreational runners. It tends to encourage them to push too hard. If the average recreational runner goes too far or too fast it will hurt too much and take too much time from his life and he will lose too often and will start to miss sessions and soon drop off at the side of the road.

The important thing is to decide what type of running you want to do and set up a training schedule you can meet consistently, which trains you but doesn't strain you, which stresses you to points of improved physical fitness but doesn't push you past points of pleasure and satisfaction. Running may not be easy. But there is no need to make it harder than it has to be.

A 10-mile run has to take the average adult close to two hours. That is fine. If it takes you longer, all right. Don't fight it. A lot depends on your age and conditioning. If you have to cut down or give up smoking, cut down (if not give up) eating; if you have a lot of wind to gain and weight to lose, it will take time to build up your running speed. Give it time.

It is possible to run almost anywhere. Bruce Dern tells about a time when it was time to take his run, but it was raining heavily outside and there was a pro football game he wanted very much to see on television. He ran 10 miles around his television set, watching the game. "I've done it a few times," he says, "especially in hotel rooms on the road. I rearrange the furniture to make room, strap on the old pedometer, and get to it."

Running in place is beneficial exercise. Done as hard as it would be out of doors, it can be as beneficial. You will be out of the rain or snow or smog, hot or cold of the outside and out of the way of barking or even biting dogs and jeering spectators and careening cars, which plague all runners. It may even put you in front of your favorite TV show, but it is as jarring as jogging and many times more monotonous. In addition, it is hard to run well in place, and it is important to run the right way.

For all running, keep your head up and your eyes straight ahead of you, unless you are going over rough terrain and have to look out for trouble. Carry yourself more or less straight up and down. At the most, lean slightly forward. Keep your hands open and your fingers relaxed and carry your elbows bent and relaxed. Let your arms swing gently back and forth in front of your body at waist level.

The poor, too-laboring runner has his head down and is gasping for air, is hunched forward, fists clenched, arms jabbing at phantom foes, and is striving for long strides, striking the surface beneath him heavily, flat-footed. Don't try for long strides. As you move past the slow running of jogging, stretch your stride only a little to a comfortable length. Land on your heels and roll forward on each foot, pushing off from your toes. Breathe naturally, but don't be afraid to gulp in air as you feel you need it. Some strike a rhythm that is helpful to them, breathing in with one stride, out with the other. Do what feels natural to you.

As I said, you should be able to carry a conversation. If you are running alone, try singing a few lines of a song you like from time to time. If you find it is a strain, slow down a little. Don't be afraid to take a break. There is no rule that you can't run a mile in 10 minutes or so, rest five minutes, then run another ten-minute mile or so.

Do not be afraid to drink while you run. Don't drink a lot and don't drink it too cold, but drink to replace the fluids you lose through sweat. Water is good. So are some of the athletic drinks now marketed, which contain glucose and potassium as well as water. One fortyish marathoner, Tim Bassler, starts with a beer at the starting line, has a cola in midrace, and says he has improved enormously with this system. Bruce Dern's wife follows him to "Coke" him during his runs. "I'm addicted to Coke and Pepsi and need it regularly to run right," he says.

Frank Shorter says, "You drink everything you can and it's still not enough. I drink decarbonated cola during races and drink more than a quart of water after a race to replenish myself. If it is hot, it is easy to get dehydrated. Runners have to take on liquids in limited amounts." Jackie Hansen, who once held the world record for women marathoners, says, "When I started running, I was told not to drink, so I was afraid to. I found out I tired a lot less and felt a lot better when I drank during long races. I don't think it's how much you drink, but how often. I've found a drink every three miles or so is best for me." A lot depends on the length and speed of the race and the heat of the day, but it is advisable to drink a little bit of whatever you like a few times during a race to replace lost fluids. Find what you can handle, but I think you will find that drinking a little is best. I'm not suggesting you run to a bar, by the way.

It is important to cool off after running. It will have brought a lot of blood and oxygen to your legs, causing a lack of blood and oxygen in other parts of your body. Because of this, there will be buildups of lactic acid, which should be dissipated. If you stop abruptly, your muscles are apt to stiffen and become sore.

After running, jog, then walk awhile, just as after races, racehorses are galloped, then walked. A bit of stretching calisthenics would do you good. Let the blood begin to circulate normally throughout your entire body, then let your body cool off. If it is cold and you are sweating, pull on a sweat suit to protect yourself from chill. When you get home get your sweaty clothes off, take a warm shower, and change into clean clothes. Once you are used to your routine of running, you should feel good afterward. You may even find it so enjoyable you will look forward to your next training session. You will have added something worthwhile to your life. It doesn't matter if you're not a world beater.

The world record for 100 meters (almost 110 yards) for men is 9.95 seconds by Jim Hines, and for women it is 11.01 seconds by Annegret Richter. The record-mile for men is 3 minutes, 49.4 seconds by John Walker, and for women, 4 minutes, 29.5 seconds by Paola Cacchi. The marathon record for men is 2 hours, 8 minutes, 34 seconds by Derek Clayton, and for women, 2 hours, 34 minutes, 48 seconds by Christa Vahlensieck. These are nice to know, but it is safe to say they are beyond you.

It is critical to realize your limitations. Strive to stretch them, but understand that the thinner you stretch yourself, the more apt you are to snap. Each of us can run only so fast, so far. Competitive running is the search for these limits. Recreational running is competing within ourselves within these limits. Recreational running at sprint distances is risky because it tempts us to go all out too often instead of staying within the safe 70 per cent limits of our routines. As we improve, our 70 per cent will be higher, but it is important to hold something back before we crash into our barriers.

One of the most dangerous things any recreational runner can do is try to catch or keep up with someone in front of him, such as on a long-distance run. The runner ahead may not look fit or fast, but may have been running longer than you have and may be better than you are. You don't know. Don't push yourself past your personal limits. The ego enters into it too often. We always want to do better. We always want to be better than the next person. A lot of us are losers in life and want to win. It's understandable. But really, we should be running only against ourselves. There will always be someone better. Most likely, there will also be someone worse. Some always will be ahead of us and some also behind us. If not, so be it.

Jack Nicklaus doesn't win every tournament. Bjorn Borg doesn't win every match. I watched Elgin Baylor make miracles for years, yet he never was a winner in a championship game. We are not Nicklaus, Borg, or Baylor. We are looking for recreation, conditioning, and health. The real game we are trying to win is the game of life.

5. OTHER LEG SPORTS: SKATING, SKIING, AND BICYCLING

While walking and running are basically the best for your body, there are other sports such as skating and cycling that are almost equally as good and may be used as an alternative by those who prefer them. Ice skating and roller skating are excellent conditioners if you push yourself to points of speed and endurance that extend you and get your heart pumping.

Generally, they are done at such a leisurely pace that they do little for you. In indoor rinks it often is difficult to go fast enough to benefit without presenting a problem to the other skaters. However, if you are in a position to skate hard, indoors or outdoors, you will benefit from it almost as much as if you were running. Skating, especially ice skating, develops your arms, legs, and trunk muscles. Ice skating demands more of you than roller skating.

It is important to get instruction so that you skate properly, especially in ice skating. If you do not develop the push-off and gliding motion necessary, you will not be able to go long distances comfortably and may strain your muscles. It is important to have skating boots fit to you, especially for ice skating. These must be high boots that can be laced snugly about your ankles to provide support for your ankles. They can be bought for about fifty dollars a pair or rented.

The risks in skating are in falling. You will fall as fast on highly polished wooden roller rinks as on ice, incidentally, and it may hurt more. You may wish to wear elbow pads.

If you are serious about substituting skating for running, you are going to have to follow similar programs of progress. You probably will not get into the sprinting, but will build up from the quarter-mile level. Eventually, you should be skating a mile in six minutes or less and skate at least five miles every skating day and ten miles once a week if you are going to approximate the benefits you can get from running.

An advantage to skating is that, like running, it is a "lifetime sport" that one can pursue into older age, slowing down, perhaps, as you pass the milestones of fifty, sixty, and seventy. Another advantage is that it usually is done with others in attractive recreational areas.

Alpine skiing is not as good an exercise, but for many it is more fun than running or skating. Most people ski only on weekends or vacations, which makes it unsatisfactory as a total conditioner. However, it is a fine weekend departure from your regular week-long program, and your week-long program conditions and prepares you wonderfully well for weekend skiing.

You need strong legs and a strong cardiovascular system to ski hard and well. Skiing at approximately 10 miles per hour will burn up 350 calories in an hour, while running at the same speed will burn up 900 calories in an hour. Anyone can learn to ski at any age, but you must learn. Skiing requires much better body control and more agility than running.

Downhill skiing is much more dangerous than running. Sometimes it seems that the skiier who has not broken a leg is rare. It is critical to get ski boots and skis that fit you properly. And you must learn to use them properly if you are going to enjoy the sport in reasonable safety. In general, downhill skiing is less satisfactory as a conditioner than running or even skating. However, cross-country skiing may be equal. The problem with cross-country skiing is that few do it, and those who do, do not do it often.

A cross-country skiier going at it hard 10 miles per hour will burn up about 600 calories per hour. Experts believe that if he and a runner did 2 to 4 miles at 6 to 8 minutes a mile, the cardiovascular result would be identical. If you live in an area where cross-country skiing is possible a fair percentage of the year it is a terrific exercise. Cross-county skiiers are among the best-conditioned athletes in the world.

If it is possible to mix some cross-country skiing in with

downhill skiing by walking parts of the way to the top of the hill, it would benefit you a good deal. Waiting for ski lifts and riding in lift chairs do not help you. If you are into downhill skiing, the more runs you make a day, the better off you are. Two or three widely spaced runs followed by an evening in front of the fireplace are not going to condition you for much.

One problem with skiing is that it is one of the most expensive sports. The basic set of skis, boots, bindings, and poles is going to cost around a hundred dollars, not much less and maybe more. The boots cost more than thirty dollars, the skis close to fifty dollars. They can be rented at ski areas. In addition, you are tempted to buy a lot of fancy cold-weather clothes. Since most of us can't ski in our backyards, just getting to and staying at ski centers can be enormously expensive. Yet skiing is one of the most beautiful sports and many people are addicted to it. And if a person enjoys his sport, it will be easier for him to stay with it as a conditioner.

Water skiing is something else entirely. It is good for the arms and legs and you aren't going to be good at it unless you are fairly fit and agile, but it doesn't do a lot for your cardiovascular system.

Bicycling is close to a match for running. Done as hard, bicycling will do as much for you. Like running, it can easily be done in most areas. The same risks of the road prevail. In fact, the National Injury Information Clearinghouse, a government agency, rates cycling the runaway leader in injuries among sporting pursuits. Three times as many people get hurt bicycling as playing football. Of course, ten times as many people bicycle regularly, a thousand times as many on the adult level. But it is dangerous—there are the spills and the highway accidents. However, it ranks right behind running and swimming as an exercise for conditioning and has some advantages over these.

You are more apt to ride your bike to the store, to school, or to work than you are to run or swim there. It is something commonly done in company with others, and it exposes you to the great outdoors. You can more easily get farther away and cover greater distances cycling than running. Cycling does not do as much for the upper body as swimming, but is nonetheless good insofar as aerobic benefits and conditioning given your cardiovascular system.

Of course, it has to be done hard. Start with a mile in ten minutes the first two days, go on to 2 miles in twenty minutes the next two days, then a mile in seven to eight minutes for two days, then 2 miles in fifteen to sixteen minutes for four days. Increase your distance after that to 3 miles in twenty minutes, then increase your speed to 3 miles in fifteen minutes. Move then to 4 miles in twenty minutes. At this point you will be moving at 12 miles per hour, which is good enough to stick with. From here, you will find you can sustain your speed while increasing distance.

If you cycle 5 miles in a half hour, it is equivalent to running 2½ miles in that half hour burning up as many calories and benefiting your body in the same way. But it is easier to bicycle long distances than it is to run them. A cyclist can exercise for an hour more easily than a runner. A skilled cyclist can cover 15 miles or more in an hour easily. Many dedicated cyclists pedal 40 to 80 miles on a weekend outing, sustaining a pace of 10 to 12 miles per hour.

You do need a good ten-speed bike, the better ones costing several hundred dollars, but after you get one you will not need a new one for many years. And bicycling is something you can do in your later years.

Older people probably should settle for a speed of 15 miles an hour and 2 miles at a time. If they pedal 2 miles in a half hour, they will have done well, burning up approximately 150 calories for each half hour.

Bicycling in place at the same pace is equally good for you, and this is fine for those who can afford stationary bikes. They can even take in some TV while exercising, and they have the advantage of getting in out of harsh weather.

It is easier for runners to run in snowy, icy weather than for cyclists to pursue their sport. In fact, the one big disadvantage to cycling, other than flat tires, is that it is so dangerous as to be undesirable on wet, snowy and especially icy roads.

It is important to set up your bike so the seat and handlebars and pedal are positioned so as to be comfortable for you. You are going to get sore legs just as in running when you start, but you do not want to create back problems by poor posture while pedaling. You should be leaning forward comfortably. Your feet should reach the pedals comfortably without cramping your legs.

Cycling is not jarring to the feet, ankles, knees, hips, and spinal column, as is running, especially slow running. The power is provided smoothly by your legs and hips. But you must pedal with power for a prolonged period so as to exert yourself if you want to get value for your efforts. Leisurely bicycling will not do anything for you. Nor will leisurely anything, as far as exercise goes.

6. THE ARM SPORTS: SWIMMING, RACQUET SPORTS, HANDBALL, ROWING, GOLF, AND BOWLING

Swimming is second only to running, provided it is done as hard. Unfortunately, most of us simply do not swim well enough to swim fast enough and far enough to get as much from it as we can from running. And we do not have a heated pool in which we can swim every day or every other day all year round. If we have a handy lake, we can only swim during the warm months.

However, if you swim well and have water in which to swim twelve months a year, swimming is a good conditioner. Although I class it with the arm sports since the arms are the main movers, you use your entire body more than in running and bicycling. Even if you swim as hard as you run, you will only burn off about half as many calories, but you will build your upper body better, and your cardiovascular system as well. It is even cheaper than running, since a swim suit costs less than a good pair of running shoes.

It may be more monotonous. Unless you are swimming in the ocean or on a lake, you are not seeing the scenery. Swimming laps, up and back, especially in a short pool, can be dreadfully dull. But if you enjoy swimming, it is wonderful exercise. You run less risk of injury than in running or cycling. In fact, the support the water provides your body enables you to do easily some marvelous stretching exercises simply by wriggling around.

Some people call a pool a backyard chiropractor. You can feel your bones and joints cracking freely—you can hear them—but you are not apt to hurt them.

If you are not a proficient swimmer, don't be embarrassed to seek out swimming lessons at any age. Most YMCAs and YWCAs and many other groups with pools provide lessons for all ages inexpensively, and you may even wish to become a member so you can use the pool regularly. If you know how to swim, there is a variety of strokes available.

The basic freestyle stroke is the one most of us know and use most easily. The backstroke, breaststroke, and butterfly strokes are harder, requiring more strength and energy. However, they do provide variety and stress different muscles. You don't have to go as fast doing the breaststroke, for example, to get as much value from it as an equal distance done freestyle.

It will take twice as long a session of swimming to get equal value with a session of running. It takes about twice as long to swim a distance freestyle as it does to run it, but for some it may be more pleasurable. You should aim for a mile in less than 45 minutes, but you may wish to hold your every swimming day distance to about 1,200 yards in 30 minutes.

Sherm Chavoor, who coached Olympic champions Mark Spitz and Debbie Meyer, recommends that the recreational swimmer start with interval training. He suggests you swim 50 yards, take a 3-minute break, swim 50 more yards, take another 3-minute break, then swim a final 50 yards to start.

Gradually, increase your distance and decrease your breaks. Go to 200 yards a swimming day, then 300, and on to 400, 500, 600, and so forth. As you go, decrease your breaks to 2½ minutes, 2 minutes, 1½, 1, and finally 30 seconds.

Once you have attained a degree of comfort with the distance you wish to swim each day, start eliminating some of the breaks. Go 100 yards without a break. Then 150. Then 200. Personally, I think it is good to level off at 200 yards a hitch with 1-minute breaks. You can, however, go on to 600 to 1,000 yards a day in total distance. You will have to measure your pool, but most are 25 yards in length. Thus, 600 yards is 40 laps. That is a lot, but not if you want to put as much into it as runners put into running.

A lot depends on how fast you swim and what stroke you use. If you swim freestyle 300 yards in less than 10 minutes, 600 yards in less than 20, 900 in less than 30, you are doing well. A skilled backstroker takes only a few seconds more than a freestyler per 100 yards, a skilled breaststroker about a fifth of the time longer. Presumably, you are not skilled. The less skilled you are, the wider the differences among your freestyle, backstroke, and breaststroke times.

World records in swimming are measured in meters. The record for 100 meters, which is a little less than 110 yards, is just under 49½ seconds for men (Jonty Skinner) and just over 55½ seconds for women (Kornelia Ender) in freestyle, 55½ seconds for men (John Naber) and almost 62 seconds for women (Ulrike Richter) in backstroke, and almost 63 seconds for men (Gerald Morken) and almost 71 seconds for women (Hanne Anke) in breaststroke.

This is at a sprinter's pace, of course. The freestyle record at 800 meters for men is 8 minutes, 1.54 seconds (Bobby Hackett) and for women, 8 minutes, 35 seconds (Petra Thumer). You are not going to swim this fast, but listing such marks shows us what is possible. If you can sprint 100 yards in less than 2 minutes and 880 yards in less than 22 minutes you probably are putting your heartbeat to 70 per cent of its maximum. At this pace you will burn up about 10 calories per minute. Swimming is good for us fatties in that we are more buoyant. However, those of us with excess weight will not have our cardiovascular system performing as well as it could, and we find that swimming can be even more exhausting than running, primarily because we do not breathe as well. Usually you will draw in a breath every time you flop to one side, and you will flop to that side on alternate strokes, and you will exhale under water, but it is not as sound a system as normal breathing.

It is said that you should not swim less than an hour after eating. There is truth to this, but it applies to all strenuous exercise. You must give your body time to digest the food you have eaten. If you feel cramps while swimming, get to safety and stop awhile. Never swim beyond shouting distance of someone. If possible, do not swim alone. If you drown, you will not enjoy the benefits of swimming.

Swimming is marvelous recreation as group fun, but if you lie about the pool or beach with friends, go into the water, and fool around, you are not getting any fitness benefits from it. You have to reserve time for serious swimming as an exercise if it is to help you. It can be an excellent alternative to other exercises on "off days" or weekends, as well as a wonderful full-time conditioner, but you have to put yourself on a disciplined program to get from it what it has to give you.

We have listed walking, hiking, jogging, running, skating, cycling, and swimming as not only excellent conditioning sports for everyone, but also as especially good for those who have not been active in physical activities and want to get going. Now we can get into games such as tennis and handball, which, along with skiing, are good for those who have been active in them, but they take more learning if you are to enjoy them.

Running, swimming, cycling, skating, and cross-country skiing occupy most of the spots in the top ten preferred conditioning activities, followed by two-man basketball, handball, tennis, and similar sports such as squash and racquetball. Singles tennis may be the single most underrated sport in the entire field of physical conditioning. Most experts do not rank it as high as it merits in my mind, but it has to be singles and it has to be played hard.

Tennis and other racquet sports are much more stop-and-go activities than running, swimming, cycling, and skating. A point may consist of a single shot and seldom more than five or six shots. You play the point, then return to get in position for the next point. Your muscles have the opportunity to recover regularly. They are at rest more than they are at work. They are not under straight stress for prolonged periods. Your cardiovascular system is subject to short bursts of stress, but does not get a prolonged workout.

In one sense, real wrestling is the most exhausting of sports because in a given hold, which may be held for minutes, the muscles are stressing without relief and the entire body may be involved. Most games, including football, baseball, and softball, are the opposite of this in that there is a flurry of activity, followed by a relaxed buildup to the following flurry. The more rest you get between bursts of activity, the less tired you are, the longer you can go, but the less it does for your body.

Tennis is a fascinating game and a lot of fun to play with friends or in any kind of competition. But to get the best benefits from it, you have to go hard. And to go hard, you have to be a fairly good player. If not, you will not keep the ball in play long enough to benefit from it. Thus, if you want to play fairly well, and you do not now, you would be wise to take lessons. This is expensive privately, but some instruction can be found in inexpensive recreation and parks programs.

There are plenty of tennis courts in most towns today, but you may find most of these occupied most of the time and may have to wait and get only a limited turn. There is a boom in the popularity of tennis today. A lot of golfers have given up their game in favor of tennis because they can get a harder workout in far less time. A lot of members of the movie colony in my Los Angeles area have turned to it for this reason. They want to stay fit. They want to present a good appearance. Don Rickles, who plays with his buddy Bob Newhart regularly, says, "I still play golf, but after golf I get in a couple of sets of tennis for exercise." The wealthy may have courts in their own backyard. You may have to join a tennis club to be able to get a court regularly, and this can be expensive.

Beyond getting a court, tennis is not an expensive game. You can wear almost anything, though you should dress lightly, giving your body the freedom to perspire. Tennis is played most often out of doors and often under a hot sun, so a cap is preferred if you do not have a thick head of hair. You will need a good pair of well-fitting tennis shoes and a good racquet. Depending on the surface on which you play, the right tennis shoe is as important to the tennis player as the right running shoe to the runner.

Shoes should be snug but not tight. The soles will be of hard rubber, more flexible than running shoes. They will wear out more often than running shoes because you slide on them and scuff the toes more often. There is a rubberized substance sold commercially and available in tennis shops that can be sprayed onto the tips of your shoes to protect them, or you can apply an extra patch of hard rubber with adhesive glue.

You should wear wool, low-cut socks that fit snugly and do not slide within the shoe, yet give the ankle and calf freedom to breathe. Again, women should wear bras.

A good warmup is more important in tennis than in most sports. This is because the first shot may turn out to be the most demanding of the day. You are thrust immediately into strenuous action. Yet most tennis players do not warm up. You should take ten minutes or more to do a variety of stretching exercises to get the blood flowing and get limber. You should practice all the strokes—forehand, backhand, serve, and overhead—with phantom swings, starting slowly and increasing speed to a full range of motion. This is especially important in the serve, which is an unnatural motion requiring an explosion of stretching.

Properly prepared, the risk of injuries is not as great in tennis as in many other games, although sore joints, pulled muscles, and cramps are not uncommon. Instruction will help you make your strokes properly. If you stroke properly the risk or pain of "tennis elbow" will be minimized, but we will get into this in depth in a later chapter on the care of athletic injuries. It is important to drink a liquid you like—most preferably noncarbonated—periodically during matches, especially on hot days. You will lose a lot of body liquid and must replace some of it. Salt tablets may help you replace lost salts and avoid muscle cramps.

You will burn up about 420 calories an hour in hard tennis. This is a little less than half the calories you will burn up in an hour of hard running. Thus you will have to play tennis more than twice as long to get a similar calorie benefit. It may be more fun for you to play an hour of tennis than to run for half an hour. Any running you do will build up your ability to get to shots, endure, and play good tennis.

If you are playing good, hard tennis, you are giving not only your arms, but also your legs and entire cardiovascular system a splendid workout. You should go for every shot, even if you can't get it. It is a good habit to develop and it is the exercise that is as important as getting the shot. Tennis is a game of winning and losing. It is important to play players on your level or just beyond so you have a fair chance to win and will not get discouraged by losing too regularly.

Tennis is popular with older players. Once a tennis player is hooked, he stays hooked. Players turn to doubles in their thirties and forties. Many older players play doubles exclusively. It is good for them. It is strenuous, but it is not as strenuous as singles, so if you are younger it is not nearly as good a game for you. You will not have to move as much, go as far for shots, stretch out as much. As a conditioner, doubles does not do half as much for you as singles.

There are also a lot more arguments in doubles. All athletes get intense in competition, and in doubles it is easy to blame a partner for a fouled-up shot or a defeat. Because you have to play an opponent, doing poorly is a lot more frustrating than in those activities in which you are essentially competing against yourself. Volleying has limited value. You have to play a hard game to get value. Play to win, but do not let losing defeat you. You may have lost a point, a game, or a match, but you can win a lot of physical fitness.

The competitive player who plays a five-set match under a hot sun is giving as much as any player in any game. In singles, he has no help. He has to go for every shot himself. He goes for three or four hours sometimes. It is tough. You do not see fat tennis players at the top. You do see them at the recreational level, but it is a good way to lose a little fat. One problem is that the average player may play only on weekends. If you can't play at least an hour of hard tennis every other day or night, you will need other exercise, such as running, to get in shape and stay in shape. Eight hours of tennis on a Saturday or Sunday is too much if you have had five days of inactivity in between and will never make up for three or four days of tennis, an hour or two at a time.

Racquetball and squash are variations on tennis. In some ways they are more strenuous. You play in a smaller space, hitting the ball off four walls. It comes at you from the side or from behind you at wild angles, and you have to react quickly. You are always on the move, and get a terrific workout. While we class them as arm sports; they are as much leg sports. It isn't long before you are breathing heavily and sweating heavily.

You can get an excellent workout in half an hour. It is something many businessmen are doing on lunch breaks. You burn up about 600 calories an hour, which puts it high on the list. You can burn up more if you play harder. The equipment is inexpensive. The lightweight squash racquet costs about twenty-five dollars. You will need good shoes that are suited to the courts and fit to your feet. The playing is expensive, however. A squash court may cost eight to twelve dollars an hour. Membership in a club may cost a couple of hundred dollars.

Racquetball is becoming much more popular today: Ten years ago there was not a racquetball club in the country. Today there are a thousand or more. Every major city has one or more: It is the hottest new recreational sport going. The boom may end and some clubs may close, but I think the sport will endure because it is a good game and excellent exercise. An increase in professional play and tournaments may help popularize it, but in the long run it seems suited best to recreational needs.

Because it is easier to keep the ball in play it is much easier to learn than tennis. Racquetball is one of those games that is easy to play, but hard to play well. You need quick reflexes and agility; thus it is being played mostly by younger players. Presumably they will continue to play as they get older. It is a good game for older players as long as they play players on their level. It is also a good family game.

The same is true of handball, which never really boomed, but always has been a passion of many players and always will be a demanding game that gives the players a tremendous amount of strenuous activity in a short time. You may have to move more as you hit the ball with your gloved hands instead of a racquet, but the ball comes at you more slowly so you do not have to move as fast. The caloric consumption is similar to that in racquetball.

Handball is a harder game to play than racquetball because it is harder to hit the ball well with your palm than with a racquet. If you play handball well, you get a terrific workout that benefits your arms, legs, and entire body. You get up to 70 per cent capacity quickly and run a risk of going beyond. The top pros in this sport are about as well conditioned as any athlete in any sport.

Anyone who plays hard handball or racquetball twenty to thirty minutes a day, three to four days a week, is getting sufficient exercise to sustain a conditioning program, but if he or she can work about an hour of hard running in one or two days a week, it will be to the better.

Although there are handball courts in some Y's and schools, there really are not many, so it is not an easy sport to pursue. It is harder now than ever, as many handball courts are being converted to or used for racquetball. Some racquetball courts are opened for use by handballers at times, but it is a lot more expensive to rent a court at a racquetball club than it used to be to use a handball court at a Y. Squash, which uses a longer-handled racquet and a slightly different court, seems to be losing out. But it, too, is a great game for fitness.

One sport that will do a lot for you but is not pursued by a lot of people is rowing. Rowing gives a hard workout to your arms, legs, chest, and shoulders—your entire system. Done hard, it is hard work. A half hour of hard rowing is equal to twenty minutes of hard running internally and it is superior externally. If you are in a position to do hard rowing regularly, consider it excellent exercise. Not many people are in this position.

Golf and bowling, with tennis, are the most popular participant sports. Golf does not do a lot for you, especially if you ride a golf cart. If you walk, you will burn up about 250 calories per hour. But it is doubtful that you will walk fast enough to benefit your body much. You will help your legs some. If you walked briskly, or even jogged from shot to shot, you would help your legs a lot more, but hurt your enjoyment a lot, too—and feel like an idiot, I suppose (although golf courses are great places to run when it is permitted).

Golfers will tell you they are tired after eighteen holes, that it is tough, but this is because they are not in good condition. A physically fit person finds a round of golf a breeze. Baseball and basketball and football players love golf and don't complain that a round is tiring.

You would have to play several rounds of golf over several days to equal the value to be gained from a half hour's hard run. You'd have to spend ten to twelve times as long at golf as at racquetball, handball, hiking, or rowing to equal these in value. Yet it is a great game, and if you play once or twice a week it helps you.

Anyone can golf, but it is a harder game to learn than most. There is no such thing as a natural grip or swing, as in baseball, for example. The proper grips and swings are unnatural and must be learned properly if you are to do well.

It is a frustrating game, too. If you average one shot over par on every hole you obviously are not a poor player, yet you wind up eighteen strokes over par, probably around ninety. It is hard for most players to break a hundred. Yet, as in tennis, there is always that great shot you hit that feels so good and that inspires you to continue.

It is important to get good instruction not only so you can hit good shots, but also so you swing without damaging your muscles or joints. It is important to warm up before playing golf, as it is before tennis, because you are going to use unnatural swings and swing hard from the first. You should do ten to twenty minutes of stretching calisthenics and practice your swings, slowly at first, increasing the tempo slightly with each swing.

The swing, itself, does some good for your muscles. A half hour on a driving range is exercise and a lot of fun, but it won't do a lot for you. Golf is a lot of fun, but it just won't do a lot for you. It is no secret that it is hard to schedule a round on public courses and requires a lot of patience and time. A set of clubs and good shoes are expensive, and membership at private clubs is extremely expensive.

Bowling is less expensive. A good bowling ball and good shoes are less expensive than golf equipment, and you can even rent shoes and use house balls at all lanes. The cost of a game or series is reasonable. Like golf, it is a lot of fun and it is easier to learn and do well. Generally, you tend to bowl in groups. Instead of foursomes, you may have a lot of people with you. Bowling leagues are available to all of us.

But, like golf, bowling just doesn't do much for you. It strengthens your hands, wrists, and arms, but it doesn't do much for your body beyond that and it doesn't do much for your cardiovascular system. You would have to bowl for twelve hours to benefit comparably to an hour's running. Bowling is a great game, but an inadequate conditioner. Other activities will condition you to play golf or bowl better.

As in golf, you would do well to put in ten to twenty minutes of stretching, your legs as well as your arms, before bowling. You can strain these muscles. Weight lifting or rubber-ball squeezing—any exercise that strengthens your arms, wrists, and hands—would be enormously beneficial to you. The average bowling ball is heavy and strains your arm, hand, and finger muscles.

Bowling and golf are lifetime sports, challenging competitions, and companionable, pleasant pursuits, but they are similar to most body sports in that there simply is not sufficient sustained effort to do for your conditioning what running, swimming, or cycling will do. You aren't forced to breathe hard enough. Your blood doesn't pump fast enough. Your lungs and heart aren't developed. Your muscles aren't developed, and your body doesn't develop. But they are great games. Which is justification enough for them.

The torso twist is excellent exercise, done here to the left, also to be done to the right, front, and back. *(Photo by Gary Ambrose.)*

The sit bend is to be done down, back, down, back. *(Photo by Gary Ambrose.)*

The hurdler's stretch is one of the best of the loosening calisthenics. Here, a gymnast demonstrates this splendid warmup exercise. *(Photo by Gary Ambrose.)*

The spread reach stresses many muscles. Can you build the elasticity of this youngster? *(Photos by Gary Ambrose.)*

The basic cartwheel, an excellent gymnastics exercise. *(Photo by Gary Ambrose.)*

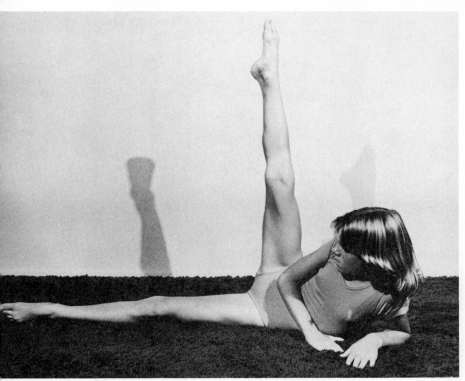

Note the stress on the leg muscles as side leg raises are employed in a calisthenics routine. *(Photo by Gary Ambrose.)*

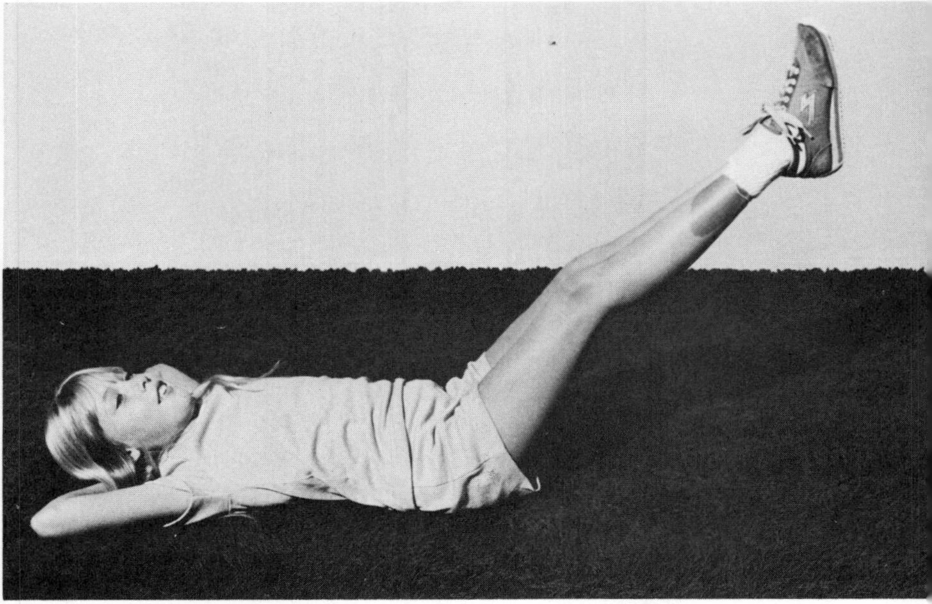

Leg raises, right, left, right, left, are demonstrated. *(Photo by Gary Ambrose.)*

Distance runner Jo Smith of Westminster, California, uses the side of a car for stretching prior to a workout. *(Photo by Gary Ambrose.)*

Jo Smith, forty-seven, is joined by Kendy Anno, twelve, in sprinter's stretch to loosen up prior to a practice run. *(Photo by Gary Ambrose.)*

She didn't start until she was forty-three, but at forty-seven Jo Smith now runs forty to eighty miles a week, hasn't missed a day in six months, and has a houseful of trophies. *(Photo by Gary Ambrose.)*

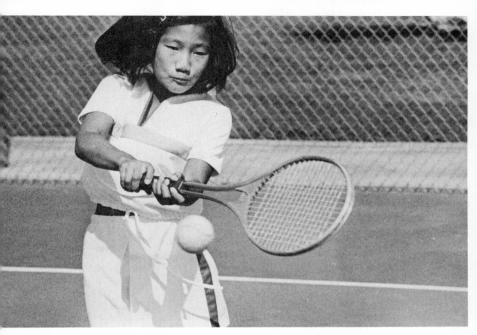

Some youngsters, inspired by Chris Evert, Tracy Austin, and Jimmy Connors, find it easier to hit a hard backhand with two hands. If this helps you handle the racquet better, fine. *(Photo by Gary Ambrose.)*

The strain on the elbow imposed by the serve in tennis is graphically illustrated here. A top-flight Southern California club tournament player, Betty Liang says she does not suffer from "tennis elbow," but this photo shows that this common court problem is a threat to her. *(Photo by Gary Ambrose.)*

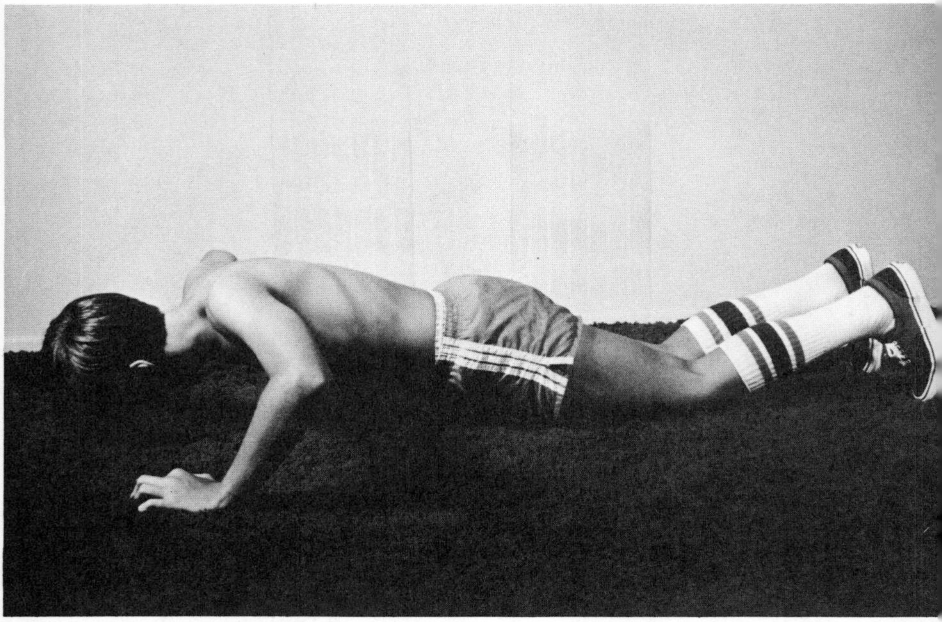

Pushups can be effective even when done with bent knee. This is the beginning position. *(Photo by Lee Payne.)*

Completed bent-knee pushup, with back kept straight. *(Photo by Lee Payne.)*

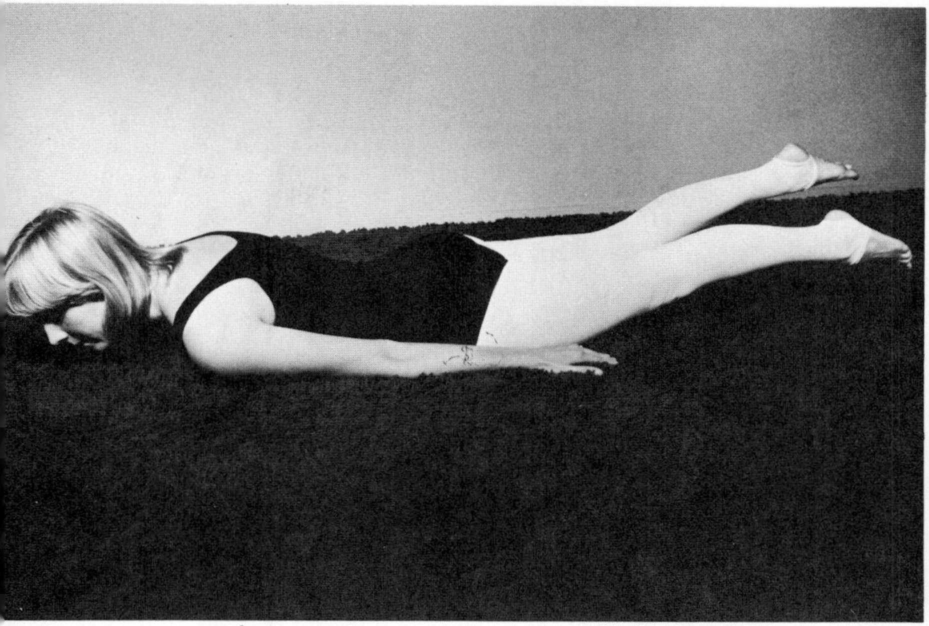

The flutter kick: A swimming exercise performed on dry land compels subject to raise head and legs, bowing back and kicking legs. *(Photo by Lee Payne.)*

Limber modern dancer Diane Breton does a shoulder stand. *(Photo by Lee Payne.)*

The forward bend: Limbering up for dance or exercise, subject drops from hips and dangles. *(Photo by Lee Payne.)*

Subject leans forward to touch floor, ke ing legs and back as straight as possi *(Photo by Lee Payne.)*

Legs spread, subject stresses back muscles by leaning head to floor. *(Photo by Lee Payne.)*

Twin stretch: Partners can help one another in some calisthenic exercises, such as this simple one, which stretches just about every muscle in the body. *(Photo by Lee Payne.)*

Situps start with arms clasped behind he
compelling stomach and groin muscles
handle the bulk of the stress. *(Photo by L
Payne.)*

Situps are completed with subject stretched fully forward. *(Photo by Lee Payne.)*

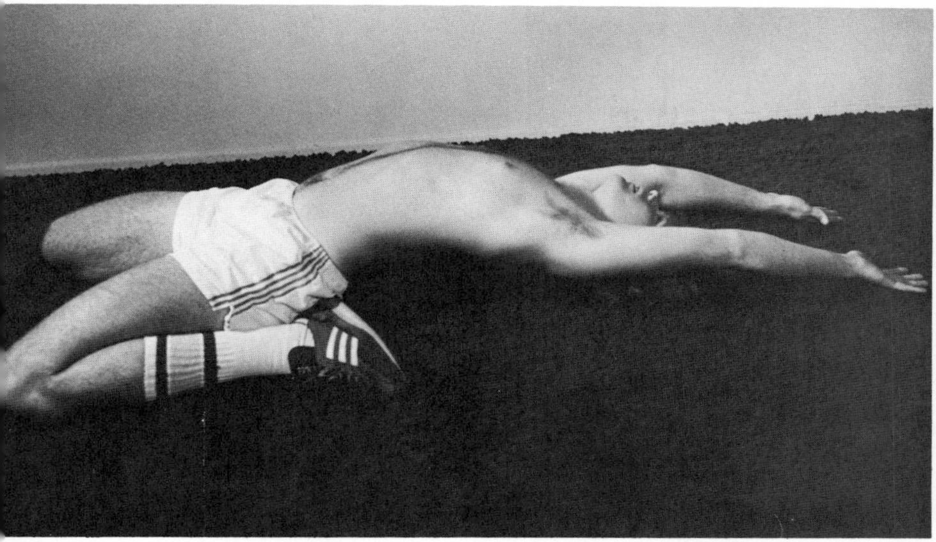

Here is a stretching exercise that really stretches the muscles—the bent-knee back bend. *(Photo by Lee Payne.)*

Leaning forward to full extension, strain shows on many of the subject's muscles as he conducts calisthenics. *(Photo by Lee Payne.)*

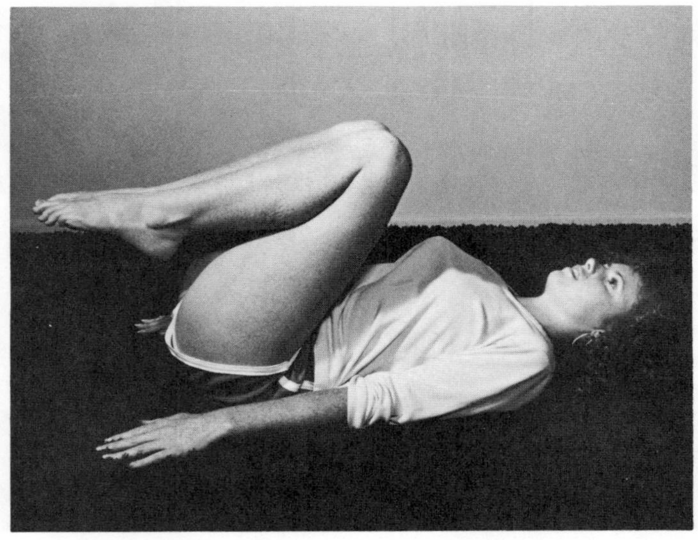

Leg raises can be effectively completed by bringing legs back as far as possible with knees drawn up. *(Photo by Lee Payne.)*

Side twists can be added to situps to increase the effectiveness of the exercise. *(Photo by Lee Payne.)*

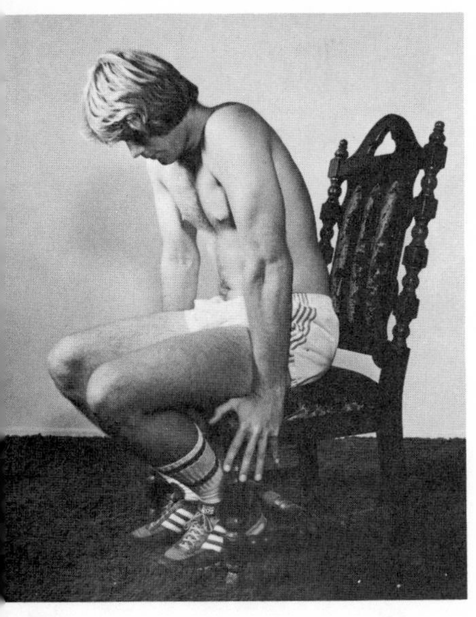

Basic isometric exercise is to push your arms down hard with your palms on chair on which you are sitting. *(Photo by Lee Payne.)*

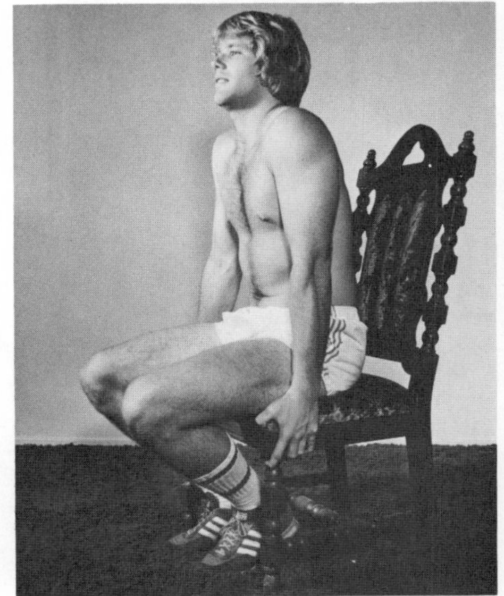

'ulling up on chair, trying to lift yourself p is another fundamental isometric exer-ise. *(Photo by Lee Payne.)*

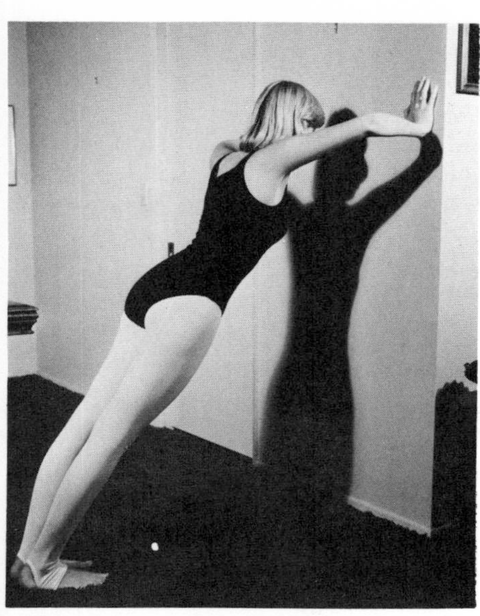

Doing pushups while angled against a wa
(Photo by Lee Payne.)

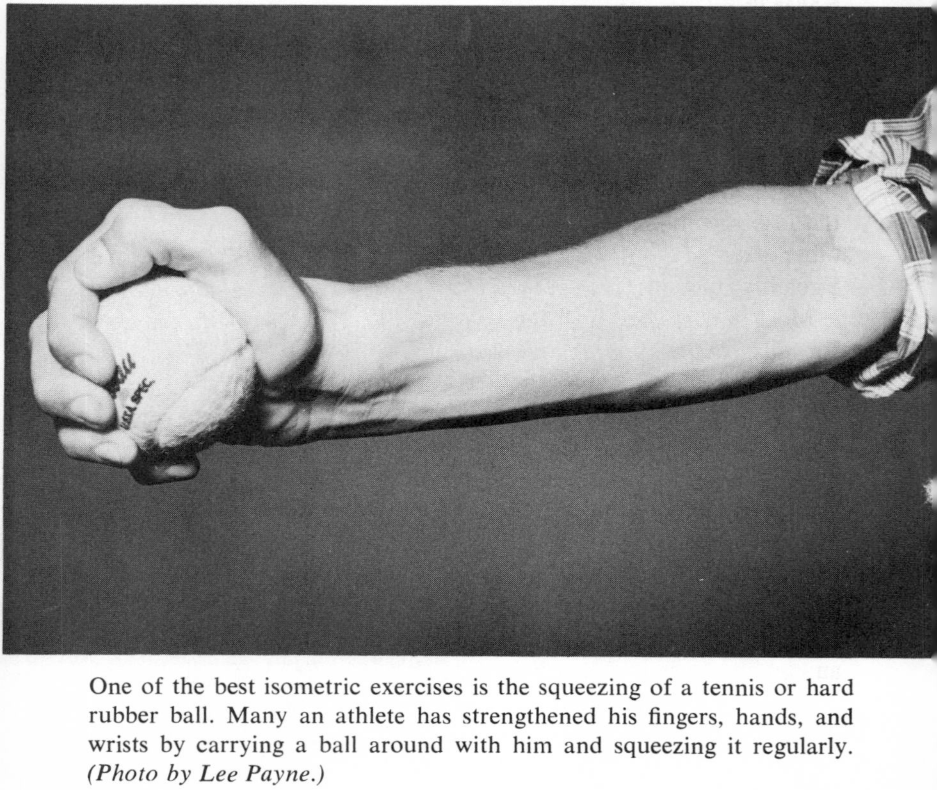

One of the best isometric exercises is the squeezing of a tennis or hard rubber ball. Many an athlete has strengthened his fingers, hands, and wrists by carrying a ball around with him and squeezing it regularly. *(Photo by Lee Payne.)*

7. THE BODY SPORTS: BASKETBALL, BASEBALL, SOFTBALL, FOOTBALL, VOLLEYBALL, AND HOCKEY

None of the body sports compares with the best of the leg and arm sports as a conditioner for the average person. Those who participate in basketball, baseball, softball, football, volleyball, or hockey with a passion have got to be in fairly good shape to compete effectively, but for the most part they must condition themselves for the sport rather than have the sport condition them.

A strong running or bicycling program will do the job. A swimming program is less effective because it does less for the legs, and the legs are critical to all of these body sports. Calisthenics and other exercises will help condition your body for these sports. Stretching and other exercises prior to participation are essential.

Most of these are high-risk sports. They are not lifetime sports for this reason, and the average adult does not continue competing in them—but there are those who do. Football and hockey are contact sports that expose the athlete to the risk of severe knee, back, and head injuries, and broken bones. You have to participate at a fast pace twice as long as in normal running to get similar aerobic benefits. You will burn off between 350 and 400 calories per hour.

Many football linemen go in for weight training because football requires strength. Running backs and defensive backs and receivers often are trim and fit, but as a group football players are among the least well conditioned in sports. You see a lot of fat football players. Many play very well, but they are not well conditioned, and they frequently get hurt. It is not unusual to have ten or more members of a pro football team require knee surgery every season.

Except for touch football, few adults will follow football as a participant sport. Better to watch your favorite teams on television or at the stadiums. Let them knock heads and bang their bodies around. The Kennedys popularized touch football to a limited extent. This is a good family sport: It's fun and it will benefit you as will any sport that requires you to run hard, even in spurts, but it is not an important part of a conditioning program.

Hockey fans are real fanatics, and I have found a few pursuing their sport as players into their twenties, thirties, and forties in leagues designed for amateurs. If you skate hard it's going to help you, but if you hit hard it's going to hurt you. The bodychecks can hurt. Tumbles into the boards can hurt. It's simply a high-risk activity and is not recommended for the average person as part of a conditioning program.

Both football and hockey are expensive sports calling for costly protective padding and other equipment. Basketball is better by far as a recreational conditioner.

If you think about it, football is the most complete of all sports in that it requires both the legs and arms, feet and hands, and combines running and hitting, throwing, catching, and kicking as no other game does. But it is rough and risky. Basketball requires you to use your legs, arms, and hands, and it calls for a combination of speed and endurance, jumping and agility beyond most games. If games are what you want, this is a good game for you.

The problem with basketball as a conditioner is that it can be played at so many different paces. If the pace is slow and there is a lot of walking from one end of the court to the other, it doesn't do much for you. You will burn less than three hundred calories off in an hour and get few aerobic benefits. However, if the pace is fast and there is a lot of running up and down the court, it will do a lot for you. A hard, hour-long game will stress your lungs, heart, and muscles, and maybe burn off twice as many calories.

The fewer the players, the better it is for you, as you must move and handle the ball that much more. Two-man basketball in which it is just you and an opponent, one on one, not only ranks with handball and racquetball as a conditioner, but may also be the most grueling game of all. Go at it hard and it will give you a great deal. Done at a top pace, it will burn off about six hundred calories an hour. But you won't be able to keep it up for half an hour. You'll run into oxygen debt before that.

Pro basketball players have the least longevity of all major-league athletes. Ten years is a long time to play pro basketball. Few players last into their thirties. Few have any excess weight. Running and jumping on the hardwood court take a lot out of your legs and joints. The sudden shifts, twists, and stops are hard on your knees. Severe knee injuries are rather commonplace. It is a fairly risky game to play as you get older, and there are few leagues for older players. Still, a good two-man game at a local gym will do you a lot of good.

Like basketball, soccer doesn't require equipment other than a ball, shorts, shirt, and shoes. You need the right shoes, of course. As with basketball, there are few soccer leagues for older players. You can't play two-man, you need teams, and you need an open field to play on. Played hard, it is a grueling game of ninety minutes, requiring a lot of running, but it is easy to play it without playing hard. Most older soccer players stand around a lot, and that doesn't do much for them. In this country at least, soccer is not a lifetime game.

Baseball is not a lifetime game either. It takes eighteen players to play a game. All have to have shoes, bats, balls, and gloves. You have to have a baseball field to play on. Usually you need a league to play in, and there aren't many for players past twenty.

There are bursts of activity, but little sustained stress put on your body. You won't burn up three hundred calories in an average hour, and if you don't loosen up properly you are apt to pull muscles or develop sore arms.

Baseball is a game of great skill. It takes timing, reflexes, speed, or power to play it well, but baseball players are the worst conditioned of all athletes. They last the longest because they do the least.

Softball is similar, but it is a more popular recreational sport. There are a lot of local leagues for older players. It's a lot of fun, it's good for you, but it won't do a lot for you.

Volleyball is better. It doesn't require running, but it demands short, quick movements such as jumping and diving. The diving is dangerous and the jumping can be hard on your legs, especially on a hard court—it is easier on sand or grass.

Volleyball has become a popular beach game. The sand will build up your legs, but on sand, grass or a hard court it is like any other game—you have to play it hard for it to help you. It is another of those sports in which it is easy to kid yourself that you are exercising.

If it's your body that concerns you, you are better off jumping in the ocean and taking a strong swim. Swimming, cycling, and especially running are your best bets for physical fitness. As games go, handball, racquetball, a hard game of basketball, and an all-out tennis match are best for young and old.

8. THE YOUNGSTER

The best way to be fit is to start at a young age and stick to a program of physical conditioning throughout your life. We can give our sons and daughters the opportunities we didn't get or didn't take. We can teach them what the schools don't.

Most schools have physical education or gym classes to provide recreation and exercise for students, but they usually do not start early enough, do not teach enough, and do not show youngsters how to take care of themselves as they get older.

They encourage the athletically able, but not the unable. As the youngsters get older, coaching is provided for school teams, but not for intramural teams. Most school intramural programs are mediocre at best.

Although the emphasis is starting to shift, most school programs still are aimed at boys, not girls. There are many more school teams for women in college than there used to be, but not so many school teams in junior high or high school.

If you have a budding Jerry West or Billie Jean King, Sue Gossick or Wilt Chamberlain, fine. Encourage him or her. But if your child is at best a bench-warmer or can't make a team, don't be discouraged. There is nothing wrong with a boy who is more brains than brawn, a girl who prefers so-called feminine things to masculine activities, or any child who is not physically strong or skilled. There also is nothing wrong with their being physically fit.

You should teach your children yourself how to run or jump or throw, catch, or kick a ball. Even those youngsters who are not interested in athletics are going to have to play punchball or kickball or some kind of game at school, and no one wants to be embarrassed. No one wants to look bad. No one likes not being picked when kids choose up teams.

Children who find fun in games are apt to continue them into their adult lives. Children who start conditioning programs early are apt to continue them as they grow older. Most kids like to run, swim, skate, and ride bicycles, and they should be encouraged to continue these exercises. These are lifetime sports.

Teach your children calisthenics. Show them how to stretch before exertion, how to warm up and cool off. Schools don't teach these things, even it they put the kids through calisthenics. They don't teach them programs of conditioning they can continue through their adult lives. What the schools do do, they often get to too late with too little. They do the same things they always have done without regard to modern methods. Teachers of PE classes and coaches of teams often compel youngsters to run laps as punishment for poor performance. Why should running be regarded as a punishment?

One veteran coach complained to me that youngsters who had trouble in school, perhaps with grades, were punished by being barred from playing on the school teams. As he pointed out, the chance to play on the teams often was the only reason these troubled youngsters stayed in school and remained where they could be helped.

On the other hand, other coaches complain that the section of the Education Amendments Act passed by Congress in 1972, known as Title IX, is a threat to athletics in this country. Essentially, this forbids sex discrimination in any educational institution receiving federal funds. It applies to the athletic field as well as the classroom.

What should athletics in this country be, then? No one is more enthusiastic than I am about high school or college football or basketball, and I realize that if funds are diverted from these boys' or men's teams to girls' or women's teams it will hurt the men's team. And the men's teams are the ones that bring in income from spectators and alumni. However, sports in schools are supposed to be amateur activities and not intended to be strictly moneymakers.

Before 1970, there were not many women's teams on college

campuses. In 1971, the Association for Intercollegiate Athletics for Women was formed as a counterpart to the men's National Collegiate Athletic Association. The AIAW started with less than 300 member schools. Now it has more than 800, and more than 100,000 athletes, some 10,000 on scholarships. The NCAA has 170,000 athletes, but most are on scholarships, and only 710 schools.

The impact has passed on to the high schools. Before 1970, less than 300,000 girls took part in scholastic sports. Now the number is nearing 1,800,000. The grade schools have also been affected. In contrast to the baseball and football teams for boys, there used to be only an occasional softball league for girls. Now there are softball and soccer leagues for girls beyond counting.

The enthusiasm with which young girls are taking to competitive sports is startling and in stark contradiction to those who thought few would be interested. And this zest extends to all ages. A few years ago, the first woman sneaked into the Boston Marathon. Now hundreds run every year. In 1972, the first all-woman minimarathon of 10,000 meters in New York's Central Park drew 78 entries. Six years later the renewal drew 4,360 women.

Boy or girl, start them young. The older they are, the harder it is to break bad habits and teach correct techniques. When they start to walk, teach them to run. Teach them the relaxed running technique we described earlier. Boys tend to be interested in sports and teach themselves techniques by copying others. Without being taught, girls tend to sway from side to side when they run. Teach them to run straight ahead and erect. Teach them to jump straight up to reach higher and higher on a wall from a crouch. Teach them to jump from a two-footed takeoff—like a long jumper, for distance. As girls become more actively interested in athletics, they will copy others and teach themselves.

Before they are one, introduce children to water. At two or three children can be taught to swim—it is best to get professional instruction for them from Y's or other recreational programs. At first they usually learn to dog-paddle themselves afloat and to swim underwater. Soon they can be taught above-water strokes. They must be watched, but children who are not afraid and know how to handle themselves in the water are far safer than those who do not, obviously.

A jungle gym or other climbing apparatus offers excellent exercise and develops coordination and agility in youngsters from four to eight.

At three or four, children will start showing sufficient motor control to be taught to throw or catch a ball. At this point they start favoring one hand over the other, but start by bouncing a large, light ball two-handed back and forth between you and your child.

At five or six a child can control a ball by bouncing it. Teach the youngster to "dribble," as in basketball, with the fingers or palms of one hand, rather than the fists or both hands. You can start to play a form of handball off a wall with the child. You can start to teach the child to kick a soccer ball correctly with the side of his or her foot rather than the toe when you roll the ball to the child.

At this point you can start to teach your child to throw the ball and catch it correctly, starting with an underhand motion and progressing to an overhand motion. If he or she is right-handed, teach the child to stride forward with the left foot pointed at the target, release the ball with the right hand pointed at the target, and follow through naturally, all in one continuous, comfortable motion. Teach them to catch by reaching for the ball, rather than pulling away from it. Teach them to watch the ball as it goes into their hands, rather than closing their eyes. Teach them to spread the fingers of both hands and catch the ball by cushioning it. Use a soft rubber ball so they cannot get hurt.

Take your time. Show persistence, but patience. Do not discourage them by shouting at them. Make it fun for them or they will not want to keep at it. Understand that they are just gaining control over their muscles and just beginning to get sufficient eye-to-hand and eye-to-foot coordination and many of them never will be especially skilled. It will take time, in any event.

At about age six you can begin teaching them to bat by using hollow, plastic bats and balls, throwing to them slowly and from short distances at first. Teach them to watch the ball as it comes across "the plate," to stand sideways, looking over one shoulder, and to stride forward with their front foot while swinging with rotating hips at the ball. Encourage them to merely make contact with the ball first, before trying to swing and hit the ball hard.

Throw underhand at first. Overhand later. Don't throw fast balls until later. Give the child time to gain confidence.

Teach children how to handle ground balls by dropping to one knee in the path of the ball to block it, and to catch it by putting a gloved hand down on the bouncing ball. Teach them how to handle fly balls by drifting toward the path of the ball and bringing their cupped hands up under the ball at about chest level. If you have to learn the correct techniques yourself, buy a specialized book on your child's favorite sport. Read it. Let your child read it. Practice.

Between the ages of six and eight, children can be taught not only baseball, but also basketball, football, and soccer. Soccer may be the best because the uncoordinated kid can at least get into the game and kick at the ball as it comes to him. As he gains agility and balance and eye-to-foot coordination, his skills, whatever they may be, will get better.

Football is harder because the ages of six to eight are too early for a young child to be exposed to contact sports, but he can be taught the correct way to spiral a pass, catch it, carry a ball protected in the arm, punt it, and place-kick it.

Basketball is hardest because smaller-size balls are not as available as in football and because most baskets are at the adult height of ten feet. Most youngsters have to learn to handle a heavy basketball two-handed. But if you can get a light ball and low basket with which to begin, your child will benefit.

Tennis is an excellent exercise that appeals to both boys and girls, but to enjoy it they must learn to hit the ball well enough to keep it in play. It may be best to start by playing off a backboard, such as the high handball boards found in most schoolyards. It takes time for youngsters to learn to get the ball over the net on a regulation court without hitting it into the next county.

Teach them a straight serve or a one-bounce hit so they can put the ball in play. Teach them how to drift into position to hit the ball at arm's length. Teach them to turn sideways and aim a shoulder in the direction they want to hit a forehand and turn with their back to the ball for a backhand. Teach them how to bring the racquet back and hit over the ball, forehand or backhand. If it is hard for them to hit a backhand one-handed, let them hit it two-handed, as Chris Evert, Jimmy Connors, and many others do these days. Again, if necessary, buy a book. Better yet, seek lessons, which are available to youngsters almost anywhere. If your youngsters show an interest in bowling, golf, or any other game, see that they learn properly so that they have a sound base on which to build and can progress properly and enjoy the game.

The key to success in getting your youngsters into athletic activities is finding games they enjoy. It doesn't matter how much you liked baseball or football or wished you had gone on to great heights with it; if your youngster takes to volleyball or some other sport, encourage the child to continue. Teaching them the fundamentals, you free them to be the best they can be, whatever that may be. There is no youngster, however able or unable, who will not benefit from calisthenics and other exercises, who will not benefit from walking, hiking, jogging, or running, who will not be the better for skipping rope, swimming, skating or cycling. Walk and hike with them. Let them jog or run with you. Swim with them. Skate with them. Go biking with them. Let them do exercises with you.

If your children prefer to do these things with their friends, fine, but encourage them to continue with those activities that will get them to breathing hard and get their blood pumping. Do not assume young bodies don't need it. In today's television society and world of two-car families, most youngsters, especially those who are not gifted athletically, need more exercise than they get, must develop endurance, and have to build habits that will help them all their lives.

If your 8-year-old can't do 6 pullups and hold each a half minute, do 30 situps in a minute, jump up a foot off the floor or out 4 to 5 feet, can't run 50 yards in less than 10 seconds and 440 in 100 seconds, then he or she needs work. Encourage them to join you in your routines. They may find it fun to exercise with their parents.

At about the age of eight, most youngsters today will be in a position to join youth leagues in various sports if they wish. If you have taught them the fundamentals of their sport they will have a chance to do well and develop properly. But if they do not wish to join a league, do not discourage them from playing games. Encourage them to play with other friends who do not wish to be in leagues, or with you. You may benefit, too.

Encourage them to seek activities they do enjoy. Gymnastics, for example, has been growing in popularity among girls ever since Olga Korbut and Nadia Comaneci starred at young ages in consecutive Olympics. Gymnastics builds balance, coordination, timing, and agility, even if one does not become really good at it. It is not important to be the best. The average person seeks conditioning, not trophies. His or her body becomes the trophy.

If you have a daughter who does not like athletic competition, let her study dancing or ballet. These can be strenuous activities that develop posture, poise, grace, and agility, as well as benefit the body. If they become stars, fine, but that is not the point.

If athletics are only for the Elgin Baylors and Bill Shoemakers and Nancy Lopezes, then we are wasting an opportunity to condition ourselves for our lives. If your son or daughter has a chance to be one of these, great. Encourage them. There are respected, well-paid professions in sports. But at no time should you expect this kind of excellence. If you push your child hard, you will more likely come up with a discontented, disenchanted, frustrated person.

Competition is important, but it is just too early to inflict it on youngsters under the age of twelve. Many develop later than others. They haven't had time to find directions.

If your youngster is athletic and anxious to improve, spend what you can so he or she can go to special schools, camps, or clinics. Take the time to check them out. Obviously, some are better than others. Find someone who knows about them who will recommend one or two. Most of us can teach only up to a point.

Obviously, some coaches are better than others. Many of the men who coach Little League baseball, for example, may be exemplary human beings but mediocre coaches. They are volunteers. Many get carried away with the desire to teach, but may lack the knowledge and experience to teach properly.

We can help by putting as little pressure as possible on them. We should make every effort to get the best qualified men or women to coach our kids, but beyond that, if they are fair to the youngsters and put together teams that are competitive and if they run games properly, we should not demand victory at all cost. Many coaches could do harm to our kids if they only care about winning. This applies to high-school level as well as the Little League level.

Try to teach your youngsters to be philosophical about sports situations just as they should be about life. Try to teach teamwork.

Within the limits of your budget, be sure your young athlete has the proper equipment and uniform for the game he or she is playing. As far as possible, stretch your budget so you can provide them with what they need to enjoy what they are doing and to do their best. A uniform doesn't have to be flashy, but I have found that a player who takes pride in his appearance plays better. The uniform should be clean, neat, and mended. It's nice to have a sweat suit, but not a sweaty one. Don't let your kid compete in soiled clothes that look like rags. When their outfits wear out, replace them.

Above all, make sure they have the right shoes and protective gear for their activities and that these fit properly. I know how easy it is to let a pair of tennis shoes do for all sports. I know how hard it is to scrape up the money for different shoes, but it is more important to have good sports shoes than good dress shoes.

Whatever protective equipment your child needs, be sure the youngster has it. Hockey and football players need heavy shoes and helmets. Hockey and soccer players need shin pads. Baseball players need thigh pads. Basketball players may need knee or elbow pads. Football players need all kinds of pads. Football and hockey players need tooth guards. Do not assume a league or school will provide these. In many cases what they provide will be worn out, or will not fit your youngster. If they do not fit or they slide around, they will not provide protection. Pads and helmets wear out just like shoes. These things are expensive, but it is critical that if your child is going to compete he or she must be properly protected.

Perhaps you can get behind a fund-raising program to provide the proper equipment for your youngsters' team. And, if you do, perhaps you can use the money for more than mere flashy uniforms, but for proper protective equipment. See that your son has an athletic supporter that fits him and your daughter a chest protector when needed.

Perhaps you can raise funds to provide health care for the kids.

Do not assume all teams have a doctor or a trainer on hand. They do not. The coach often does the job, and not always well. Perhaps you can get a doctor or a trainer to serve the team part-time and provide instruction on how to tape players and bandage injuries, offer first aid, and provide emergency service.

There should be someone on every team and at every game who knows how to tape and bandage. There should be all the antiseptics, tapes, and bandages that might be needed available at all times, at practices as well as games. There simply is no point taking chances with children and regretting an accident later.

Experts disagree on it, but I am in the majority when I suggest your youngster stay away from contact sports until he or she has matured physically to at least the level of the average teen-ager. While it is true that young bodies are flexible, it also it true that young bones are soft. I understand that your youngster may be rough and ready, eager to get going, and I am not against contact sports, but I know that there is a real risk of injuries in these games. I do not believe a youngster of eleven or twelve is ready to run these risks reasonably.

I prefer flag football or touch football to tackle for youngsters in their formative years. The risks of broken bones or head injuries in youngsters are simply too great in tackle football. Later, when they are more mature, better equipped, and well coached, there will be time enough.

Similarly, I know I am in the majority in believing that a youngster should not attempt to throw a curve ball or any other breaking pitch that requires him to bend his arm unnaturally or snap his wrist or arm sharply when pitching. Just throwing a ball hard takes a lot out of an arm. The number of sore arms among major-league pitchers points to this. Dr. Kerlan points out that the art of pitching requires stress on an arm it was not designed to endure. Blood vessels pop and the arm swells. I have long advocated ice on an arm immediately after pitching, and most major leaguers subscribe to this these days.

Major leaguer Jim Lonborg says, "I've had arm trouble since I broke into pro ball fifteen years ago. It's always tender and needs ice after every game." Tom Seaver says, "I worry so much about my right arm that if I roll over on it in my sleep I immediately wake up."

Catcher Johnny Bench says, "I caught balls for Gary Nolan for ten years and I watched his face and I don't think he ever threw a pitch that didn't hurt." The lesson is clear. The tendons, ligaments, and muscles in the shoulder, elbow, and wrist, all along the arm, are constantly twisted, pulled, and threatened. If major leaguers have so much trouble, it makes no sense whatsoever to allow your youngster to snap off curve balls or any other breaking balls. It is not even clear that you should do so when he is in high school. If he can't get by with straight pitches, so be it, but the majors are full of pitchers who didn't throw breaking balls until they were seventeen or eighteen.

The biggest and strongest kids usually excel on the Little League level, but they often are not the best later on. Some mediocre Little Leaguers become major leaguers. George Foster couldn't make his high-school team and couldn't hit in college, but he is just about baseball's best hitter now. Youngsters mature physically and develop their potential at different rates.

Never make snap judgments on a youngster's ability at an early age and don't discourage the child if he or she is determined to carry on. But encourage them to take care of themselves. If their arms are tired, don't let them pitch. Most lower leagues have limits on how much and how often kids can pitch, but high schools may not. Don't assume a coach has your child's best interests at heart. The coach wants to win. Coaches take chances. You set the limits.

Up to the age of twelve, I would say six innings a game, nine innings a week, and at least three or four days off between pitching appearances. From thirteen through sixteen, I would say seven innings to nine innings a game, fourteen innings a week, and three to four days off between appearances for all pitchers on all levels through the majors, and I hate to see a pitcher pitch more than nine innings a game.

It depends, of course, on how many pitches he throws in a game. If your pitcher is wild, perhaps you should keep count. Once a pitcher throws more than a hundred pitches in a game, his arm is apt to tire. In any event, all pitchers should ice their arms after appearances, keep their arms warm after the ice, perhaps applying a little heat. They should rest entirely the following day, not throw again until the second or third day, and then start slowly.

It is important for all pitchers to warm up properly before throwing. Start throwing softly to a catcher who is close in, and gradually increase the speed and distance of your throws. Do not throw all out until it is time to throw all out. Even then, never throw harder than what comes easily to you. All of this applies to football passers, as well. A football is heavy, and it is not easy to throw it well. A passer should not throw hard every day, he should ice his arm after hard throwing, and he should limit the throwing he does every week. He should warm up properly. All of this applies especially to youngsters. A football player should not tackle, nor should a baseball player slide before his body is ready for it and he has been taught the proper way to do it. Otherwise, broken bones are real risks.

If I sound overly cautious, I would simply rather be safe than sorry, especially where youngsters are concerned. Studies show that about half of all football players will suffer serious or fairly serious injuries at some point in their careers, as will many baseball and basketball players.

The protective padding itself produces injuries. Blows from hard helmets provide almost a third of football's serious internal injuries and half of all fractures of the hand. Almost 40 per cent of the injuries compiled in a survey conducted by the Stanford Research Institute were the result of blows received from helmets and shoulder pads. A reported one hundred thousand young pitchers annually suffer elbow strain and go on to develop chronic conditions.

Be alert to signs of fatigue, especially in hot weather. According to an article by Dr. James Keane in the Wisconsin Medical Journal, heat stroke is the second highest cause of death for football players, and more than one thousand athletes annually are stricken with heat prostration. Be sure your child drinks plenty of water as cold as he wants it when playing football or tennis or exerting himself in any way in summer temperatures. Don't argue with the coach, but if the coach forbids drinking during games or practice, tell him he's wrong.

If your child does suffer an injury, don't rely on a doctor assigned to the team. Find out in advance which doctors specialize in athletic injuries. These are specialists, and they are not apt to make mistakes in treating your child's particular injuries. Dr.

Kerlan will tell you that many doctors make mistakes in the care of athletic injuries, and this is why he helps conduct weekend clinics designed especially to teach the proper application of athletic medicine.

Encourage your child to embark on an exercise program or to be active in athletics. Teach your youngsters as much as you know about these activities and join them as much as possible. Exercise caution where it is needed. It is fine for a youngster to run, swim, skate, and cycle year round, but if he or she is participating in competition in a specific sport, be sure the child takes time off between seasons and spends several weeks preparing for the particular sport prior to each season. As a parent, it is your job to see that your children are prepared and protected properly. If your youngster has the ability to become a top-level athlete, fine, but encourage also the one who does not do well. Winning games is wonderful, but if we can condition ourselves to lead a long, healthy, and happy life through athletic activities we will have scored no small victory.

9. THE ACTIVE ADULT

You can condition yourself and stay in condition at any age. Conditioning will help keep you in good health. Age is physiological and psychological as well as chronological. All forty-year-olds are not alike. Many well-conditioned fifty-year-olds can do physical feats that poor conditioned thirty-year-olds cannot. But the years are relentless and do take a toll.

Before the age of six and after the age of sixty we are limited in the things we can do physically. Between six and sixteen we develop the quickest physically. Between twenty-five and thirty we are at our physical peaks. After thirty-five we slow down noticeably. From fifty on, we are wearing out. These are averages. The surge upward and the slide downhill are inevitable, but we can speed the one up and slow the other down.

The newborn infant has all its parts. Its brain will attain almost full size within one year and full size by puberty. Its nervous system will be complete within a few months. Its cardiovascular system is fully developed, but the heart and lungs will grow for about twenty-five years and can continue to be developed through exercises. The bones, soft at first, will harden and develop for sixteen to eighteen years. Girls begin puberty at about ten, boys at about twelve. Then there is a growth spurt during which girls reach final fusion of their bones at about sixteen, boys at about eighteen. Seldom will either grow much taller after this.

Between the ages of twenty-five to thirty, when the body reaches its physical peak, it also starts to turn downhill. The eyesight has developed to its full potential at this time and starts to weaken little by little. If the muscles are not steadily stretched and strengthened, they will start to lose their elasticity and power. The bones will gradually become brittle. A conditioned person can hold his peak or close to it for about ten years, but he is fighting time.

Studies suggest that the seeds of disorders such as hardening of the arteries and other cardiovascular problems, cardiopulmonary problems, adult diabetes, and the like are planted by the time we are twenty-one and develop from then on. Obviously if we smoke cigarettes, eat fatty or rich foods, or inherit illness we are more prone to these problems. Elements in the muscles and bones that govern their elasticity and sturdiness, respectively, harden or stiffen, especially without exercise.

Because the cornea becomes increasingly rigid, from forty on more and more people lose the ability to focus their eyes. With this and muscular deterioration, eye-to-hand coordination decreases. There are similar losses in hearing and the sense of smell. Slowly but surely the cells cease to function effectively and the body cannot rid itself of poisons as well as it once did. Over the years, illness and injury will have left effects on various parts of our body that will inhibit their functions. It sounds dreadful, but that is life—and death.

The older you are now, the longer you are apt to live on the average. Census statistics show that at age thirty you can expect to live to the age of seventy-four, at age forty to seventy-five, at age fifty to seventy-six, at age sixty to seventy-eight, at age seventy to eighty-two. On the other hand, at ages thirty to forty your chances of having a heart attack within ten years are about fifteen to one, but at fifty to sixty they are only about half that. If you smoke regularly, are obese, are inactive, or have bad hereditary factors, the odds are much worse.

The things that accelerate aging can be controlled. If you stop smoking, go to a good diet, and become physically active you can slow drastically the deterioration of your body and prevent, postpone, or recover from major killers such as heart disease and stroke, arteriosclerosis, cirrhosis of the liver, and lung cancer. If you never began bad habits, that's best of all. You are in a fight, a fight for life, and a long life.

You do not slow down suddenly one day; you have been slowing down all the weeks and months and years of your adult life. You do not die suddenly one day; you have been dying throughout your life. You are the result of not only what has been done for and to you, but also what you have done for and to yourself all of your life, and if you have not done what you should have been doing by the time you are an adult it is time to do it now. It is never too late, and if you already have started, don't stop.

I was struck by something a Connecticut housewife, Carolyn Bravakis, said recently in a newsmagazine article on physical fitness. In her thirties, she had come no closer to exercise than when she was a cheerleader for her high-school football team. She said, "All my life, I never did anything. The only time I went outside was to hang the wash." Then her brother organized a ten-thousand-meter road race and she decided to enter. When she found she had to stop halfway, she said, "I was so disgusted with myself that I started running seriously."

Within one year she was running fifty miles a week. She even entered the Boston Marathon and finished twenty-ninth among women entries. This prodded her to do even more. By 1978, she was twelfth among two hundred women who finished the twenty-six-mile run in less than three hours. She said, "I have more self-confidence and more energy than ever before. When I run in the rain, I feel about six years old."

This reminds me of Dr. George Sheehan, a New Jersey heart specialist, who, with his books, has become a sort of guru to middle-age runners. He ran in school, but laid off for about twenty years before resuming in his midforties. Fifteen years later he can't say enough about exercise in general and running in particular as a benefit to you, not only physically, but also psychologically. "It is important for the adult to rediscover the child that remains in all of us. It is critical that we find games to play if we are to keep our sanity as well as our health," says Dr. Sheehan.

It is sad that so many women missed the fun of games both as youngsters and as adults. It is a joy to see them getting into games at all ages today. Those women who go out and participate are finding it easier every day because there are more of them, and more men are used to having them there. Women are running, swimming, skating, and cycling alongside the men, and many women do better than men. Women are playing basketball and softball. In bowling, mixed leagues are becoming popular. In tennis, mixed doubles is popular. Professional tennis and volleyball leagues require women competitors.

There is no question that it is better to be an active adult than an inactive adult. No matter what your age, you should do some calisthenics, especially stretching exercises, ten to twenty minutes every day. You should be walking, hiking, jogging, or running, swimming, skating, or cycling, or playing games of some strenuous sort at least twenty to thirty minutes every other day. Your body will be the better for it, you will slow down the deterioration of aging, and you will better be able to perform comfortably such everyday tasks as walking, bending down, reaching up, and so forth.

There is some risk. If you have not been active you will have to take up activities gradually and develop your body's ability to handle increased stress. In a formal statement, the American Medical Association has said, "There is one tried and true rule for all those who are out of shape and want to start training: Start slowly and increase the vigor and duration of the activity as your fitness improves. In time you will be able to do with ease what was hard for you in the beginning."

However, there are limits to what one can do. It is as dangerous to overdo as it is to underdo. Even if you have been active, there comes a point when your body can only handle comfortably less activity than before. If you have any health problems you will have to accomodate your athletics to them. If you are uncertain of your physical capacity or are past the age of thirty-five it is essential to have a medical examination before embarking on a program of exercise.

An EKG will help to determine the health of your heart, but this is a test at rest and may not show possible problems. A stress test, such as the treadmill test, will help pinpoint problems and determine your physical capacity. It is important to remember that there is risk in any strenuous activity, and people have suffered heart attacks or other serious ailments running, swimming, cycling, and playing games. What is not known is how many would have died anyway, doing something else.

More important than age is the amount of activity you have been participating in. The less active you have been, the more slowly you will have to start. The more active you have been, the more you can do. Although I believe it will endure, the problem with the physical-fitness era we are in is that it oversells the product. Buying the ideas of happiness and health, people are plunging over their head.

Few of us have the proper patience. If we want to stop smoking, we want to quit "cold turkey." If we give in to temptation and take a cigarette now and then, we are annoyed with ourselves and start to smoke again. Despite false starts, persistence will pay off. If you are hooked, the habit will not be broken easily. But if you keep trying to stop, eventually you will. It is an addiction for many of us and hard to stop. If you want to quit, you will have to work at it.

If you are addicted to junk foods, it takes determination to shift to a better diet. If you want to lose weight, it takes will power to cut down on the amount you eat and to stay away from harmful foods. Unless you go on a crash diet, the pounds will not disappear quickly. And crash diets can be dangerous. The body needs the proper nourishment to perform properly. Many popular fad diets have been labeled dangerous. You should get a good diet going and help burn up calories with proper exercise. The more exercise you do, the more fuel your body will need. The less exercise, the less fuel. The formula is simple. It takes patience to go on a weight-losing program and stick to it until it pays off.

It also takes patience to go on a physical-conditioning program and stick to it. You have to start slowly and progress gradually. Too many get "the message" and expect to run four-minute miles and twenty-six-mile marathons and play basketball with the boys and tennis with the girls before they are ready. They want to beat their buddies and do better than their neighbors before their bodies are equal to it. You have to take the time to build up your body. It may take a month or six months or a year before you show the sort of progress you want, but you must stick to a sensible plan. You are really competing only with yourself and your own well-being.

If a physical-fitness program is to pay off, you have to schedule it into your life and follow it every day. Every day off you take makes it easier to take the next day off. Either you are willing to make the time and sacrifice some other aspect of your life for it, or you are not. If you are willing, you exercise for twenty minutes or a half hour or an hour from day to day. You have to do something every day, but you don't have to do everything every day. You can be a weekend athlete if you wish, and it is better than doing nothing physical seven days a week, but you had better limit what you do on Saturday or Sunday if you have done nothing on Monday through Friday, or you may not be able to do anything any day. You will be far better off spreading three to six hours of real exercise over a week than you will be jamming six to eight hours in on a weekend.

Years ago we wouldn't let youngsters run more than a mile in track meets. Today kids run in marathons before they are ten. While their bone and other development are insufficient for certain stress, we have found the capacity of kids for physical activity to be far beyond what was once believed to be best. Similarly, we have found that the capacity of older people for strenuous exercise is far greater than what was accepted at one time.

The best time for a person to get into a conditioning program is any time he or she is willing to start seriously. I like to encourage those in their twenties because it is at this time that they get out of school, stop playing games, go to work, start driving to and from work, and start sitting at desks or doing housework. It is at this time that it is easiest to get them going on an exercise schedule they can continue through their adult lives. But if they have missed their twenties, let them start in their thirties. Or in their forties. Or fifties. But the older they are, the more caution they must practice.

Athletes such as football's George Blanda, baseball's Hoyt Wilhelm, golf's Gary Player, and hockey's Gordie Howe have remained effective into their forties on the demanding professional level because they continued to prepare properly for and play their games year after year. Many others who retired between the ages of thirty and forty could have continued to perform skillfully, but perhaps could not have kept up with the younger stars. There is no doubt that we slow up with age no matter how hard we work out.

A University of Minnesota study showed that the maximum oxygen intake of moderately active men decreased from the age of twenty by about 8 per cent at age thirty, 16 per cent by age forty, 26 per cent by age fifty, and 35 per cent by age sixty. Another study shows a person who could run a hundred yards in ten seconds flat at twenty is almost a second slower at forty and three seconds slower at sixty, even if the runner has kept up his running. A four-minute miler has added fifteen seconds from age twenty to forty and more than a minute by the age of sixty. A 2½-hour marathoner has added close to ten minutes by forty and more than an hour by sixty.

Yet it is incorrect to assume older people can't perform marvelous feats with proper conditioning. In a recent survey veteran cross-country skiiers in the fifty-to-sixty-year-old bracket surpassed some twenty-year-old students in tests of endurance. Since the jogging craze began, many older persons have built themselves up to where they do well in twenty-six-mile marathons. The best sixty-year-olds do not beat the best thirty-year-olds, but they do beat the worst thirty-year-olds. Recently, a sixty-six-year old man ran the Boston Marathon in less than 3½ hours. That's less than eight minutes a mile for twenty-six miles. At his age, that was comparable to a four-minute mile for a fellow of thirty-six.

Jack LaLanne, who has made a business out of physical fitness, practices strenuous activities on his birthday annually for the benefit of television and newspaper publicity. Such stunts as swimming through water while towing a boat with your teeth are hardly typical activities, but for a man in his sixties they are remarkable and indicative of what is possible. Almost anything is possible for almost anyone at any age, but there are limits to be observed and cautions to be practiced.

The Masters programs are marvelous, but possibly there comes a time for all people when practice is preferable to competition, when conditioning yourself for life is sensible and striving to win events is not. The Grand Masters tennis program has shown that stars who have had to drop from the top level can continue to compete on their own level, but these contestants are exceptional.

Beppe Menlo, fifty, says, "I practice more now than ever before. To keep yourself in shape you must practice really hard. I realize now I should have practiced more when I was younger." Frank Sedgman, fifty, says, "You've got to play a lot to keep in shape. And stretching exercises are very important because the muscles are not what they used to be." Rex Hartwig, forty-eight, says, "I've learned to warm up more than I ever did before. I used to just go out and play. Hitting the ball has never been a problem, but getting to it is. I don't hit the ball as hard as I did and I tire sooner." Sedgman adds, "My reflexes, speed, and power are not what they once were, but I'm smarter than I was and I can still play a good game by playing strategically." Pancho Gonzales, forty-five, says, "A player on any level who keeps playing can keep playing well but he has to prepare harder than when he was younger and can't take time off and come back as well."

Whitney Reed, forty-five, says, "I'm a competitive person and I've been in one kind of competition or another for a long time, but there comes a time where you are competing more with the years than with anyone or anything else."

So do, but don't overdo. Train, but don't strain. Play to stay trim, not to win. Try to win, but accept defeat. Strive for flexibility, strength, and endurance, for health and for happiness. Condition yourself for your exertions, prepare properly for your games, warm up properly, and cool down correctly. Find those things you like to do, and do them. Try not to go two days in a row without doing something.

If you're a skiier, don't sit out the summers: Turn to tennis or swimming. If you're a tennis player, try skiing in the winters. Bicycle in the summers and skate in the winters. Run year round. Find your own formula. You are aiming at a long, good life. Chances are that exercise will help you get there. Chances are you will find it fun (which does not mean it sometimes will not be hard). Sometimes it will hurt. You may injure yourself at times. You may have to overcome obstacles and bounce back from setbacks. Remember, the race is not always won by the swift. Dedication and determination win in the end.

10. THE CARE AND PREVENTION OF INJURIES

If you are going to be physically active, you are going to run the risk of injury. If you are going to extend yourself, you are apt to suffer aches and pains, cuts and bruises, strained or torn muscles, twisted or sprained joints, even broken bones. The odds are in your favor that you will not suffer serious injuries, and if you condition and care for yourself properly you can hold the minor ailments to a minimum.

Aside from boxing, in which the goal is to injure one another, or car racing, in which sheer survival is a victory of sorts, football has the highest rate of injury in sports and is the only one that has a statistically significant rate of fatalities. Close to one million players compete in tackle football at the college, high-school, and lower levels. Of these about 20 per cent will suffer an injury, 8 per cent a serious injury. Less than two out of one hundred thousand will suffer a fatal injury. Another one will die from noninjury problems such as heat stroke and heart attack, but all athletes, including runners, are subject to these.

Most of the fatal injuries occur to the head, neck, or spinal column. About 65 per cent occur to the head. About 10 per cent stem from internal injuries. Tackling accounts for about a third of fatal injuries, being tackled a sixth, blocking or being blocked about a tenth.

Because of the contact, football also has the highest rate of serious joint injuries and broken bones. Because of the sudden stops and sharp turns, basketball has a high rate of joint injuries.

Hockey has a high rate of injuries because it is a contact sport, but because the legs slide on ice skates and do not jam against turf fields or hardwood courts, hockey's incidence of joint injuries is not high.

There are clues available we can use to reduce injuries in football. More than half of the fatalities happen to boys between the ages of sixteen and eighteen. More than half occur outside of games, such as in practice and scrimmage. Most occur in the first half of the season. This would suggest that if players learned the fundamentals and were conditioned and prepared properly, the risks would be lower.

Football players trained in gymnastics and tumbling suffer a far lower rate of injuries than those who have not been taught to "roll with the punches." Training can be undertaken and sports can be pursued that help condition athletes for other sports. Stretching exercises are critical in the avoidance of pulled and torn muscles so common in basketball and track. I spoke about some of these in earlier sections.

Among popular participant sports, basketball ranks second to football in serious injuries, though few are fatal. Although designed as a noncontact sport, basketball does have considerable contact. Large players are confined to close quarters as they battle for the ball and the basket. Basketball players suffer heavy falls more frequently than in any other sport except hockey and are less well padded than hockey and football players. However, the heavy, hard helmets and pads in hockey and football sometimes produce injuries in and of themselves. While they are shields, they also are weapons. In a given collision they may protect one player while doing damage to another.

Most serious injuries in basketball occur to the knees and ankles, wrists and elbows, feet and hands. Most serious injuries in hockey occur to the back, and head, and the eyes. Flying sticks and pucks have cost many a player his eyesight. Since most players have started to wear helmets, the incidence of head injuries in hockey has decreased sharply.

More than a million players are active annually in baseball, and the injury rate is low. Blows to the head and chest from the bat or ball are responsible for many injuries, especially among younger players whose skeletal development is not complete. Improper sliding techniques account for broken legs, the hands and fingers can be hurt in catching the ball and the arm and elbow suffer from throwing it. Young players no doubt try to do too much too soon.

Of the other sports, skiing may be the most dangerous. A skier must learn how to handle his skis and himself on his skis. This takes time, and many won't take the time. Too many novices try too much too soon. Even experienced and skilled skiers run great risks. Broken legs and damaged knee joints are not uncommon.

Skating and cycling are relatively injury-free sports. Pulled muscles are common in tennis and track. Sore elbows are common in baseball, tennis, and bowling. Bad backs are created or worsened by improper form in tennis and golf.

There are a few fatalities annually from heat prostration or infection, and these can be prevented by taking proper precautions. One should be careful about prolonged exposure to the sun, and lost liquids must be replaced. Cuts and scrapes should be treated antiseptically.

A large percentage of schools do not have doctors or trainers on hand at all times, and provision must be made for prompt and proper care of all ailments and injuries. The proper protective equipment and other clothing, including the right shoes for the sport, must be used and fit to the individual.

You must guard against going back into action after injury before you are ready. As a professional athletic trainer my job has been to get the players back into the games as soon as possible. Often they were well paid to run reasonable physical risks and felt they owed it to their team and teammates to play in pain at times. However, there have been times when teams asked more of individuals than they should have given. Bill Walton protested that the Portland Trail Blazers concealed a broken bone in his foot from him, gave him a pain-killing shot, and encouraged him to compete. There are those who feel Detroit has pressed Mark Fidrych to pitch despite a shoulder ailment that has not totally healed.

In any event, no matter how gung-ho you may be, the average recreational athlete should not rush back into action before an ailment or injury has healed. If you have a young athlete in your care, it is your responsibility to see that he or she does not return to action too soon.

Preventive medicine should be practiced wherever possible. Most injuries in competitive sports occur in the first three or four weeks of the season. The athletes have not prepared properly and are using the sport to get in condition rather than conditioning themselves for the sport.

The athlete should do daily conditioning and should continue to condition himself in one way or another during the off-season. The athlete should take six to eight weeks to prepare for the season. Most preseason practice periods are too short and the athlete is put into contact or scrimmage activity too soon.

The athlete should warm up for practice as well as for competition. He must build the strength needed for endurance in advance of activity and do flexibility exercises daily and ahead of activity. He must build up gradually to all-out effort. It is more important for the activity to be intense than long. No practice period should exceed two hours. A tired athlete is more apt to get hurt—his strength and coordination have been sapped.

Earlier, in the chapter dealing with exercises, we described the best ones to build up each part of the body and to warm up properly. The purpose of a warmup is to raise the body and deep-muscle temperatures and to stretch the ligaments and other tissues that permit flexibility, which reduce the possibility of muscle strains and tears. Most will not take the time, but a ten-minute warmup has been found to be far better than a five-minute warmup, and twenty minutes has been found to be best. Warmups should include stretching exercises, light running, and the use of those movements you will employ in the activity. You may need more or less warmup depending on you, your sport, and the weather, but the nearer to the activity it takes place, the better it will serve you.

Cooling off is as important as warming up. You must take time to allow your blood circulation to return to normal. Walking, light running, and stretching exercises often help here. You must allow time for your body to relax and regain strength both during and after exertion. Just stopping is not the best way to go about it.

If you have suffered injuries of any sort during your activity you must tend to these properly. Different ailments call for different treatments. I will get into this shortly, but first let me explain the different modalities that are available. A modality is simply that tool that can be used to condition or recondition the body.

I always have felt that the finest modality was simply the hands. There is no substitute for the laying on of hands.

I have found massage a marvelous conditioner, but it must be done in the right way at the right time. One should seldom massage a recent injury, and never where there is bleeding beneath the surface of the skin, because this will increase the bleeding. Never massage where there may be infection that might spread. Never massage a numb area, because the lack of feeling could stem from a serious injury.

Massage is meant to stretch, loosen, and warm muscles and to increase circulation. It both soothes sore muscles and helps heal injured ones. Massage should be applied firmly, but not painfully. You do not want to maul muscles, bruise them, or irritate injuries. Some men and women have marvelous hands and apply the proper pressure. They have a feel for it. It takes a touch.

I can tell you how to apply massage, but it is really something that should be taught in person by someone who knows how. It takes practice to get good at it. If you are a beginner, begin gently and slowly. Do not do too much. Most massages should be limited to five to fifteen minutes.

The person to be massaged should be seated or lying down in a comfortable position. Your hands should fall comfortably on the area to be massaged. Always use an oil or a powder as a lubricant on the skin so your hands will slide smoothly over the skin. To reach the muscles you must go through the skin and you do not want to irritate it. Alcohol is an excellent lubricant. It is an anesthetic and is cooling, yet it evaporates swiftly. Analgesics such as camphor, ethyl chloride, menthol, methyl salicylate, and Ichthyol work well, too. They also serve well as soothing, cooling agents when applied to sore muscles before going into action. Massage serves well in loosening and warming sore muscles before going into action.

There are two types of massage: theraputic and stimulating. Theraputic massage is meant to heal. It involves stroking (technically called effleurage) and friction.

In stroking, you rub with the palms and heels of your hands. As much as possible, stroke in the direction of the heart. Work on an area surrounding the soreness. Work steadily in a circle that starts at one point from the soreness and proceeds back to that point. Work in ever-diminishing circles. Use a pushing, pulling stroke.

In friction you use your fingers and thumbs over similar circular areas, gathering and lifting the muscles, pulling them gently, stretching them. Friction works successfully in any area where there is little soft tissue, such as joints. It works well where there may be accumulated scar tissue, such as in a pitcher's arm, or adhesions, where muscle or other tissue has stuck together, often from lack of use of that part. Joints should be rotated gently to increase their elasticity.

The other type of massage, stimulating massage, is meant to give the body a feeling of well-being. It increases circulation and warmth, which feed the muscles. You play the body as you would a drum, but you don't want to pound on it as if you were Buddy Rich. You shape the muscles as if they were made of clay, but you don't want to tear them apart.

The strokes include percussion (tapotement), in which the hands cup or clap the area to stimulate the tissue; kneading (petrissage), in which soft tissue is rolled or twisted gently between the thumb and forefinger to stimulate fluid drainage; and vibration, which can be done with tapping fingers or a vibrating machine.

There are many machines available to trainers and in training rooms. Electrotherapy machines should be used only by qualified people. They can easily be misused. Used properly, they can be helpful.

In ultrasound therapy, radio-frequency electrical energy is converted into vibrations that are transmitted onto the body through a liquid like heavy mineral water. The head of the machine is applied in circular or stroking motions to the area to be treated, penetrates about two inches, increases the temperature of the tissue about eight degrees, and has a massaging effect. It eases muscular pain and irritation considerably

In diathermy you apply high-frequency electric current to the tissue beneath the surface of the body. Short-wave diathermy penetrates about an inch, raises the tissue temperature close to ten degrees, and increases blood flow through the dilated vessels. It is used on a wide area. Microwave diathermy is more intense and used on a more specific area, penetrates deeper, to about two inches, raises temperature higher, and creates greater blood flow.

Infrared lamps have been devised to warm the lower tissues

without blistering or burning the outer skin, but there is a danger of blistering or burning in the misuse of any electrotherapy machine.

Thermotherapy, which is the application of heat, is the most widely used of modalities in athletic training. Heat speeds circulation and drainage and helps healing. Aside from diathermy and ultrasound devices, and the dry heat of infrared lamps, there also is the moist heat to be found in whirlpool and water packs.

Moist hot packs are thermostatically controlled pads that are placed on towels over the area of the skin to be treated. They contain a silicon gel and retain a constant heat for up to a half hour. As with electrotherapy, you should not apply heat to sensitive or recently injured parts of the body.

Hydrobaths are taken in hot tubs. Hydromassage is taken in whirlpool tubs of heated water. Temperatures up to 120 degrees can be used safely for up to a half hour. The buoyant, hot water has a soothing effect and permits mild exercise of sore muscles and joints. The whirlpool adds a massaging action. A stinging shower at temperatures up to 105 degrees will do some of the same. Some of us have access to Jacuzzis, a device to create strong water circulation in our own tubs. Some of us have access to saunas, which are steam rooms similar to the old Turkish baths. In using these you often move between icy baths and steam rooms.

One should never jump right from a hot activity into a hot tub or hot room. In exercise, you will have built up your heartbeat, expanded your blood vessels, and sent an increased flow of blood, rich with oxygen, circulating through your body. Unless you give your cardiovascular system time to cool off and return to normal you may be asking more of it than it can take. Wait awhile until you have cooled off before relaxing in a whirlpool or sauna, and then don't linger longer than twenty to thirty minutes.

These do soothe sore muscles and aching joints and help rehabilitate an ailing or aging athlete.

Normally, if you are not treating an injury, you would do well to stick to a warm shower.

Cryotherapy is the use of cold to treat physical ailments and injuries. Cold penetrates deeper tissue with greater effect than heat. It constricts superficial blood vessels, producing local inhibition of circulation. Where trauma has taken place, cold combined with pressure tends to slow internal hemorrhage and assists in faster clotting. It also has an anesthetic value.

Cold can be applied with immersion in ice-water tubs of sixty-five degrees F. or less, by the use of ice bags or commercial chemical cold packs, or by the use of spray coolants, such as ethyl chloride. These have only short-term value. Generally, I believe in applying cold to twists, strains, sprains, pulls, tears, bruises, and other injuries where bleeding beneath the skin is present from the moment of the injury, through repeated applications for twenty-four to forty-eight hours. After this, you should turn to heat. Stabilize and limit the swelling and hemorrhaging of injuries with ice or other cold treatment first, before promoting healing with heat.

Many medicinal drugs are available that are valuable in the treatment of ailments and injuries. Antiseptics inhibit the growth of micro-organisms, and disinfectants kill organisms that cause disease. These are used to avoid infection or combat infection. Since most scrapes, cuts, and punctures in sports take place on playing fields and courts that are not clean, the use of antiseptics and disinfectants, as well as protective coverings, is critical.

Antiseptics and disinfectants that feature phenol, formaldehyde, halogens, silver or mercury compounds, oxidizing agents, and alcohols such as ethyl and isopropyl are excellent. If you wish to get specific, consult your physician or pharmacist as to which apply best in different situations. Learn them and read the labels before buying bottles of compounds. Soap and warm water are as good as any cleansing agents. You should always start with these. Use basic soaps that are not loaded with exotic ingredients or heavily perfumed.

Alcohol is the basic antiseptic. Since it evaporates quickly it does not have long-lasting effect as with a disinfectant. However, it works well as a cleansing agent and has an anesthetic effect, so it lessens pain. Hydrogen peroxide also cleanses an area effectively, but it decomposes so rapidly it also has little lasting effect. It foams up, dislodging and raising infectious debris to the surface of a wound. It also has a styptic effect that stops bleeding. Because it is nontoxic, a fifty-fifty hydrogen peroxide and water solution is effective in treating sores and cuts of the mouth and throat.

Tincture of benzoin is an effective disinfectant. It is composed of 20 per cent benzoin in a solution of alcohol. Mercury compounds such as Merthiolate, Metaphen, and Mercurochrome are antiseptics, germicides, and fungicides that work well, especially in the treatment of skin cuts and abrasions. Tinactin is a medication that is effective as a fungicide. Astringents that are helpful for their styptic work in stopping bleeding are alums, zinc oxide, tannic acid, and boric acid.

Boric acid is soluble in water and works well as an ointment to protect open skin wounds or as a rinse for irritated eyes. Boric acid is effective as a cleansing agent. Tannic acid, tincture of benzoin, and zinc oxide are effective agents for toughening skin. Soaking hands or feet in solutions of these helps prevent blisters. A combination of tincture of benzoin and storax is an effective antiblister agent. This combination also serves well as a protective base for adhesive tape. Brown-colored, it stains and sticks and builds up on, say, an athlete's ankle over a season. Thin protective wraps and plastic sprays can be placed on the skin ahead of adhesive tape to prevent damage being done to the skin when the tape is removed.

Analgesics and anesthetics such as simple ice, alcohol, camphor, menthol, and methyl salicylate stop pain temporarily. Many are used in the spray coolants. There is a danger in these in that pain warns us of possible serious injury and should not be disregarded. These freeze the injury and ease the soreness, but if you do not feel the pain of an injury, you will not protect it. A sore knee, for example, might be overextended, resulting in serious injury. Use the pain killer to kill the pain, but use the pain to tell you when to stop play.

Protect surface injuries by cleansing them, applying antiseptics and disinfectants, and dressing them. Dressing protects wounds from further damage and infection, acts as a compress, controls bleeding, and supports or immobilizes an injury. Have gauze, cotton cloth, elastic wrap, sterile pads and plastic coatings and tapes, pressure bandages, and adhesive tape available.

Gauze can be used as a sterile pad and as padding, as well as a bandage to hold compresses in place. Cotton cloth is used as a wrap and a bandage. Elastic bandages are used as wraps because they conform to the part being bound and exert even pressure.

Plastic coatings and tapes are waterproof and especially protective to wounds treated with wet modalities. Pressure bandages are used to contain and support an injured part while permitting motion. Adhesive tape is less flexible but offers more support, and also is used to bind down bandages.

Do not use tape or bandage directly on a wound, but use it to hold down a dressing. When a wound occurs, cleanse it thoroughly with antiseptics or disinfectants, apply a protective coating or pad, then wrap it with bandages and tape to hold the dressing in place and to protect it.

Never apply an elastic or any other wrap so tightly as to cut off circulation. It has to be tight enough to be effective, but if any numbness starts, loosen the wrap until it is comfortable. It is difficult to tape too tightly, but taping is the most restrictive type of wrap. It is useful in that it provides more support than a cloth or elastic bandage and should be used when you want an area immobilized or protected.

Use half-inch-width or one-inch-width tape for hands and feet, one-inch or one-and-one-half-inch tape for wrists and ankles, and two-inch or three-inch tape for thighs and other large areas. Place the body part in the position in which it is to be stablized and start to tape. Tape and tear off a turn at a time to avoid constricting the area. Overlap the strips about half their width. Try to turn the tape to fit the contour of the area being bound, and smooth and mold it as you apply it. Start with an "anchor" strip from which the subsequent strips will flow. Finish with a "lock" strip across the wrap. Never tape on the bare skin. Always apply a spray base and protective wrap under the tape.

I believe in taping ankles in sports such as football and basketball because I believe that in these sports ankles are subjected to terrific stress and are easily turned, strained, twisted, or sprained. Most coaches believe in it. Some penalize players who do not do it. Some players never have done it, don't like it because they believe it restricts their movement, and won't do it. But it is important preventive care.

Of course, you could tape every part of a person's body as part of a program of preventive medicine, but I don't believe other parts are as vulnerable as the ankle. The knee may be, but a taped knee really is restrictive much more so than a taped ankle. I do believe in taping knees where there has been strain or sprains or other serious injuries. I believe in taping thighs where the athlete has been found to suffer from or be subject to pulled or torn muscles. I do not believe in taping wrists or elbows unless injuries make it necessary because it is restrictive.

Whenever possible, use a sort of "figure eight" form when elastic bandaging or taping a foot, ankle, thigh, groin, wrist, or whatever for protection. This sort of wrap supports itself. Weak parts can borrow strength from stronger parts. As you work, let the athlete move the part being bound to the degree you wish to permit it to be moved. The pros I have taped always flexed their ankle or whatever to be sure I was limiting them no more than necessary. They always will want it looser. The trainer will want it tighter. You can compromise only so much. If it is not tight enough, it will not do the job it was designed to do, yet the player must have some motion, too.

The pros would always jump off the table and test a taped ankle immediately. If they were happy with it, you probably had it too loose. They had to be warned that the taping would loosen with use, that it had to be tight in the beginning so as not to be loose at the end.

I can tell you how to tape and show you in pictures how to tape, but there is an art to it and you really learn it only by doing it. If possible, find a doctor, trainer, or coach who can teach you, and keep practicing. Taping is the guts of a trainer's job.

If there is any thought that an injury may be serious, the injured person should see a doctor. If there is any thought that a wound may be infected, see a doctor. If there is any thought that a strain, twist, or sprain may be covering up or really be a broken bone, immobolize the area, apply a splint, and see a doctor. Splints can be improvised or purchased commercially. A well-equipped team has finger, arm, and leg splits available. Slings will help immobilize possible broken arms or wrists.

If braces, supports, or other protective devices have been recommended, by all means use them. They may restrict your movements and may be uncomfortable, but they may enable you to continue in action and may prevent more serious injuries. Knee and back braces often are recommended in bowling, golf, or tennis when the person has a problem. Hinged or laced leather braces will provide support while allowing some movement.

The most common injuries are those to the surface skin. Scrapes, cuts, and punctures should be cleansed carefully with soap and warm water before a mild antiseptic is applied, then a medicated ointment. Hemorrhage can be controlled with a cold compress or ethyl chloride. A solution of hydrogen peroxide can be used as an antiseptic. The wound then should be covered with a pad or gauze and other bandage. It should be changed and checked regularly for signs of infection. Any infection should show up within a week and will reveal itself by the wound becoming red, hot, tender, or swollen. It must be washed briskly and dried and new antiseptic and bandage applied at least once a day. If infection persists, a doctor's treatment is called for.

Contusions or bruises result from traumatic blows to the body. These can cause injuries ranging from minor to major, depending on the severity of the blow and the part of the body struck. Most commonly, blows to the muscles cause bleeding, swelling, and soreness, with a consequent loss of action in the affected area. The blood flows into the tissues, causing discoloration.

Cold and pressure should be applied for up to an hour immediately after the injury and continued on and off for twenty-four to forty-eight hours, depending on the severity of the bruise. If it is severe, the sore part should be elevated as much as possible and subjected to some mild stretching. An elastic support bandage should be worn.

As soreness and hemorrhaging decrease, brief warm baths or hot packs of no more than ninety degrees F. are prescribed, as well as stretching, on the third or fourth days following the injury. Then hot whirlpool baths and massage are recommended. The elastic support bandage should be worn until you return to action. Back in action, sponge protective padding should be taped over the injury to prevent a recurrence.

In "floor burns," which occur when a player slides on a hard or abrasive surface, such as in basketball, the skin usually is rubbed off so the player suffers both cutting and contusion. The affected area has to be cleansed completely, antiseptic applied, and a protective, padded bandage taped on, and the individual then usually can continue. This is much the same treatment used for "sliding strawberries" suffered in baseball.

A contusion to the thigh muscle commonly is called a "charley horse." A severe blow to the tissue of the thigh compresses it against the hard surface of the femur—the thigh bone. This is painful and there usually is loss of function in the leg for a short time. The treatment is the same as with other bruises, but this injury sometimes is so deep it will not readily respond. Rest for a week or more may be required before it heals.

If someone tells you to "walk it out" or "run it out," tell them this is an old wives' tale. There is a real risk of increasing internal bleeding if you subject the injury to additional stress. You should not return to action until the pain no longer persists and the leg begins to look good again.

A severe blow may produce a contusion so deep that it causes a bone bruise. This is especially incapacitating, and the affected area is difficult to reach with treatment. Still, it is treated as are other bruises, starting with cold and ending with heat, with pressure and protective bandaging until it heals.

The shin is especially vulnerable to bruising because it lies just under the skin and is not as protected by the padding of flesh and muscle as are other parts. A kick in the shin is especially painful, of course, because it is one case where the blow is delivered directly to the bone. The usual treatment is called for, but the shin does not heal easily, especially the lower third, which has a smaller supply of blood than the upper part. A bruised shin has to be padded and protected.

Although the heel is well padded, sudden hard stops often bruise them. It is then impossible to walk or run without pain. If possible you must stay off your feet for a few days to enable the bruise to heal. Apply ice immediately for an hour. Apply it on and off for twenty-four hours. Then start cold baths several times a day for several days. Then switch to warm baths. Ultrasound is helpful. And tape on a protective padding.

A heavy blow to the stomach may knock the wind out of a person. This is common in football, for example, but can come with any kind of collision. It is one of the most painful things that can happen to an athlete, but it is not as serious as it seems and the pain disappears quickly. What has happened is that the air within the body has been forced out suddenly and the person is starving for oxygen. As the air returns, the pain subsides. Normally, less than a minute is required before the individual has gasped enough air back into his body to have recovered fully.

There really is little you can do for people in this situation, except to see that they have not swallowed their tongues. Open the mouth and if the tongue is not visible, pull it out with your fingers. Beyond this, simply see that the person is on his back with his clothes loosened. Never move him unnecessarily, since some more serious injury, such as a broken rib, may have occurred. Be especially cautious with blows to the head, neck, and back.

You have to beware of concussions or broken bones, serious injuries that I will deal with in the following chapter. Injuries to the eyes, ears, or nose must be considered with caution. If there is any thought that they might be serious, a doctor's care is called for.

When the injury is around the mouth, check to make sure that the teeth are not involved. Chipped or broken teeth will need dental care. Lightweight mouthpieces to protect teeth are recommended for football and hockey. Also check the tongue. Commonly, kids bite their tongues. As far as that goes, Rudy LaRusso of the Lakers used to do it all the time. Once he almost bit his in half.

Not much can be done for injuries inside the mouth. You can't apply antiseptics internally, but a doctor may administer an antitetanus shot for a severe cut. He may wish to sew stitches to insure the proper healing of any severe cut. If a cut is severe, consider that it may call for stitches.

Cuts in the mouth and on the tongue tend to heal fast, though they are sensitive as long as they last. Perhaps the fast healing is nature's way of making up for the fact that you cannot treat the wound extensively. Do not apply antiseptic close to an eye, for it might get in the eye, where it would be an irritant and perhaps create a real problem.

When an injury is around the head, make sure the eye is not involved. If there is any hemorrhaging within the eye, have a doctor check it. Some blows to the eye may cause at most minor discomfort and can be treated successfully with cold compresses for about 24 hours, followed then by hot packs, but caution must be exercised in deciding the extent of an eye injury.

So-called "black eyes" are a result of a blow that has bruised the surrounding tissue and produced bleeding that has gone unchecked. An athlete should never "blow his nose" following such an eye injury, as this will increase the bleeding. The old-fashioned treatment of laying a piece of beef on a black eye had merit because the beef usually came from an ice box or refrigerator and was cold. It is the cold you want. Treat an eye contusion with a cold, damp cloth or ice pack for an hour as soon as possible. Continue on and off for twenty-four hours. After that, apply hot, moist packs.

Frequently, we get foreign bodies in our eyes. If you do, do not rub it no matter how sensitive it is because you may scratch the surface of the eye. Do not try to remove the substance with a finger or a swab because you may poke the eye and damage it. Gently draw back the eyelids to see if the substance has stuck to the upper or lower lid. If the substance is located on the lower lid, it may be removed by rolling the lid down and carefully wiping it out with a sterile cotton swab. If on the upper lid, it may be washed out by pulling the upper lid over the lower one, causing tears to be produced. This may wash out the substance even if it has stuck to the eyeball. If it does not, you will need a doctor to remove it safely.

The eye is protected in many ways. It is held within an oval socket formed by the bones of the head. It is surrounded by soft fatty tissue and the thin skin flaps of lids. The eyelashes screen out most foreign substances. Lubricating organs keep the eyeball moist and help wash out foreign substances. Yet it is delicate and can be damaged easily. The socket can be cracked. The eyeball can be injured. If an athlete suffers any harm to his eyesocket or extensive bleeding within the eyeball or is troubled by faulty vision, he must cover the eye at once and seek medical care.

If you wear eyeglasses and engage in any athletic activity in which the glasses may be struck, by all means use glass guards, glasses made of unbreakable glass or plastic, or contact lenses. Obviously, broken glasses can damage the eyes. Few people wear eyeglasses in competition—most wear contacts.

Most injuries to the ears occur to the outer-portion and are seldom dangerous or severe. Repeated wrenching of and blows to the outer ear have caused a condition known as "cauliflower ear," primarily to boxers or wrestlers. Greasing the ear with petroleum jelly prior to combat will lessen the likelihood of this condition developing. If the ear becomes swollen from blows it should be compressed with a cold pack. If an ear becomes infected or is in danger of infection, it should be cleansed with a mild solution of alcohol, dried, and plugged with lanolin and cotton.

"Swimmer's ear" is an infection created by exposure of the inner ear to cold, damp foreign matter. It may be sore or may itch, fluid may seep out, and there may be some loss of hearing. Medical treatment is required to clear up the condition before it harms the hearing, but the swimmer will have to stay out of the water and keep the ear clean and dry for a while.

Some people are subject to nosebleeds. Others suffer them from blows. Usually, these present only a minor problem and the bleeding will stop spontaneously. If not, there are several corrective measures that can be taken. The individual can sit with his head lowered between his legs or lie on a slant so his nostrils point upward. He can apply finger pressure or a cold compress to the nostril for a few minutes.

If the problem persists for five minutes or more, an astringent or a styptic such as tannic acid can be applied at the point of the hemorrhaging and a gauze or cotton pad applied to promote clotting. After the bleeding has stopped, the person can continue activity at little risk, but should avoid blowing his nose for a while rather than risk a recurrence of the problem.

If the bleeding continues or is heavy, doctor's care is called for. It is always possible that the nose has been broken. Unprotected as are eyes and ears, the nose sticks out there, exposed and vulnerable, as we head into action. A broken nose may be the least serious of broken bones, but it is serious, and I talk about treatment in the next chapter. Here, too, I will cover serious injuries to the neck and back, as well as the joints of the body.

A "crick in the neck" is not serious, though it is painful and limits movement. It is caused by holding the head in one position for a prolonged period, or in an awkward position, or by a sudden wrench or twist that causes abuse to muscles in the neck. Sometimes this happens in sleep, when we are not aware of it. It is a muscle spasm that can be reduced swiftly with care, but can linger a long time without care.

Apply heat for about fifteen minutes. Follow with gentle massage and rotation of the head and neck. Then, standing behind the person with the problem, with your right hand cupped under his chin and your left hand on the back of his head, apply a slow, steady upward pull and rotate the head slowly to stretch the muscles. If relief is not complete, repeat the whole process and conclude with a traction pull away from the sore area. If the soreness is to the right, pull gently to the left. Some of this movement may be painful, but the worst thing a person with this problem can do is hold his head stiff. No matter how sore they are, the muscles must be moved and stretched. As they regain their form and elasticity, the pain will disappear.

The shoulder, elbow, wrist, hip, knee, and ankle joints are intricate, delicate mechanisms that normally hold up under stress, but easily suffer serious injuries. The wrist and ankle joints are freely movable hinge mechanisms that nevertheless are easily strained, twisted, or sprained with sudden, violent, or awkward turns. Often, stabilizing connective tissue is torn.

A strained muscle has been stretched until torn. A sprained muscle is more of the same, only more severe. The more severe it is, the more painful and immobilizing. Although not nearly as serious, it may hurt more than a broken bone. It may swell and bleed. Knee and shoulder joints are sometimes strained or sprained, too.

The first thing to do in treating strains or sprains is to apply a cold pack and pressure bandage to the joint for one to two hours. Depending on how severe it is, continue for twenty-four to forty-eight hours. Don't use the injured limb, even if you have to use crutches, and keep it elevated as much as possible.

If the sprain is severe, apply ice massage and cold whirlpool for ten minutes at a time. As the severity lessens, start mild exercise of the injured part. Keep an elastic bandage on it to limit movement. The third or fourth day you can begin therapy with moist heat, whirlpool baths, an analgesic balm pack, and an infrared lamp.

If it has not started to respond by the third or fourth day, see a doctor. If there is any thought that the injury might be more serious than a strain or a sprain, see a doctor. Torn muscles, connective tissue, or damaged joints sometimes have to be repaired surgically, and there always is the possibility of broken bones.

When you do return to action, tape the injured part for a while, limiting its motion, to avoid restraining an injury that may not have healed completely or to avoid reinjury of a weakened part. Strains and sprains are commonplace problems, but even if not among the more serious injuries, they can be serious.

When I was at USC, the great pole-vaulter Ron Morris sprained an ankle between major meets. It was the ankle with which he pushed off, and he needed strength in it. He figured he was finished as far as the forthcoming meet was concerned, but I talked him into trying treatment on a crash basis. We iced the ankle for days, then applied heat treatments. The day of the meet I taped it heavily. He went out and won with one of his best-ever vaults.

On the other hand, when I was with the Lakers, Elmore Smith was troubled by persistent ankle problems. These may have started with a sprain, but persisted long after that had healed. At least he complained of pain. X rays revealed no break or other damage. Neither I nor Dr. Kerlan nor the finest medical minds in the country could discover a problem. Elmore went to every doctor but Marcus Welby.

You can't treat what isn't there, but I treated it as a sprain. Elmore claimed we weren't doing anything for him, and I took the blame. It cost me my job. Frankly, I feel the problem was psychological rather than physical. Elmore was having a bad season and blamed it on a bad ankle. The fact is he has blamed a lot of bad seasons on a lot of bad ankles on a lot of teams since.

As the replacement for Wilt Chamberlain, Elmore was more important to the team than I was.

Wilt had bad hands. Passes would catch him on his fingertips, jamming his fingers. Rudy LaRusso was another Laker who was always catching passes on his fingertips, jamming them. When Hot Rod Hundley was with the Lakers his passes always were catching teammates on the fingertips, jamming them. Any quick, hard passer, like Pete Maravich, is going to catch his teammates by surprise and jam their fingers.

Baseball players and softball players catch the ball on their fingertips a lot and jam their fingers. Jammed fingers are painful. They swell up and sometimes hemorrhage, and you can lose the use of them. They have to be iced and splinted so they are kept immobile. You can play with some fingers splinted and you can't with others, but you can't use a jammed finger until it recovers.

You often need X rays to determine if a jammed finger is really a broken finger. Usually it is only badly bruised. Ice and compression will reduce the bleeding until whirlpool and other hot baths and heat treatments help the healing process. A sponge rubber pad sometimes can be taped to the affected area to protect it.

Sprained fingers, especially sprained thumbs, are common from catching balls or from attempts to tackle opponents, but these are so similar to fractured or dislocated fingers that you should have a doctor diagnose the injury. As with most sprains, there will be pain from damage done to the tendons or muscles, and swelling and discoloration from internal bleeding. Over the years these may have been the most neglected or mistreated injuries. Proof can be found in the many old players, particularly catchers, left with bent or misshapen fingers from lack of care at the time of their injuries.

Generally, ice and compression applied for at least an hour will control the bleeding. After seventy-two hours, heat will help. The finger must be splinted, or at least immobilized by taping it to the next finger.

Cuts and tears between the fingers are not immobilizing, but they bother the players and they can become infected. They have to be cleansed completely, treated antiseptically, and disinfected regularly because it is difficult to apply protective bandaging between the fingers.

If a fingernail or toenail has been mashed, causing blood to gather under it, you have a painful condition to deal with. Immersing it in ice water immediately will usually halt the hemorrhaging, but it takes a long time to heal and must be protected with padding.

As with a blister, it is dangerous to puncture the wound to release the fluid. Someone skilled in this may release the blood and relieve the pain created by the buildup of pressure under the nail by applying antiseptic to the nail and a sharp-pointed instrument, such as a needle, and gently penetrating the nail to create an opening through which the pent-up blood will spurt. Heat often helps the instrument penetrate the nail.

Sprained wrists, often suffered when you fall forward on your hands, are among the most common wrist injuries. The usual cold and hot treatment is called for, but because of the greater need for freedom of motion you can't tape a wrist the way you can an ankle. Muscle soreness or stiffness may follow exercise, especially early in a new program. When you begin, you will suffer sore legs, for example. If you start to throw a ball hard when you have not been throwing, you will suffer sore arms. If you bowl a heavy ball when you have not been bowling, you will suffer sore arms and fingers.

There may have been tissue damage done, such as tears of muscle fibers or connective tissue, especially if the individual did not stretch properly prior to the activity and had not attained a good degree of elasticity.

Fluids that collect in the muscles during exercise are absorbed slowly into the bloodstream, causing the muscles to contract, to become shorter and thicker than usual, and to swell up, making them more resistant to stretching.

If your body can handle your program of exercise, the soreness and the stiffness that usually goes along with it should not last more than a few hours. After rest, stretching exercise the following day will condition the muscles to handle the load imposed on them. If the problems persist twenty-four hours or more, you will have to re-evaluate your program and progress more slowly. Soaking sore muscles in cold water will help at first, followed later by warm baths, preferably whirlpool baths.

"Shin splints" are characterized by sharp pain in the frontal, lower leg. What has usually happened is that the tendons have been irritated and become inflamed. It often comes from running on hard surfaces, but can be caused by switching from soft to hard surfaces or even hard to soft surfaces, or by poor posture or running technique. In any event, the tendons have been stressed to points of pain.

The condition is not easily corrected. You have to figure out what faults in your running or what changes in your running could have caused it, and you have to avoid that situation, or condition yourself to it. Rest eases the pain, heat will help, and taping can keep the tendons from further stress. If pain persists and there is swelling, the shin must be checked for fracture.

The "sore arm" occurs when the muscles and attachments of the arm and sometimes the shoulder and elbow have been subjected to excessive stress. "Pitcher's arm," "Little League elbow," "tennis elbow," "golf elbow," and "bowler's elbow" all fall into the same category. I consider them serious injuries and will go into them in detail in the following chapter.

Any part of a muscle or its tendons may be partially or fully pulled or torn. Most often this occurs where the muscle joins the tendon, but it may occur in the muscle or tendon separately. The person will feel a "pull" and may even hear a "pop." He may feel like he has been struck at the point of pain. When this happens he should stop at once so as not to tear the muscle further.

This happens most often when the muscles have not been warmed up properly and stretched, but it may happen any time the muscle or tendon is stretched past its limits, such as in a sudden stressful thrust. It happens often to sprinters, no matter how much they may have warmed up and stretched, no matter how good their condition. However, it does not happen much to most athletes who have warmed up and stretched and are fit.

When it does happen, get off the injured part. Use ice and pressure bandages to treat it for at least seventy-two hours. As it heals, start to treat it with heat and massage. Rest it as much as possible until all pain has disappeared. Give the injury time to heal. If it is a severe injury, such as a pulled hamstring muscle or groin muscle, it will take time to heal. Keep it bound with an elastic bandage.

The hamstring runs from the buttocks across the back of the thigh. A pulled hamstring does "pop" and the injured person often goes down as though shot. The groin muscle may be the one that heals the slowest because it involves rotating muscles. A person suffering from it cannot get in and out of his car without discomfort. An athlete can run straight ahead, but cannot turn and move from side to side easily. The muscles from your upper thigh have separated from those in your lower abdominal wall, and there is no way to properly support this area with tape.

The careers of the two greatest guards who ever played basketball, Oscar Robertson and Jerry West, were curtailed by groin pulls. They simply would not heal. Jerry tried to come back too soon from his and suffered a reinjury that ended his season. And the problem persisted and pestered him the rest of his career.

In Jerry's case, he was one who never took the time to warm up properly. I never knew him to use stretching exercises. Ironically, he allowed Del Tanner to institute stretching exercises on the

Lakers that reduced muscle pulls markedly. Jerry learned his lesson, but too late.

Jerry hated to be called "injury prone," but he may have missed more games from muscle pulls and tears than any player ever. I can't say for sure that there is such a thing as being "injury prone" because someone's muscular or skeletal structure is inferior in some way, but I can say that some athletes get hurt more regularly than others.

Jerry did play with a reckless abandon that led to injuries, but I believe that his hesitance to warm up, stretch, and tape himself led to his many muscle problems.

Every sport has specialized injuries as a result of specialized movements, such as sore arms, "pitcher's arm," "tennis elbow," and so forth. There are a lot of pulled muscles in basketball. Also a lot of "jumper's leg" problems. The legs and feet, the hip, knee, and ankle joints are subjected to shock when landing off a jump. The takeoff exerts extreme stress on these parts too. Athletes should be taught to jump properly, but jumping takes a toll on legs that eventually costs them their strength and elasticity.

Soccer produces something called groin strain. It happens when you hyperextend your body and abduct your legs at the same time. This pulls the sheet of connective tissue on the inside of your thigh over your lower abdominal muscles and it attaches to the little bone over your pelvis. Overstressed, these little fibers become inflamed. The player may retain freedom of movement, but suffer pain. Ice baths followed by heat treatments will help.

The most common soccer injury is the tearing of cartilage due to twisting the body on a fixed base. This happens a lot in basketball too, but groin strain is peculiar to soccer. Hyperextension of the elbow, wrist, or knee joint is not uncommon in any sport, however. This happens when the joint hinges are forced against their natural movement, stressing and tearing the muscles.

Leg cramps are common to tennis. These are really muscle spasms, sudden and violent. They come mainly from fatigue and the loss of fluids and salt through sweating. Sometimes they are suffered in sleep. The muscles bunch up painfully, and it can be corrected by stretching. This will increase the pain temporarily, but erase it swiftly. Either point your toe and stretch your leg out as much as possible or have someone pull it. Spread a thin layer of analgesic balm over the affected area to soothe it before resuming action. You will have had to stop temporarily, anyway. In addition, you should take salt tablets and drink lots of liquids to replace what was lost.

Foot cramps sometimes occur, but these are not common. A lot is asked of our feet. Almost any athletic activity is done from the feet up. The foot is composed of twenty-six bones bound by ligaments and designed for flexibility and stretch, but we subject it to extreme stress. We do not do much for our feet. Most "full" physical examinations stop at the feet. Fortunately, there is an increasing interest in medical circles in foot care.

Many feet have structural faults. The bones are not aligned properly, or growths have begun on the bone. Some people suffer from "flat feet": Their weak muscles have permitted their arches to drop. Running on hard surfaces sometimes increases this problem.

Specialized activities produce particular conditions. For example, the way surfers kneel on a board while propelling it out over the waves causes their weight to rest on the instep of one foot, and a growth may begin at the head of the first metatarsal bone. This is "surfer's foot."

There are no easy cures for these conditions. Wearing the proper shoes, perhaps padded, with good arch supports will help whenever possible. But these are things one has to live with.

Wearing the wrong shoes, or shoes that are not properly fit to our feet cause many problems. Rubbing may cause blisters to form on our feet and toes, as well as on our hands and fingers. Friction separates the epidermis and the dermis, and fluid can form between the layers. Never puncture a blister unless you feel you cannot carry on with it the way it is. Simply protect it with a pad and bandage and let it dissipate on its own. You must be careful of infection.

If you insist on puncturing it yourself, use a sterilized needle, make a small opening, press the fluid out, cleanse the area with soap and water, rinse it with alcohol, apply an antiseptic, and cover the area with a sterile dressing. After the underlying tissue has hardened, trim away the dead skin. You can toughen your hands and feet by soaking them daily in an astringent such as tannic acid.

Calluses are caused when there is rubbing over a bony area, often by shoes that are too tight. Calluses can be painful and can crack or tear, and possibly cause infection. Soak these in warm, soapy water and rub a little lanolin into them several times a week to soften them.

You can use an emery file to keep them in control. Cover calluses with felt or sponge rubber pads to protect them and save you discomfort. But, again, start to toughen your feet with soakings so calluses will not form.

Corns can be soaked in warm, soapy water, treated with keralytic ointment, and protected by pads until they disappear. With toughened feet, corns will not reappear.

"Bowler's toe" is an ailment which may afflict as many as twenty million of the sixty-five million bowlers. Stress placed on the big toe and the second toe of the rear foot the bowler drags behind him as he makes his delivery creates misshapen toes and thickened toenails and causes calluses behind the toes. It is so painful that even wearing shoes becomes a problem. It is caused by the stiff cap of the bowling shoe as it bends over the foot. Bowling shoes with soft caps or no caps would not create the ailment, but would wear out, as do the toes of tennis shoes dragged during serving. Tennis players seldom suffer this type of ailment. Bowlers who do, have to switch to soft-toed shoes.

Athlete's foot is a sort of rash of pimples and blisters that stems from a fungus or bacterial infection. Commonly we consider that it is created in openings in the skin of the feet that have been exposed to soiled water, such as in the shower room. The openings may come from failure to dry feet properly and keep them dry. Wet feet tend to crack, especially between the toes. Athlete's foot itches, so we scratch, causing more cracks. A doctor or a dermatologist can prescribe a lotion with which to treat it. I've had good luck with aerosol sprays available on drugstore shelves—tincture of benzoin works well. The best bet is to avoid it by wearing shower shoes going to and from showers, by drying your feet thoroughly after showers, by keeping them dried and powdered, and by wearing clean, sweat-absorbing white cotton socks in athletic competition. There are no telethons to raise money to cure athlete's feet. It is a common problem and can be bothersome, but it certainly is not serious in comparison with bad backs, broken bones, and torn knees.

11. SERIOUS INJURIES AND HOW TO RECOGNIZE THEM

The most dangerous injuries are those to the head, neck, and back. Blows to the head can cause concussions. What this means is that the head has been shaken severely, and, with it the brain. The violent movement of the brain within the container of the skull can cause damage. There may be dizziness and disorientation, headache and a "ringing in the ears." There may be a loss of consciousness.

No one knows precisely what causes a "knockout," as when a boxer strikes a foe on the chin so sharply as to render him unconscious, but it is presumed that the blow has caused a shaking of the brain that has constricted the blood vessels leading to it. Any blow to the face or head, as in football or other sports, can cause this condition.

Mostly, blows to the head are minor matters, causing only momentary, if any, unconsciousness and doing no damage. But they are dangerous because the whole of the brain has been threatened and because the life-giving flow of blood has been threatened. If unconsciousness persists, if the flow of blood to the brain has been interrupted in any way, the danger of fatality or loss of function is great.

Dilated or unequal pupils, nausea, vomiting, any convulsions or paralysis, any fluid escaping from the nose or ears are warning signs that have to be heeded. Any person suffering a blow to the head that has hurt him in any way should be removed from the activity and rested at once, and if his symptoms continue he should be turned over to a doctor immediately.

One simple test that can be administered is to have the person stand up straight, feet together, hands at his side, eyes closed. If there is no swaying or loss of balance and if the person feels all right, he probably is all right, but if there is any persistent problem, even a headache, a doctor's care is called for.

Most people who suffer minor blows to the head can return to action within a few minutes, but many will require twenty-four to forty-eight hours of rest and one to two weeks away from contact sports. A few will require one to two weeks of rest and three to four weeks away from their sport.

Apparently some damage is done to the brain in trauma to the head causing unconsciousness because a person who has suffered such an injury once is statistically more likely to suffer another than someone who has not had one. Thus, any person who has been knocked unconscious for as much as a minute two or three times probably should be retired from that activity, even if no other problems appear.

Blows to the jaw frequently fracture it because the lower jawbone is not well protected. The lower jaw has a wide range of movement and often also is dislocated. It usually is displaced and will not move well. It will be tender to the touch, painful, and there may be bleeding around the teeth. Cold compression should be applied, the jaw must be immobilized as much as possible, and a doctor's care sought. In severe cases of fractured jaw it may have to be wired shut to be stabilized and all nourishment for a month or more must come through a straw. It is not among the easier injuries. Fractured cheekbones are less troublesome. They are not easily immobilized, but tend to heal rather rapidly.

Fractured noses are annoyances as much as anything. They are commonplace and the main problem with them is once you have one, you are apt to have another. Jerry West had six or seven—he did not have corrective surgery until he completed his career. This surgery is primarily cosmetic.

In the case of a nosebleed you must check for a broken nose. If the nose is broken, you can stuff the nostrils with cotton, ice the nose to control bleeding, then tape splints onto both sides of it. Usually the athlete can return to action almost immediately, and in West's case I devised face guards he could wear to protect his nose while he was playing and still recovering from the injury.

Kareem Abdul-Jabbar wears a plastic mask or goggles to protect his eyes, having had them poked by fingers once too often to suit him.

Sometimes a severe shaking or twisting of the neck can cause a shaking of the head and brain that creates a condition similar to a blow to the head. Sometimes a severe shaking or twisting of the spinal column can cause this shaking and twisting of the neck. Both the neck and spinal column have a wide range of motion and are not twisted easily beyond this range, but it does happen. A blow to the top of the head may jam it down, compressing the neck muscles. The head may be snapped back so hard that the neck becomes hyperextended, or the neck may be twisted severely. This can happen from blocking or tackling in football, for example, or in any kind of collision or fall. It happens if a diver's head hits the bottom of a swimming pool.

Such an injury may result in compression or cervical fractures or, more commonly, dislocations. A dislocation is a separation of parts of a joint. Although not as serious as a fracture, it is still serious. The outward signs of a cervical dislocation are similar to that of a fracture. The injured part suffers muscular spasm and becomes contorted, there is pain and, perhaps, partial paralysis. Usually it is a dislocation if the head and neck are tilted to one side with the muscles tensed on the long side and relaxed on the short side. However, this is not a condition for the average person to diagnose. A doctor's diagnosis is called for. Often, spinal cord and nerve injuries may be involved, and these can be extremely dangerous.

The spinal cord is well protected, and dislocations and fractures resulting in paralysis are uncommon, but to be feared. The spinal cord and nerve roots may be twisted so as to cause a fracture or dislocation. Normally, no irreparable damage is done, but jagged ends of fractured bones may cut into the cord, and hemorrhaging interferes with the circulation within the cord. Paralysis, sometimes permanent, can result.

A "pinched nerve" is just what it sounds like, resulting in a burning sensation from the neck through the arm, followed by numbness and loss of function. A pinched nerve will pass, but a slipped or cracked disc, which is much more serious, may have similar symptoms. Whenever there has been a head, neck, or spinal cord injury, extreme caution should be exercised. If there is any thought that it is serious, a doctor's care is called for. In the case of neck or spinal cord injuries, the injured person should not be moved except under medical care.

Ordinary neck strain or sprain calls for rest, traction, heat, massage, and manipulation, but X rays are in order to make sure there has been no fracture or dislocation. The traction should be a steady but mild stretching applied two or three times a day. Moist heat should be applied to the sore area. The massage and manipulation should be mild.

There are back conditions that are not caused by specific injury but are the result of sustained insult. The spine is composed of thirty-three individual bones, called vertebrae, twenty-four of which are moveable and nine of which are immovable, all joined by ligaments and encased in a network of muscles. It is a complex network.

Damage can be done to the spinal column in normal living, let alone athletic activity. Frequently, people are born with disorders of the spine. If the bones are not aligned properly, or get out of alignment, there is a problem. If the muscles are strained, there is a problem. There is pain and loss of freedom of motion in a part of the body that was designed to be flexible.

We know some things about disorders of the back. We know that tall people suffer from them more than short people. We know that the older you get, the more subject you are to these problems. Poor posture is a sign that such a problem is present or may develop, and contributes to the problem.

We know that most back problems lie in the lower spine. It is this area of the back that carries the heaviest load in sports that require twisting movements. Thus the muscles, tendons, and ligaments in this area are most subject to tension and stress.

We know how to help with the problem. Initially, rest helps. You should stay away from those situations that stress the spine, such as swinging golf clubs or raising windows. As the condition improves, application of damp heat and deep massage will help.

You must improve your posture. Stretching exercises will help. Sleeping on a board may help straighten out your back. Exercises that strengthen your abdominal, hip, buttocks, and thigh muscles so they can help carry the load will help.

The sports that will help most are swimming, running, and

cross-country skiing, in that order. Sports that will do the most damage are water skiing and bowling. I'm not sure a bowler with a bad back can continue. Tennis players and golfers may have to modify their strokes to continue. Taping your back or encasing it in a brace to restrict its movement may be cumbersome or bothersome, but it will enable you to continue in your activity. We can help, but for the most part we cannot heal.

In extreme cases, a doctor may decide corrective surgery is possible and necessary. The discs that act as shock absorbers for the spinal column may have slipped or been cracked or crushed. Hockey players who have crashed into the boards have at times damaged these discs in this way and have had to have them removed. Players such as Stan Mikita and Rod Gilbert have had their careers prolonged by spinal fusions.

In most cases, those persons troubled with back problems can do for them only what I have suggested they do. Beyond this, they simply must learn to live with their conditions and limit those activities that aggravate them. A U. S. Public Health survey suggests that seventy million adults have had severe and prolonged problems with their backs. The National Center for Health Statistics estimates that two million more are added every year. Back problems are second only to feet problems in athletic activity.

Before I even broke into big-time sports, I worked with Jill Kinmont in her rehabilitation from that spinal injury suffered in skiing that resulted in her permanent paralysis.

Another brave gal with whom I worked, one of many referred to me by Bob Kerlan, enabling me to have a productive private practice, was Sue Gossick, the diver.

She had strained lower back muscles. I treated her with heat in the form of hot packs and ultrasound, plus massage, and set her on a routine of stretching exercises. The pain passed.

The 1968 Olympics trials were held at Long Beach. I went as Sue's guest and sat with her parents. Her back held up, but, as fate would have it, she hit her hand on the board during one of her dives.

She was in pain and worried. Weeping, she came to her family for consolation. I examined her hand. It was bruised and the skin was broken, but I couldn't feel any fracture. She asked if it was broken. I said I was sure it wasn't.

I said, "It's going to be sore awhile. We could ice it."

She said, "I've got to dive. I'm only two dives away."

She had two dives left, and two bad ones would drop her from the lead and off the Olympics team. I said, "Well, the hand will hurt you, but you don't dive with your hand."

She looked at me, sort of surprised, as if she hadn't thought of it that way, and started to smile through her tears. She said, "You're right."

She went out and did two terrific dives, made the team, and went on to win the gold medal in the three-meter springboard event at Mexico City.

Sometimes psychological help is as important as physical help.

Another referred to me was Sharon Stouder, the swimmer, who had pain over her entire back. I treated her with heat and massage, sometimes twice a day, for months before every major meet in 1964. And she went on to win the gold in the hundred-meter butterfly event at Tokyo.

So you can overcome obstacles, even bad backs.

Bill Toomey suffered severed tendons in one hand as a boy as a result of an encounter with broken glass. He has very little feeling in the hand. As a decathlete he had to perform ten widely different events in two days, which led to widely different physical problems. He suffered a lot of leg and back problems and many muscle pulls.

He was having trouble with a shoulder when Dr. Kerlan treated him, and I provided the therapy as Bill recuperated. And he won the gold in Mexico.

It is the athlete who overcomes the obstacles. Doctors may make miracles, but trainers can only help. I take pride in the small part I played in the success of some, but the real success belongs to the athlete.

Lionel Rose, the Australian bantamweight boxer, began to have back spasms while in Southern California for a title fight with Chu Chu Castillo of Mexico at the Forum in December of 1968. In his roadwork Rose had done some downhill running, which had strained his back. Dr. Kerlan turned him over to me for therapy.

I treated him with heat and massage, and the soreness eased. He came in every day for almost a week, and on the day of the fight asked me to work with him at the Forum. I massaged and stretched him. He went out and won the fight, but it was a bitter battle in which a bad back could have beaten him.

Actually, the partisan Mexican crowd thought Castillo had won, and rioted, doing damage to the Forum in its first year from which it has not totally recovered. Rugs and drapes that were ruined were never replaced. It was scary. Getting to the dressing room with the Rose party I exchanged swipes with an angry fan, and there I treated Rose's manager, Jack Rennie, for cuts he suffered on his scalp and leg when bottles broke around him.

Terry Sawchuk, the great goaltender, who came to the Forum as the first star of the Los Angeles Kings' hockey team near the end of his career, had an arthritic back, causing curvature of his spine. Dr. Kerlan, himself, has this condition. Dr. Kerlan worked with him and I worked with him, but we could not do much for him because his was a chronic condition.

Bob Rosburg, the great golfer, had arthritis in his neck and shoulders, and I worked with him. He was helped and went on awhile, but eventually his career was curtailed. I worked with Casey Tibbs, the rodeo cowboy, who had neck problems, shoulder problems, back problems, knee problems. These bronc riders take a terrible beating, but they go on.

I worked with Sandy Koufax. Years of stress had done damage to the great Dodger pitcher's elbow, and an arthritic condition had developed. You can only do so much for arthritis, which is an inflammation of a joint and tends to be chronic. Sandy took pain-killing injections, but you can only take so many before their effectiveness wears off, so he pitched in pain until he called it a day. In his last seasons he was treated every day.

Most of the sore arms of pitchers occur when the muscles and attachments of the arms and sometimes the elbow and shoulder joints have been subjected to severe stress. Sometimes this stems from improper warmup and lack of stretching exercises. Sometimes simply from overwork.

Sore arms often develop simply because the arm has been asked to do something it was not meant to do. Dr. Kerlan says, "The human arm is not constructed to throw a ball overhand and hard. You have only to swing your arm to see that the underhand motion is more natural. So softball pitchers suffer far fewer sore arms than baseball pitchers."

Throwing hard, throwing awkwardly, throwing with a twisting motion pulls and twists the muscles and tendons. Small tears take place. No matter how tiny, they must have time to heal. Usually there is some hemorrhaging and it takes time for the bleeding to stop, so pitchers take three or four days off between starts.

Sandy Koufax used to say that the pain was so bad after starts that he sometimes couldn't comb his hair. He quit for fear he would be permanently crippled. Pitching coach Billy Muffett says that sooner or later every pitcher is going to hurt his arm. Jim Palmer, the Baltimore Orioles' ace, says, "The only cure for a sore arm is to take a year off. Then retire."

Over a period of time there is an accumulation of damage within the arm. Depending on the physiology of the arm and the stresses to which it has been subjected, there comes a time when the muscles and tendons no longer can take stress without pain. As the tears heal, scar tissue develops. As this hardens, it breaks off into flecks of calcium, like grains of salt, which remain within the area, acting as an irritant on it. Bits of bone may break away, acting in the same way, or spurs may develop on the bone, irritating tissue. These flecks and spurs can be removed surgically, but the scraping sometimes does more harm than good.

The stress of hard or awkward motion may do damage within the wrist, elbow, and shoulder joints. The rotator cuff muscles of the shoulder and other muscles may be torn. Adolescent bones and muscles are immature, so Little League and high-school pitchers in particular are vulnerable to damage to their joints, which may linger the rest of their lives.

Young pitchers should not throw past any power that comes easy to them and should not throw curve balls or any breaking balls that require them to twist their arms or snap their wrists. Rules limiting the amount they can pitch should be enforced, but damage is done when the youngster goes right out and throws on his own or his dad decides he needs more work.

It is important that a pitcher be taught to throw properly so there is as little strain as possible on his arm and the burden of throwing is borne as much by his body as by his arm. Tom Seaver says, "If you strengthen your lower body and leg muscles so you can push off properly and follow through to a finish correctly you will take a lot of strain off your arm."

I was one of the early believers in the use of ice to rehabilitate an arm after each effort and am happy that today most major leaguers soak their arms in ice vats immediately after a game and for as much as a half hour to help the healing process. Later heat and massage are helpful. Little Leaguers and high schoolers should pursue this practice too, but seldom do.

I believe a pitcher should take off four days between starts and should not throw at all for two days after a start. On the third day he can start to stretch his arm out again by throwing easy. He should start easy, but throw a bit harder on the fourth day. He should never throw hard until loosened up thoroughly.

Relief pitchers can throw more often because they throw less each outing, but they start throwing every day or every other day or two days out of three and soon their arms get sore. Relief pitchers seldom last long. For that matter, you can count on the fingers of one hand the number of major leaguers who have pitched as few as fifteen victories for as few as five seasons in a row.

Major leaguer Jim Lonborg says, "Pitchers have to look out for themselves. Most managers will overwork them. Even if you have a sore arm, they'll let you rest it awhile, then send you right back out there before you're ready. And the way they overwork young pitchers is criminal. A lot of talented young pitchers never make the majors because their arms are ruined before they're ready."

"Tennis elbow," "golfer's elbow," and "bowler's elbow" problems develop similarly along the lines of sore arms. Stress damages the muscles within the arms and joints. Any kind of unnatural stress can contribute to it. I discovered I had developed a bad elbow simply from the strain of reaching in and lifting my "little black bag," a heavy bag full of my trainer's tools, out of the trunk of my car.

"Tennis elbow" problems stem primarily from the stress of the serve, which is an awkward, explosive motion, but sometimes stem from other strokes and from the shock of hitting the ball. The faster the court, the more probable the problem because the more apt you are to make a fast, awkward swing at the ball. You must warm up properly and do stretching exercises, especially those that will imitate the motions you will use.

You must use correct strokes that will involve as little twisting of the elbow as possible. Most serves are unnatural, and you may have to turn to a straight-on serve. If your backhand does not feel comfortable, turn to a two-hand backhand, which may relieve strain. Learn to get your body and especially your shoulder into your swing so the stress is lessened on your arm and elbow.

Use a tubular metal racquet and gut strings, which absorb impact better than wooden racquets and nylon strings. Use a racquet that has the largest grip you can handle easily and a handle that is heavier than the head, as these seem to reduce strain on your elbow. Do not use old, dead balls, which are heavier than new, lively ones.

"Golfer's elbow" develops similarly, but in golf most correct strokes are not natural. You may need to be taught strokes that put as little stress on your elbow as possible. "Bowler's elbow" stems not so much from an unnatural delivery as from the weight of the ball being thrown, which strains the arm and the elbow.

In all elbow cases, ice will help but not heal. Heat will heal, but not help permanently. A doctor may administer some anti-inflammatory agent, such as cortisone shots, which will reduce any swelling and hasten healing. Occasionally, cortisone injections effect a lasting cure, but not consistently. Surgery can be corrective, but is called for only in extreme cases.

When the condition is acute, it must be rested. After rest, return to the activity, but you may have to do so in moderation, and you may have to modify your motions. You must do exercises that stretch the arm and flex the elbow and warm up properly before exertion. Beyond this, you may simply have to learn to live with the problem.

The most serious injuries I have dealt with in team training have been with the knees, especially those suffered by the three Laker superstars of my time. Elgin Baylor suffered his knee injury in April of 1965, Wilt Chamberlain in November of 1969, and Jerry West his in March of 1971. It is ironic that all three suffered the same general type of serious injury, though each was different in its specifics.

The knee is a hinge joint, and although formed by only two bones, the tibia and the femur, it is supported on all sides by ligaments and muscle tendons and is quite complex and damaged easily. It does not have the range of motion of the wrist or ankle joints, for example, and in athletic competition is subject to the sort of twisting it was not meant to endure. The knee is vulnerable to blows, especially when extended.

Baylor suffered from an arthritic condition in his knees. Midway in the 1964–65 season he fell and banged his knee on a hard court that had been laid on a cement base in Cleveland. Later, X rays revealed a crack in the kneecap that might have been suffered at that time. Then he banged kneecaps with another player, which could have done damage. Finally, in the playoffs, he went up to shoot and came down hurt. There was a loud pop we could hear all over the court.

Elg had fractured his left patella, which is the kneecap. Essentially, he tore away about the upper eighth of the kneecap. In a ninety-minute operation the next day, Dr. Kerlan removed the broken piece of the cap, drilled holes in the remaining portion, and attached the torn and stretched tendons to it. Later, he said that it was by far the worst of the three Laker knee injuries and that at the time he wondered if Elg would walk naturally again, much less play again.

Elg was on his back for a week, in a cast and on crutches for six weeks, and limited to walking for a month after that. Then he was put on recuperative therapy. On the doctor's advice, I had Elg attaching heavy weights to his legs, lying on his back, and raising his legs a hundred times a session. He had to jog up the steps of the bleachers at a nearby field. He had to ride a real bike and a stationary bike.

It hurt. And he had fears for his future. The recovery rate from knee operations is getting better all the time, but where a career is concerned the individual has to worry. Much depends on how hard you work and how much pain you can endure in rebuilding the strength and flexibility in the joint. Frankly, we had to beat on Baylor to get him going. He is not by nature a hard worker.

In preseason camp he favored his left knee so much he strained the ligaments in his right knee, which had to be encased in a cast for a month and then had to be built back up, too. When he returned during the regular season, he held back. I called Dr. Kerlan and told him this. He said the knee could take any test and he told Elg that if he wasn't going to go all out he might as well use one of his seats on the sidelines.

Angry, Elg went out, all out, and came all the way back. He was all right until he ruptured the Achilles tendon of his right foot in November of 1970. He was out the rest of the season and played only a few games the following season before retiring.

The Achilles tendon binds the heel to the ankle. It is delicate and damaged easily. With age it loses its elasticity and is subject to injury. Strains or other minor injury to this tendon are not uncommon, especially after a sprained ankle has created awkward activity. There usually isn't much hemorrhaging, so the application of cold and a pressure bandage usually are all that are needed initially. The patient will have to stay off the foot for a day or two and it will have to be treated with hot packs. When the player returns, the heel will have to be padded and the foot and ankle strapped.

The condition can become chronic. A stretched tendon can rupture, limiting your athletic activity for a long time. Torn Achilles tendons must be repaired surgically and immobilized for up to eight weeks if the athletic activity is to be resumed. These torn tendons don't respond as well to surgery as some other injuries. If the tendon has been stretched, you may not be able to stand on the balls of your feet, raise your heels, or jump properly from then on.

Like Baylor, Chamberlain also suffered from arthritic knees. He ruptured the patellar tendon of his right knee. It just simply gave way on him in a game. He lay down and it was a while before we realized he was really hurt. He was cursing when I got to him. We got him to the dressing room, and Laker owner Jack Kent Cooke rushed in to ask if it hurt. Wilt lied that it didn't, but he was sweating from the pain. The next morning another ninety-minute operation, this one by Dr. Kerlan's associate, Dr. Frank Jobe, repaired the damage, and the torn tendons were reattached to the bone.

It is not commonly known that there was conflict between Cooke and Kerlan over Chamberlain's knee. Like most doctors, Kerlan was conservative in estimating how long it would take Wilt to recover and didn't want to put him on a timetable. Cooke, an optimist by nature, believes in mind over matter. He wanted Wilt to get back into action as soon as possible, called Chamberlain an extraordinary man who would not need as much time to recover as an ordinary man, and predicted he would be back by mid-March, which was about twenty weeks after the injury and a couple of weeks before the playoffs.

Challenged, Chamberlain responded. I have never known an athlete to work as hard to come back from an injury. He did all the weight lifting and bike riding and running you have to do and more. He ran on the soft sand of the beach. He played volleyball. He was back playing basketball just when Cooke had said he would be and he played well in the playoffs. And when some criticized him for not playing as well as he had in the past, I wondered if they realized how remarkable it was for an athlete to return to action successfully only five months after such an injury.

West tore the medial collateral ligament when hit from the side by another player. I saw it was serious, but didn't know if it was torn. The doctor in Buffalo didn't say it was, either. Sometimes you strain the ligaments, but the cartilage is not involved. The muscles tighten up and go into spasms, so it is difficult to determine the extent of the injury. But Dr. Kerlan, an outstanding diagnostician, saw what it was as soon as Jerry flew to him. Jerry went into surgery with Dr. Jobe.

West was hurt late in the season, so he had all the off-season to do recuperative therapy. He worked hard to rehabilitate himself and played three hard seasons after his injury before he felt he no longer could play as well as he should and suddenly quit at the start of the next season.

Jerry normally wasn't a good patient because he was too anxious to get back in action and too impatient to treat himself properly. If you work hard at rehabilitation those first few months after the cast comes off knee surgery—and this is the critical time to work hard—you can come back as if you hadn't had an accident. But Jerry never did the things you should do to avoid or recover from muscle injuries, and in the end I think these nagging problems pestered him into retirement.

Jerry had a severe muscle pull in his groin, and these injuries are among the slowest to heal and hardest to play with. You are in pain and lose lateral motion. Sometimes they conceal or create hernias, which Jerry may have suffered. A hernia is a rupture in which, usually, the intestine has pushed through the abdominal wall. It is created by a blow or by strain. It is serious in that it can't be contained well or treated well and has to be corrected by surgery.

Hernias occur in the pelvis, a bony ring formed by the sacrum and coccyx, which supports the spine and trunk and serves as an attachment for the upper legs. The pelvic girdle can be cracked, which must be mended as is any fracture.

A "hip pointer" is a severe pinching of soft tissue caused by a direct blow to the relatively unprotected hip bone. It is extremely painful and difficult to correct. The athlete is unable to rotate his trunk or flex high thigh muscles without pain. He may require bed rest. Cold and pressure must be applied immediately and continued on and off for at least forty-eight hours. A doctor's care is required, and the athlete may be sidelined a week or more. He should be provided protective padding when he returns to action.

Dislocated or broken bones are serious injuries, of course, calling for a doctor's care. It often is difficult to determine if an injured part may be dislocated or broken, but in any case where this situation arises the area must be immobilized immediately. In any severe cases, such as a compound fracture, in which the jagged end of a bone penetrates the skin, the patient should not be moved except by qualified personnel. Fractures may result in bones being broken into sharp ends, which could do severe damage within the body, so extreme caution is called for.

These injuries usually produce hemorrhaging, which can be controlled with cold packs. The injured area must be stabilized with a sling or splint. The doctor will bring the break together and set the bone straight. Usually he will cast it. Then nature takes over for the healing process. Except in extreme cases, bones will knit together firmly and there will be no lingering or lasting aftereffects. However, there may have been muscle damage. Enclosed in a cast, muscles will atrophy, anyway. Rehabilitation exercise to restore free, flexible movement will be necessary after the injury has mended.

Jockeys are rugged guys whose frequent falls from their racehorses often result in fractures of their shoulders, chestbones, and pelvic areas, as well as their arms and legs. The most serious injuries I dealt with were Walter Blum's and Bill Shoemaker's.

Blum was thrown over his horse's head and trampled in the small of his back by a trailing horse. Blum had a compression fracture of the fourth, fifth, and sixth cervical vertebrae and was bedded down and in a brace for a while. I treated him with heat, massage, and exercise during his recuperation, went with Dr. Kerlan to the track for Walter's comeback, and watched Walter win the first race of his return with special pleasure. Shoe, who has won more races than any rider ever, also has come back successfully from more major injuries than any other.

The one I particularly recall came when a horse fell on Bill, fracturing his femur—the thigh bone. It was severe and he had to have a pin placed in it to hold it together and had to live and ride with this for about a year. I had to devise an exercise program that would keep him fit for racing without putting undue stress on the injured area. Deeply dedicated, he worked at it. He, too, returned victoriously.

The shoulder girdle consists of two bones, the clavicle or collarbone and the scapula or shoulder blade. These form four joints, three of which are movable. Shoulder movement is part of arm movement. Shoulder muscles can be strained, sprained, or torn, just as can any muscles. Fractured clavicles are not uncommon, usually resulting from a direct blow or from a fall, sometimes when an athlete falls on an extended arm, stressing the collarbone. These usually occur in the middle third, where there is less support from ligaments.

It is difficult to tell fractures from shoulder separations, which are sprains of the joint, usually resulting from straight-arm falls. There are varying degrees of these ranging from stretched or partially torn ligaments to rupture of the supporting ligaments. In the worst of these, surgery is required to correct the damage. The area is difficult to contain and usually is strapped.

Because the shoulder joint is a loose mechanism and not well protected, injuries are commonplace. Fractures of the upper humerus, the bone that connects the arm to the shoulder girdle, resulting from a direct blow, a dislocation, or a straight-arm fall, are fairly commonplace. There is a lot of danger of internal damage being done by broken bones in this area. There will be tenderness, pain, swelling, discoloration, and inability to move the arm, but it is difficult to diagnose, and an X ray is required. The area where it may exist must be strapped.

When an arm is rotated violently, severe shoulder dislocation or sprain may result. The athlete suffers pain and large loss of shoulder motion. Because of the possibility of fracture, the area must be immobilized and examined by a doctor. If it is determined to be a dislocation or sprain, recurrences may be treated with traction applied by qualified people. Studies show that anyone suffering these once, especially those under the age of twenty-one, will suffer them again; hence the term "trick shoulder." Thus the shoulder will have to be held in place with strapping in an effort to avoid recurrences in athletic competition.

Most broken arms occur in the forearm or lower half of the arm, to the humeral shaft. Like other breaks, they may stem from a direct blow or compression, but sometimes stem from severe twisting. There will be pain, swelling, and deformity, the latter resulting as the muscles tend to pull the break apart. There is also the danger that the broken bone ends may do damage to the tissue and nerves. Splinting is in order, followed by the setting of the injury, and casting.

Elbow fractures are not uncommon. The elbow joint is composed of the humerus, radius, and ulna bones, bound and reinforced by ligaments. Any of the elbow bones are easily fractured in the usual ways, often from falls. These bones are not well protected. Dislocations are always possible, and a doctor's diagnosis is called for. Cold should be applied at once, the arm immobilized in a sling, and the patient taken to a doctor. There should not be any massage or movement of the joint prior to healing. Even in rehabilitation forced stretching is to be avoided.

Bursitis of the elbow is a common complaint. The bursa is a small fluid-filled sac located within the joints; the bursa helps cushion the bones against friction. The bursa in the shoulder is especially susceptible to acute or chronic injury, especially from direct blows. It becomes inflamed, swells up, is tender and painful. The usual cold-hot treatment is called for, but in chronic conditions constant heat is called for and the elbow must be padded for protection.

The wrist is a complicated mechanism formed mainly by a variety of carpal and metacarpal bones. Its strength stems from the tendons that cross it rather than from the ligaments or bone structure. Like the ankle joint, the wrist has a wide range of movement. Unlike the ankle, the wrist is used widely so usually is more flexible. The ankle is less complicated, formed by the meeting of the tibia and fibula with the talus. Like the wrist, it is quite strong. In the ankle's case, this stems from the bone structure, mainly.

However, sprains and fractures are commonplace in both. Severe sprains should be treated as possible fractures. The joints should be treated with cold and compression, encased in slings or splints, taped, and taken to a doctor. The usual setting and casting will follow, followed by extensive rehabilitation. At times it is possible to play with a casted wrist, if not a casted ankle, but it is not recommended. One problem with fractures of the ankle or leg is that you cannot keep in condition by running.

Fractures of the metacarpals, those bones just below the surface of the back of the hand, occur frequently from a blow to the hand, a blow delivered by the fist, or having the hand stepped on. Often there is no deformity and you can move the hand, so the fracture is concealed. It may seem no more than a bruise. But applying pressure to the fingers sometimes produces pain in the hand, revealing the fracture. If the possibility exists, an X ray is required. The hand has to be splinted, sometimes set and casted. Healing may take a month.

Fractures of the fingers may be the most common in sports. The thumb, by the way, is classified as a joint, rather than a finger, but can be considered in the same category as the fingers. Obviously, there are many ways in which fingers are fractured. Often what appears to be a jammed, strained, or sprained finger is fractured, so caution must be taken in diagnosing the injury. Cold and compression are in order, but care must be taken not to extend or stretch the injured member. Splinting, setting, and casting are called for.

The jammed finger or thumb really is a dislocation, caused usually by a blow directly to the tip. It is commonplace in all sports, especially in baseball, where the ball may strike the tip while being caught. The injured member must be treated with cold to stop hemorrhaging and must be immobilized, sometimes for as much as a month, sometimes even splinted. A jammed or sprained thumb poses special problems, since full use of the hand requires full use of this hinge mechanism.

Fractures of the foot, usually caused by the force of a jump, or a direct blow, or being stepped on must be iced, immobilized, and casted. Fractures and sprains of the toes, usually caused by kicking an object, are troublesome in that they cannot be immobilized or casted effectively, so they must be splinted or taped. They may take up to a month to heal and obviously limit your mobility in that time.

The most common leg fracture occurs to the fibula in the middle third of the leg or the tibia in the lower third. The distortion that usually takes place stems from muscles pulling apart the broken ends, but this would not be true in hairline or lesser fractures. To mend properly, the leg will have to be set and casted, and in the more severe cases immobilization may be required for three months or more, requiring rehabilitation extensively later.

Most broken bones do heal well, so they are not serious in the sense that they are not a threat to your future participation in physical pursuits, but they are serious in that they limit or more probably prohibit your participation during the recuperation period and may require extensive, rigorous, and perhaps even painful rehabilitation of the muscles later. Whenever possible, continue conditioning during recuperation. Someone with a broken arm can run, for example. You will have plenty to do in simply strengthening the injured member later.

One broken bone stands out in my mind above all others I've cared for. When he was with the Eagles, defensive back Tommy Brookshier, now a broadcaster, suffered a compound fracture of the tibia and fibula bones of his leg on a rain-soaked field. His broken bones literally were stuck in the mud, and he had to be gathered up with considerable care and had a terrible time trying to get the wound cleansed before doctors could begin to work on them.

Wilt Chamberlain, who hurt his fingers so often on the rims and receiving passes, often played with broken and taped or splinted fingers. Few realize he played brilliantly with a broken bone in his hand the year the Lakers won the championship in the playoffs of 1972. I remember that Doc Kerlan went to the dressing room before the final game to see if Wilt could play. Unexpectedly, Doc threw him a basketball. Wincing, Wilt caught it. "You can play," Kerlan laughed. And Wilt did, without complaint. And we won. He was a moody man who felt unfairly maligned as a loser and sometimes refused to take up the burdens he was capable of bearing, but there also were times he carried heavy loads and showed me he was quite a man.

Rudy LaRusso suffered a hairline fracture of one foot during the playoffs one season. X rays revealed a mild condition with which he could continue to play, though in pain. Possibly this was similar to the circumstances surrounding the Bill Walton situation. This was the playoffs and our manager at the time, Lou Mohs, figured LaRusso had all summer to mend and talked LaRusso into playing.

Mohs teased LaRusso. I was with them when Mohs told LaRusso he knew a doctor who could fix the fracture: "This doctor is the greatest. He has the strongest thumbs of any man I've ever known. He can press into your foot with his hands, break off the fractured part with his thumbs, push it right up through the skin, and take it right out."

Rudy went pale. He looked at me. I didn't say a word. I didn't disagree with Lou in those days. Rudy turned back to Lou and asked, "Are you kidding me?" Lou said, "No, I'm serious. I've seen this guy in action. He's been doing it for years. He'll do it for you." Rudy said, "I got to think about it."

Later, he got me to one side and said, "Hey, Frank, there's no way I'm gonna let some guy break off a piece of bone in my foot and push it up through the skin. What do you think?" I said, "I'm with you. It can't be done. If it could, it wouldn't heal the fracture anyway."

Rudy said, "I want to play and I don't want to cross Lou." I said, "I think I can put a pad over the area of the fracture and tape it in such a way that it will be supported and protected. It will hurt until it's warmed up and it may hurt like hell later, but you should be able to play without too much pain."

Relieved, Rudy went to Lou and said, "Frank said he can tape it in such a way I can play with it. I'd rather do that than let your doctor do anything to it." Lou said, "Well, all right, as long as you can play. We really need you."

Rudy looked at Lou and you could see Rudy's brain beginning to work. He said, "Well, Lou, it hurts like hell, and it will be hard to play, but I want to play. It would help if I had a little incentive." Lou made a face and asked, "How much incentive?" LaRusso said, "Let's talk about it."

They left me and went off to talk. After a while, LaRusso returned and I asked him if he'd gotten his incentive. He grinned and said, "Yeh, I got a little bit." I asked him if it was enough for him to play. He laughed and said it was enough for him to play.

The pros play for pay, of course, and the incentive Rudy got to risk his health came in cash. Careers and cash ride on pros' performances, of course, and they play in the kind of pain the average person would not endure and run the sort of risks the average person should not.

Hockey players may be the toughest of all athletes. They get severe wounds stitched up and return to action after a few minutes. Boxers battle while bleeding and dazed, of course. Car racers risk their life and limbs. Football players play battered. Most pros play in pain. The average young athlete and adult recreational athlete does not have to do so and should not.

Take care of yourself.

12. FOOD FOR ENERGY

The feeding of athletes is full of myths. For many years, steak and milk was the accepted diet. It still is at many training tables. For years, mothers have been sending their children out for activity on hot meals, and they still do. They holler at them for grabbing a peanut-butter sandwich or a candy bar.

The fact is, steak is one of the hardest foods to digest. It sits in your stomach for as long as four hours before even entering the intestinal tract. It converts slowly into the sugar we need for energy. Candy does give you a quick lift, but the body swiftly produces insulin to keep the blood sugar in balance and you have a letdown. Peanut butter is better.

A peanut-butter sandwich is a good pregame meal. But milk, while it may taste good with it, does not go well with it. Milk does not digest easily. Many people don't digest it well at all. The older you are, the less you need. A starch, such as spaghetti, may actually be the best pregame meal. But cooking takes much of the food value out of it and the heat is lost long before your body absorbs it. Hot meals are really overrated. Let's look closely at what we eat, especially as it applies to the active person.

While most professional athletes are trim, most of us carry around much more weight than we should. A survey shows almost 60 per cent of us are overweight. The average person is 10 to 20 pounds overweight. Many of us are much more overweight, and some are 10 to 20 pounds underweight. Height-weight charts are misleading because they are averages and do not take into account our varying body types. Most of us know when we are overweight.

Our pot bellies and double chins give us away. If you have any doubt, pinch the skin on the back of your upper arm. If you pull more than a half inch or so away from muscle, you have too much fat content in your body.

Much depends on what you want to do. Runners tend to do best at the lowest possible weight, while football players are most effective with extra pounds. If the extra weight is muscle, it may help you more than it will hurt you.

Track coaches say you should carry no more than 2 pounds of weight per inch of height. This means a person who is 5 feet, 10 inches in height should weigh only 140 pounds. Most top runners are really skinny and gaunt. Actor-runner Bruce Dern says, "If I looked like the runners coaches tell me I should look like, the only parts I could get would be as a refugee from a concentration camp and the only film I could have made lately would have been *Holocaust.*"

It isn't the weight that matters as much as the way we look and feel. If we look trim and feel good, we are all right. If not, we are not and should do something about it. It is not healthy to have excess weight. It makes the body's systems work too hard to perform properly.

As a general guide, here is a height-weight table:

Height	*Men* (Ages 25–40, medium frame)	*Women*
5-0		102
5-2	124	112
5-4	130	116
5-6	137	120
5-8	145	135
5-10	153	144
6-0	162	152
6-2	170	
6-4	180	
6-6	190	

Many athletes use sweat boxes to keep their weight down. Track doctors prefer steam rooms to the use of diuretics or water pills because these deplete the body of vitamins and minerals. Most tracks ban appetite depressants, too. I'm also against these things. The natural ways of controlling weight are best, but some jocks are trimmed down so fine they can't eat a bite without picking up poundage. Most of us do have to lose weight to be healthy, but most of us can take the time and the effort to trim down properly.

Life insurance studies show that if you are even 10 per cent over the "table weight" for your height, you are twice as apt to develop high blood pressure, three times as apt to develop diabetes, and five times as apt to get gallbladder problems. If you are more than 20 per cent overweight you are regarded as obese. The more overweight you are, the more obese. What an ugly word! Obesity by itself does not kill us, but it creates complications that do. The ideal in a good conditioning program is to provide diet that trims us as well as provides us with the energy we need for exercise. Exercise and diet go hand in hand not only in losing weight but also in maintaining the proper weight. You have to cut down on your caloric intake while stepping up your athletic activity.

A calorie is a unit of heat, a measurement of the energy in different foods. In your activities, you burn up this energy. However, we usually take into our bodies more calories than we can burn up. What is left over is stored in the body and becomes fat, so we gain weight. The key is to take in just what you need, less if you want to lose weight, but enough to provide your body with the fuel it needs to perform properly. A person can perform well while on a diet because his body fat will provide fuel, but once he is trim, he will need more fuel.

Every pound of weight represents about 4,000 calories that you must burn off if you are going to lose the weight. The average person needs 2,000 to 3,000 calories per day to function well. If you cut to 1,500 calories a day you can lose weight while still functioning effectively. Once you are down, you can stick to 2,500 a day and maintain your fitness. If you go to 3,500 or 4,500, you are going to gain weight.

Earlier in the book, I listed the amounts of calories that are burned off by amounts of activity. Here I'll list some major calorie counts:

Item	*Measure*	*Calories*
Apples	1 medium	60
Applesauce	½ cup	115
Asparagus	6 stalks	23
Bacon	2 slices	90
Bananas	1 medium	85
Beans, lima	½ cup	100
Beef, lean	1 ounce	58
Beets	½ cup	31
Beer	8 ounces	100
Brandy	1 jigger	110
Biscuits	1	90
Bouillon	1 cube	5
Bread, French	1 slice	82
Bread, rye	1 slice	55
Bread, wheat	1 slice	65
Bread, white	1 slice	70
Broccoli	1 stalk	26
Brussels sprouts	8 medium	26
Butter, salted	1 teaspoon	33
Cabbage	½ cup	18
Cakes	1 slice	140–275
Candies	1 ounce	110–60
Cantaloupe	½ medium	60
Carrots (cooked)	½ cup	23
Carrots (raw)	1 large	20
Catsup	1 tablespoon	15
Cauliflower	½ cup	14
Celery	1 piece	5
Cereal, cold	1 cup	100–55
Cheese	1 ounce	105–15
Cheese, cottage	1 cup	260
Chicken	1 ounce	49
Cookies	1	50–150
Corn on the cob	1	91
Corn, creamed	½ cup	101
Crackers	2	25–80
Cream	1 tablespoon	20–55
Cream subs	1 tablespoon	10–20
Eggs	1	80
Fish	1 ounce	22–32

Item	*Measure*	*Calories*
Frankfurters	1 ounce	85
Grapefruit	½ medium	58
Grapes	½ cup	85
Ham	1 ounce	50
Honey	1 tablespoon	65
Ice cream	small serving	165
Jams and jellies	1 tablespoon	55
Lettuce	1 head	20
Liver	1 ounce	65–75
Luncheon meat	1 slice	65–175
Macaroni	½ cup	78
Margarine	1 teaspoon	33
Mayonnaise	1 tablespoon	100
Milk	1 cup	160
Mushrooms	½ cup	34
Mustard	1 tablespoon	11
Nuts	½ cup	425
Olives	4	15
Onions	1 tablespoon	4
Orange juice	½ cup	55
Oranges	1 medium	60–90
Pancakes	1	60
Peaches	1 medium	35
Peanut butter	1 tablespoon	95
Pears	1 medium	100
Peas	½ cup	70
Pickles	1 large	15
Pies	1 slice	285–365
Popcorn	1 cup	40
Pork	1 ounce	71
Potatoes (baked, mashed)	½ cup	95
Potatoes (fried)	10 slices	155
Pretzels	5 sticks	20
Raisins	1 tablespoon	30
Rice	½ cup	70–90
Salad dressing	1 tablespoon	65–80
Salt	1 teaspoon	0
Sauerkraut	1 cup	45
Sausage	1 ounce	87
Shellfish	1	180–210

Item	*Measure*	*Calories*
Soft drinks	8 ounces	95
Soup	1 cup	30–145
Spaghetti	½ cup	78
Spinach	½ cup	24
Strawberries	1 cup	55
Sugar, white	1 tablespoon	45
Tea	1 cup	2
Turkey	1 ounce	50
Veal	1 ounce	45
Whiskey and gin	1 jigger	0
Wine	4 ounces	100–55
Yogurt	1 cup	125

Although a third of our population admits to being concerned dieters, doctors' and dieticians' surveys show that almost half will quit a diet within one year, 70 per cent after two years, and 98 per cent within five years. Almost no one sticks to a diet. Only 5 per cent of dieters are successful, so you can see that it takes unusual determination to limit your eating over your lifetime. There are a thousand diets, and most are faddish. Many produce weight loss rapidly, but in the form of loss of liquids, which just as rapidly return to the body, discouraging the dieter. Many are downright dangerous. The only diet of value is the one that cuts down on calories combined with an increase in exercise, so long as the body is being fed what it needs.

Let's get into types of foods. The four basic food groups are meats, fruits and vegetables, dairy products, and breads and cereals. A balanced daily diet should include some foods from each of these groups.

Essentially, this is so. However, vegetarians will tell you that you do not need meat, and you do not. You can have a healthy diet without it if you prefer. Most adults do not need much if any milk, which hardens the bones and makes them brittle, and which is not easily digested. Milk and eggs are heavy contributors to the killer cholesterol. Skim milk is much better. Refined sugars, such as can be found in white bread, are really junk foods. You have to carefully consider such a basic daily diet and you may wish to make exceptions. For really balanced diets you will have to make additions and may wish to make subtractions.

Let's break the foods down into more specific categories. Carbohydrates are complex sugars and starches the body converts into fuel for the body. They may be the basic sugars, which are all pretty much the same, whether white or brown or those contained in candies, potatoes, or grains, such as wheat, rice, corn, and oats, or the foods made from them, such as spaghetti and other macaronis, and bread.

A recent trend in athletic training has been "carbohydrate loading." The main source of energy for short-term exercise is glycogen, a starch that is converted from carbohydrates within the body and stored in the muscles and liver. The amount of glycogen the body has available for use will determine how long it can function effectively before fatigue. Accordingly, athletes have been loading up on carbohydrates for as long as a week before competition.

Studies show that conditioned athletes can store more glycogen than others. However, they also show that no one can store more then two to four hours' worth, and this can be added in a day or so. Thus spaghetti, say, is a good pregame meal, but eating spaghetti for seven days is not going to do you any good. In fact, it may do harm because the body cannot absorb excesses of anything. And excess carbohydrates simply will be turned into fat, which converts into energy, but cannot be converted fast enough to help the athlete.

Carbohydrates are necessary for an active person. But raw sugars overload the bloodstream and do harm. Along with refined breads and cereals, they are empty calories without nutritional value. The body uses starches better, especially the macaroni and rice dishes, but it is best to include these as part of a regular diet rather than load up on them. They can be eaten effectively for three days prior to exertion, including the day of exertion.

Fats are a more concentrated source of energy than carbohydrates and take over as the prime source of fuel when the body has exhausted the limited amount of carbohydrates that can be stored. However, fats have a higher caloric count and present weight problems. It is estimated that we take on more than 40 per cent of our calories in fats, and dieticians believe half that would be best. We do need fats, not only for energy, but also for their acids, which maintain the quality of our tissues, especially the skin and kidneys, and for their high content of vitamins A, D, and others.

Meats, dairy products, nuts, and vegetable oils are fatty foods. The problem with regulating the amount of fats we absorb is that so much is concealed in meats, salad dressings, and cooking oils. If you trim off all the outer fat from meat, it still will contain 10 per cent or more fat. Some meats are leaner than others, of course. Frankly, I feel lean meats are the best sources of fat needed in the body. I believe in eating beef, but it would be best to include it in your regular diet and limit it the days immediately before activity, especially in the pregame meal.

Because of their high cholesterol content, dairy products must be limited. Two to four eggs a week are plenty, and if you have a cholesterol problem, one to two would be sufficient. Limit the butter you spread on your bread, as well as the bread. Preferably, use margarine rather than butter. As you get older, limit the milk you drink. Stick to skim milk and stick to unsaturated fats and oils.

Proteins are the prime material for the building of all living matter. They are not energy builders, but they build and repair muscle tissue, regulate the body's functions, and provide vitamins, antibodies, and enzymes necessary to health. Proteins are composed of amino acids. Surveys have shown eggs to be highest in essential amino acids, followed by meat and fish, milk, rice, corn, potatoes, peanuts, and milk.

A few athletes, such as basketball's Bill Walton, have survived on a vegetarian diet. It has become clear that you can do without meats of all kinds without missing them. You can also do without eggs, but experts believe that if you in addition exclude milk and cheese, rice, potatoes, and corn, you will not be getting the amino acids you need for your body to be healthy and for it to function properly.

Frankly, I feel you should have meat. Fish and poultry appear to be better used by the body than beef, veal, lamb, and so forth. Fish and poultry are less fatty. You can stick to fish and poultry if you prefer, but I believe that if you simply alternate them with beef you will do well. High-protein diets have been popular and have value, but the problem with them is that they are not balanced and do not include sufficient food the body needs from other groups.

Minerals and vitamins are not direct sources of energy, but do help the body process and use energy sources. They also help the body's systems function properly and aid growth. To the athlete, the most important minerals are calcium, iron, magnesium, phosphorus, chloride, potassium, and sodium, while the most valuable vitamins are A, B, C, D, and E.

Minerals govern, among other things, the salt and water balance in the body. Sodium, potassium, and chloride are the main minerals that contribute to this. Salt, which is sodium chloride, passes through the body unchanged, feeding it en route. Excessive salts work harshly on the body, and many persons live healthily on medically prescribed salt-free diets. Sodium chloride is found in so many foods that no diet is completely salt-free. Studies show that it is not so much the sodium in salt that is lost through sweat during competition as it is magnesium and potassium. Thus salt pills may help make up for this loss, but fruits and vegetables may make up for it more completely. Bananas are a good source of fruit sugars, minerals, and vitamins, by the way, but solid food is not as easily absorbed during activity as are liquids.

We must replace liquid lost during exertion. We lose so much water through sweating during extreme exertion or on hot, humid days that we cannot replace it all reasonably. The body cannot comfortably carry excess liquid so take days to properly replace the full amount of liquid lost in long, extreme exertion.

Fresh water is the ideal liquid. Fruit juices, especially orange juice and tomato or other vegetable juices are also excellent, and they are some of the best ways to bring energy-producing sugar into the body. Some of the commercial compounds offered as athletic drinks have value but will not do the job by themselves. Milk has its importance, but it should not be taken near a time of exertion. Many people are allergic to milk without knowing it.

Coffee causes acid in the stomach, and stimulates bowel activity, so it is bad at a time of competition. Tea is milder, but has similar effects. Either is all right in moderation, but does not contribute to effective exertion. Soda pop is loaded with sugar and of no real value. Diet drinks are healthier, but of no real value, either.

Calcium comes in milk, cheese, and leafy green vegetables, among others. Leafy green vegetables also provide magnesium, as do nuts, fruits, and whole-grain foods. Other vegetables, including tomatoes, beets, and beans, are excellent sources of potassium. Sodium and chlorine come from all vegetables, certain fruits, such as apples, as well as from meat, milk, and salted snacks. Milk provides phosphorus. Lean meat, dried fruits, nuts and egg yolks provide iron. Women need more iron than men, nutritionists tell us. Interestingly, 10 per cent of the women and 20 per cent of the men in the world are said to be suffering from an iron deficiency.

Vitamins are organic combinations present to different degrees in natural foods. Originally, they were identified by the letters of the alphabet because it was felt there were only a few. Now we know there are many, and many are similar, and we have had to divide up some names, as, for example, in vitamins B_1 and B_2.

Vitamins A and D are found in dairy products, such as milk, butter, cream, and egg yolks, and also in liver, cod-liver oil, green vegetables, and carrots. The body also manufactures D from sunshine. Vitamin B is found in milk, cheese, meat, beans, and whole-grain foods. Vitamin C is plentiful in citrus fruits, tomatoes, and green vegetables, as well as meat, potatoes, and grains. Vitamin E is found in green, leafy vegetables, whole-grain flour, and vegetable oils.

All vegetables should be cooked lightly in a minimum of water, if cooked at all. Fresh, raw fruits and vegetables are the most nourishing. Cooking robs vegetables of their nourishment. Freezing and canning adds substances that are not needed and sometimes are harmful. Cooking takes the most out of vitamin C.

Vitamin A promotes vitality. Lack of it lowers resistance, leads to skin disorders and infections and poor eyesight. Vitamin B aids growth and endurance. Lack of it lowers the effective working of the heart, other muscles, and nerves. Vitamins C and D promote healthy bones and teeth. Lack of them hinders the mending of broken bones and promotes tooth decay. Vitamin E promotes energy and some say fertility, too.

I cannot say whether vitamin C does or does not combat the common cold. Recent studies suggest that Linus Pauling may have been right in saying so, but scientists still are split on it. After years of research, they do not know how to prevent the common cold. We have been told only to treat the symptoms, provide rest, and drink lots of fluids to promote recovery.

Laker Keith Erickson used to take massive doses of vitamin C. He swore by it, but it seemed to me he used to suffer as many colds as anyone else. The rest and liquid diet I put him on when he came down with a cold probably helped as much as the vitamins he took.

Elgin Baylor had a lot of bad colds. I had a lot of luck rubbing Vick's Vapor Rub into his chest, as I did with other athletes. It seems to break up the congestion within the chest and open up the breathing.

The only vitamin the body manufactures itself, from sunshine, is D. However, most vitamins can be manufactured synthetically, and the body can use these as well as it does natural ones gotten in the diet.

While I do believe a balanced diet will provide most of the vitamins and minerals we need, I do not believe most of us eat a balanced diet every day. So I also believe that one of the well-known multivitamin tablets should be taken daily to assure us of getting what we need, as well as special ones for special problems.

Beyond that, do not load up on such pills unless your doctor decides you need it. It simply is not true that taking ten vitamin pills is ten times as good for you as taking one. The body can absorb only a limited amount and the rest will be wasted. Some vitamins taken in excess will interfere with the functions of the body.

The rules of the leagues I worked for limited the use of pills. It is just as well because I wouldn't have wanted to use many. On the Lakers we were limited to pills prescribed by our doctors. Most of these were prescribed in particular cases. The only ones I had with me at all times were sleeping tablets, and Dr. Kerlan carefully instructed me on the circumstances under which these could be given out. I don't think I gave out ten in my time with the Lakers. I was not even allowed to provide the players pills to soothe upset stomachs before and after games. I know some players took these, but they got them on their own. Upset stomachs are common, especially before games, even among veteran pros.

I know many athletes today take "uppers" and other pills designed to get them "up" for games, but none ever got one from me. Schedules in professional sports are rough and players get hurt and tired. I presume such pills might help, temporarily, but in the long run I think they have to hurt terribly, reducing the effective function of the body and putting the person's psychology out of whack. Youngsters who experiment with pills are risking their future fitness. They have to be strong enough to resist the temptation of taking what their buddies may be taking.

The great Olympians Harold and Olga Connolly told me an athlete might take anything if he thought it would help him run faster, or jump or throw farther. But they are fooling around with their futures. A woman athlete may increase the efficiency of her muscular activity with injections of male hormones, but she runs the risk of being barred from competition.

I really want no part of any of it, guard my teams against it, and never have been willing to risk my professional future by providing pills to players, over or under the table.

There are some liquid food supplements being produced that seem to work well. They are not too expensive and supply about five hundred calories a serving. They may be a useful part of the pregame meal as they seem to soothe the stomach and aid digestion, curtailing the cramps and nausea and other disorders that pester athletes prior to competition.

Frankly, some athletes survive junk-food diets. It makes no sense. I suppose some are so sound physically they can handle it. Wilt Chamberlain used to gobble down hot dogs before games. I never will forget one time when Fred Schaus was coaching the Lakers and he walked into the dressing room and found Wilt wolfing down a dog. Fred had banned dogs before games. Wilt didn't bother about bans. He looked up and saw an angry Schaus standing over him.

"Want a bite?" Wilt smiled, holding the hot dog out to his coach.

I have seen players eat awesome amounts of frightening foods, beer for breakfast, french fries and milk shakes for lunch, hamburgers and onion rings for pregame meals. One player, Ray Felix, liked hot root beer three meals a day. I remember one time he had scrambled eggs, whole wheat toast, and hot root beer for breakfast.

Wilt and Elgin ate more than anyone else, and Elgin was a fast eater. It was nothing for Wilt to have a large steak, three eggs, a stack of pancakes, a pile of toast, a rasher of ham and bacon, and three or four glasses of orange juice for breakfast. Elgin might have more.

Of course, a lot of time, tight schedules require professional athletes to eat on the run, grabbing sandwiches and soft drinks as they race for airports. Many drink beer to relax after tense games. It's simply not the best way to go, but sometimes you go any way you can. On the other hand, the average person has a choice.

We are a nation of junk-food eaters, which is why we are overweight and under par in health. While they have their place, we rely too much on vitamin pills and food supplements to replace a balanced diet. There is no replacement for a balanced diet of the right foods eaten at the right times.

If we want to lose weight, we should cut down on the calories and step up the exercise. Studies show that if you add a half hour a day of hard exercise to your regular diet you can easily lose twenty pounds or so a year. Cut down your diet, and most of us should, and you will lose more.

If we want to gain weight, we should increase the consumption of good foods, not junk foods. Whole- or cracked-wheat bread instead of white bread, meat and fruit instead of candy and cake, starches instead of sugars. The "quick lift" foods such as candy bars taken just before exertion won't act fast enough or last long enough to help.

A balanced diet of 2,000 to 2,500 calories a day is best. A younger person may need a little more, an older person a little less. The more active you are, the more you will need. Some top swimmers and runners burn off so many calories they require 6,000 to 7,500 calories a day, but you have only to look at them to see that they really are burning it up. The average recreational athlete won't burn up 3,000 to 3,500 a day, so adjust your diet to your requirements.

I'm not going to load you down with diets, the way so many

"experts" do. We all like different foods and follow our tastes. But within the caloric limits you set for yourself include a variety of the carbohydrates, fats, proteins, minerals, and vitamins that I have stressed as desirable. Avoid snacking between meals. If you have to snack, eat peanuts, fruits such as raisins, wheat germ, and honey. Do not eat honey with other foods because it inhibits digestive juices. Fresh fruits and vegetables and dried fruits such as raisins are splendid snacks.

On the days preceding major physical activity, increase your consumption of carbohydrates and fruits. On game days eat macaroni meals, perhaps lean meat like chicken, peanut-butter sandwiches on whole-wheat bread, fruits, and fruit juices. Avoid milk, coffee, and tea. During games, drink water. During breaks, drink water and fruit juices, or suck on oranges. Eat your pregame meal at least three hours before games and wait at least an hour after games before eating again.

Eat well, play hard, get in condition, and stay trim, and you will enjoy good health and a long life.

INDEX